Bloom's Literary Themes

Alienation
The American Dream
Death and Dying
The Grotesque
The Hero's Journey
Human Sexuality
The Labyrinth
Rebirth and Renewal

REBIRTH AND RENEWAL

Bloom's Literary Themes

REBIRTH
AND RENEWAL

Edited and with an introduction by
Harold Bloom
Sterling Professor of the Humanities
Yale University

Volume Editor
Blake Hobby

BLOOM'S
LITERARY CRITICISM
An imprint of Infobase Publishing

Bloom's Literary Themes: Rebirth and Renewal

Copyright © 2009 by Infobase Publishing
Introduction © 2009 by Harold Bloom

Bloom's Literary Criticism
An imprint of Infobase Publishing
132 West 31st Street
New York NY 10001

Library of Congress Cataloging-in-Publication Data
Rebirth and renewal / edited and with an introduction by Harold Bloom ; volume editor, Blake Hobby.
    p. cm. — (Bloom's literary themes)
  Includes bibliographical references and index.
  ISBN 978-0-7910-9805-9 (acid-free paper) 1. Regeneration in literature. I. Bloom, Harold. II. Hobby, Blake.
  PN56.R37R43 2009
  809'.9338—dc22   2008042992

Bloom's Literary Criticism books are available at special discounts when purchased in bulk quantities for businesses, associations, institutions, or sales promotions. Please call our Special Sales Department in New York at (212) 967-8800 or (800) 322-8755.

You can find Bloom's Literary Criticism on the World Wide Web at
http://www.chelseahouse.com

Text Design by Kerry Casey
Cover design by Takeshi Takahashi

Printed in the United States of America

IBT EJB 10 9 8 7 6 5 4 3 2 1

This book is printed on acid-free paper and contains 30 percent postconsumer recycled content.

Contents

Series Introduction by Harold Bloom:
Themes and Metaphors

1. TOPOS AND TROPE

What we now call a theme or topic or subject initially was named a
topos, ancient Greek for "place." Literary *topoi* are commonplaces, but
also arguments or assertions. A topos can be regarded as literal when
opposed to a trope or turning which is figurative and which can be a
metaphor or some related departure from the literal: ironies, synec-
doches (part for whole), metonymies (representations by contiguity)
or hyperboles (overstatements). Themes and metaphors engender one
another in all significant literary compositions.

As a theoretician of the relation between the matter and the rhetoric of high literature, I tend to define metaphor as a figure of desire
rather than a figure of knowledge. We welcome literary metaphor
because it enables fictions to persuade us of beautiful untrue things, as
Oscar Wilde phrased it. Literary *topoi* can be regarded as places where
we store information, in order to amplify the themes that interest us.

This series of volumes, *Bloom's Literary Themes*, offers students and
general readers helpful essays on such perpetually crucial topics as the
Hero's Journey, the Labyrinth, the Sublime, Death and Dying, the
Taboo, the Trickster and many more. These subjects are chosen for
their prevalence yet also for their centrality. They express the whole
concern of human existence now in the twenty-first century of the
Common Era. Some of the topics would have seemed odd at another
time, another land: the American Dream, Enslavement and Emancipation, Civil Disobedience.

I suspect though that our current preoccupations would have
existed always and everywhere, under other names. Tropes change
across the centuries: the irony of one age is rarely the irony of another.
But the themes of great literature, though immensely varied, undergo

transmemberment and show up barely disguised in different contexts. The power of imaginative literature relies upon three constants: aesthetic splendor, cognitive power, wisdom. These are not bound by societal constraints or resentments, and ultimately are universals, and so not culture-bound. Shakespeare, except for the world's scriptures, is the one universal author, whether he is read and played in Bulgaria or Indonesia or wherever. His supremacy at creating human beings breaks through even the barrier of language and puts everyone on his stage. This means that the matter of his work has migrated everywhere, reinforcing the common places we all inhabit in his themes.

2. Contest as both Theme and Trope

Great writing or the Sublime rarely emanates directly from themes since all authors are mediated by forerunners and by contemporary rivals. Nietzsche enhanced our awareness of the agonistic foundations of ancient Greek literature and culture, from Hesiod's contest with Homer on to the Hellenistic critic Longinus in his treatise *On the Sublime*. Even Shakespeare had to begin by overcoming Christopher Marlowe, only a few months his senior. William Faulkner stemmed from the Polish-English novelist Joseph Conrad and our best living author of prose fiction, Philip Roth, is inconceivable without his descent from the major Jewish literary phenomenon of the twentieth century, Franz Kafka of Prague, who wrote the most lucid German since Goethe.

The contest with past achievement is the hidden theme of all major canonical literature in Western tradition. Literary influence is both an overwhelming metaphor for literature itself, and a common topic for all criticism, whether or not the critic knows her immersion in the incessant flood.

Every theme in this series touches upon a contest with anteriority, whether with the presence of death, the hero's quest, the overcoming of taboos, or all of the other concerns, volume by volume. From Monteverdi through Bach to Stravinsky, or from the Italian Renaissance through the agon of Matisse and Picasso, the history of all the arts demonstrates the same patterns as literature's thematic struggle with itself. Our country's great original art, jazz, is illuminated by what the great creators called "cutting contests," from Louis

Armstrong and Duke Ellington on to the emergence of Charlie Parker's Bop or revisionist jazz.

A literary theme, however authentic, would come to nothing without rhetorical eloquence or mastery of metaphor. But to experience the study of the common places of invention is an apt training in the apprehension of aesthetic value in poetry and in prose.

1

William Butler Yeats's "The Second Coming" is possibly the central poem, in any Western language, of the twentieth century. Nearly a decade into the twenty-first century, it has not lost its relevance. Composed in January 1919, ninety years ago (I write on January 30, 2009), it began as Yeats's exultant outcry in response to the counter-revolutionary invasion of Russia-Poland by the *Freikorps*. This force of German officers and men was organized, paid, and directed by the Allied high command, in an attempt to overthrow Lenin's Russian Revolution. Direct ancestors of Hitler's Nazis, the *Freikorps* were to be thrown back by Leon Trotsky's Red Army. But when Yeats drafted his poem, under its initial title, "The Second Birth," Irish rightists had the mistaken conviction that the Bolsheviks would be defeated by a Prussian mercenary army.

Nothing could be more arbitrary than Yeats's altering this poem's title from "The Second Birth" to "The Second Coming". Yeats believed neither in the First Coming of Christ nor the Second, as prophesied in the Revelation of Saint John the Divine. A Gnostic occultist, Yeats celebrates the Second Birth of the Egyptian Sphinx of Memphis, one-eyed Divinity of the Sun, a shape with lion body and the head of a man. The Greek Sphinx of Thebes, Riddler and Strangler undone by Oedipus, has a woman's head on a lion's body, and is excluded by Yeats from his fierce poem. This Yeatsian Sphinx recalls Shelley's *Ozymandias* and Blake's Urizen, who will emerge from twenty centuries of "stony sleep" until his second birth as fallen man, that is to say, as ourselves.

In his systematic treatise, *A Vision* (1925, 1937), Yeats assimilated "The Second Coming" to his prevalent esotericism:

> At the birth of Christ religious life becomes *primary*, secular life *antithetical*—man gives to Caesar the things that are Caesar's. A *primary* dispensation looking beyond itself towards a transcendent power is dogmatic, leveling, unifying, feminine, humane, peace its means and end; an *antithetical* dispensation obeys imminent power, is expressive, hierarchical, multiple, masculine, harsh, surgical. The approaching *antithetical* influx and that particular *antithetical* dispensation for which the intellectual preparation has begun will reach its complete systematization at that moment when, as I have already shown, the Great Year comes to its intellectual climax. Something of what I have said it must be, the myth declares, for it must reverse our era and resume past eras in itself; what else it must be no man can say, for always at the critical moment the *Thirteenth Cone*, the sphere, the unique intervenes.

> Somewhere in sands of the desert
> A shape with lion body and the head of a man,
> A gaze blank and pitiless as the sun,
> Is moving its slow thighs, while all about it
> Reel shadows of the indignant desert birds.

A strange power is shared by Christ and Sphinx, both revelatory of opposed rebirths. But what is Rebirth? For Yeats it was a repetition of the Romantic incarnation of the poetical Character, from the odes of William Collins on through Blake, Wordsworth, Coleridge, Shelley and Keats. The American heirs of this iconography include Walt Whitman, Hart Crane, and Wallace Stevens.

2

The rebirth of a person as a poet is akin to the emergence of the hero, a transmemberment of the unknowing into tragic knowledge that tends not to be wisdom. Edgar in *King Lear*, punishing himself for having been his half-brother Edmund's gulled victim, descends to the abyss of impersonating a Tom O'Bedlam wandering, mad beggar, and then ascends to the role of an unnamed avenger, who cuts Edmund down. The pattern of rebirth concludes more unhappily in Cormac McCarthy's *Blood Meridian*, where the Kid augments in moral strength until he is able to confront the monstrous Judge Holden, only to be destroyed by the preternatural Judge in an ill-matched contest.

As the heir of Romantic tradition, Yeats gained much from its characteristic substitution of the poetic genius for the saint or hero. The rebirth of anyone as a saint or a hero is no longer rhetorically and spiritually persuasive. Yet the renewal of the self when Walter Whitman, Jr. became the rough Walt captivates us. It does seem now, seventy years after Yeats's death in 1939, that he was the very last poet in the old, high line of Blake, Shelley, and Nietzsche. Reading them, and Yeats as their son, we come to believe in imaginative rebirth, even if the poet of the Second Birth only can attain the apotheosis of being able to assert, as Yeats did: "I shall find the dark grow luminous, the void fruitful when I understand I have nothing, that the ringers in the tower have appointed for the hymen of the soul a passing bell."

THE AENEID, "BOOK 6" (VIRGIL)

❦

"Introduction: The Sixth Book of the *Aeneid*"
by H.E. Butler
in *The Sixth Book of the* Aeneid (1920)

INTRODUCTION

In his introduction to The Sixth Book of the *Aeneid*, H.E. Butler argues that this book "is the very heart of the poem viewed as the National Epic of Rome." Describing how Virgil (or Vergil, his preferred spelling) "for the first time gives a definite picture of the life after death," Butler focuses on renewal and rebirth. As Butler argues, "In the response to the enquiries of his son Anchises sets forth the doctrines of the fiery World-soul that permeates all creation and the wheel of rebirth: how the earth-stained soul must be purified of its sins ere it can come to Elysium, and how thence, all, save a happy few, when they have rolled the wheel of a thousand years, return to live on earth anew." Thus, Butler describes how a journey to the underworld, which he calls a "Nekyia," leads to a symbolic rebirth, not only of Aeneas, but also of Troy in the future greatness of Rome.

∾

Butler, H.E. "Introduction: The Sixth Book of the *Aeneid*." *The Sixth Book of the* Aeneid. Oxford: Blackwell Publishing, 1920. 1–18.

The Sixth Book of the *Aeneid*, together with the Second and Fourth Books, holds a special place in the affections of all lovers of Vergil. Some will prefer the sombre tragedy of Troy, others the pathos of Dido's passion and self-slaughter. But be his personal predilection what it may, for the reader who considers the *Aeneid* as a whole and regards it as something more than a mere literary epic, the Sixth Book must hold a unique place. It is the very heart of the poem viewed as the National Epic of Rome, the *Gesta populi Romani* as it was sometimes known in ancient times.[1] Hitherto the national element has only been shadowed forth, in a few vague prophecies and in the dying curse of Dido. The atmosphere thus far is Greek, and the poem no more than the greatest of Hellenistic epics, while its hero is almost as colourless as the Jason of the Argonautica of Apollonius. But with the Sixth Book comes a change. We are on the soil of Italy in a region familiar and very dear to Vergil's heart. He describes scenes that he has known and loved, and the verse begins to glow with a richness of descriptive colour that it has hitherto only revealed in glimpses. The Sibyl, the guide and instructress of the hero, is a figure closely linked with Roman history, and the position which her dark oracles and the worship of the god whom she serves are to hold at Rome are unconsciously foretold by Aeneas.[2] To enter the world of the dead he needs the talisman of the Golden Bough, which, though its significance and nature are obscure, may well reproduce a picturesque feature of Italian folklore.[3] But ere he can visit the shades of the dead he must be purified from the stain of death, for his comrade Misenus lies a corpse on the seashore. And thus is introduced the description of the familiar rites of funeral, no mere echo of the burials of Hector and Patroclus, but a Roman funeral such as a Roman mourner for his dead could scarce have read without tears.[4] The descent to the underworld takes us for a while into a purely Greek atmosphere. Heroes and heroines, ghosts and goblins, hell and purgatory, the grouping of the spirits, and the doctrine of rebirth, all are Greek.[5] That it should be so is inevitable. Roman beliefs as to the existence of the dead were too impersonal and colourless to permit of poetic treatment, and from the horrors of the Etruscan Hell Vergil rightly stood aloof. Minos[6] alone appears in Roman garb, as the *quaesitor* with the urn whose lot decides the order in which the dead shall appear before him, and, it may be, with a Roman jury of spirits to assist him. And in the list of crimes that

doom to eternal pain there are echoes of the sheer simplicity of early
Roman law and dark hints of more than one unnamed criminal of
Roman history.[7] But when we reach Anchises, the whole spirit of the
poem changes. It is not that we feel an atmosphere of greater beauty;
for the book has been full of mystery, romance, and colour. Suddenly
there dawns on us the vision of the grandeur of Rome, and a deeper
note is sounded than Roman poet had sounded before or should
sound again. One by one the spirits of the unborn pass before us, the
heroes who are to make Rome the mistress of the world. The gallery
of portraits is not complete: the canvas must not be overcrowded,
and the gaps are to be supplemented later in the no less magnificent
description of the Shield of Aeneas.[8] But from the mythical builders
of Latium, through the warrior Romulus, the priestly King Numa,
the founder of the Republic who sacrificed his own sons to the public
weal, to the heroes of recorded history, Fabricius, great amid his
poverty, Regulus at the plough, the conquerors of Greece, and those
who broke the power of Carthage, Fabius who "by his delaying saved
the State," and the Scipios, the thunderbolts of battle, and finally the
two great protagonists of the civil war, every verse is instinct with the
Roman spirit, every name wakes an echo. If a slightly more artificial
note is struck in the vision of Augustus, we must remember that the
poet was on more difficult ground. It is hard to praise the living hero
without exaggeration or artificiality, and the judgment of posterity
may destroy the whole effect of the poet's art. And yet Augustus,
perhaps the most unheroic of heroes and the least of the great men
of history, has stood the test of time not ill. For if in sober truth he
had little of the true hero, he was more than one of the most astute of
statesmen. He had a great and unique work to do, and he knew not
merely how to do that work and to restore the shattered fabric of the
State by the most grandiose compromise of history, but he knew also
how to play the rôle of the second founder of Rome. And that he was
accepted as such we cannot doubt. A world sick for peace and order
may have been uncritical in its judgment of the man who gave it what
its soul desired. Horace and Vergil may have been the most dexterous
of Court poets. But *securus iudicat orbis terrarum* is not an utter lie, and
neither Horace nor Vergil was a fawning fool. Their flattery is inspired
not merely by genius, but by sincerity as well. And if the modern
reader cannot feel the thrill that Vergil's own age must have felt at

the words *hic Caesar et omnis Iuli progenies*[9] introducing the romantic pageant of the new Roman empire, even to-day there is no feeling of anticlimax, though the words follow on the superb picture of Rome of the seven hills, whose realm is conterminous with the bounds of earth, whose spirit with the sky's, a "fresh Cybele"[10] riding in pomp through all the cities of earth, with nations and kings nestling to her breast. It is at worst the apotheosis of Court poetry; but for most students of Roman history it is something more.

The vision draws to its apparent conclusion with the immortal comparison between Greece and Rome. The worldly greatness of Rome has been described; the poet seems to close on a note of moral grandeur.

> *tu regere imperio populos, Romane, memento*
> *(hae tibi erunt artes) pacisque imponere morem,*
> *parcere subiectis et debellare superbos.*[11]

And there, perhaps, the vision was intended to close.[12] But the end is not yet. Marcellus, the victor of Clastidium and Nola, advances bearing the *spolia opima*, and with him moves a younger spirit over-shadowed by the cloud of night, the young Marcellus, son of Octavia, the destined heir of Augustus, who died untimely, ere his promise could become reality, and left the throne of the Cæsars to fall into other and perhaps less worthy hands. Whether, as seems probable, this is a later addition to a book that was virtually complete, cannot be said with certainty. It comes as an unexpected addition (cp. *haec mirantibus addit*), but the addition is effected with consummate art. If the praise of Augustus rings artificial to the ears of some, who cannot render to Cæsar what they cannot conceive to be his due, here all forget that they are reading the utterance of a Court poet. For the pathos is intensely human, and the spirit of the boy who was born for the purple is still duly subordinated to his great ancestor who fulfilled in deeds what destiny did not suffer his descendant to perform.

From this point the book draws to a rapid close and with the magical exit through the gates of sleep Aeneas is once again in upper air, and proceeds without delay upon his appointed task, a man new-nerved for his great task, and, as the subsequent development of his character shows, a hero indeed.

So much for what is the predominant feature of the Sixth *Aeneid*, the feature which gives it special significance and power. But it is not with the Roman element that its greatness ends. Through almost every passage runs that haunting and romantic beauty of which Vergil was a supreme master. The mysterious priestess and seer, the gloomy woods of Avernus, through which the golden bough sends its unearthly shimmer, the dark cave and the solemn sacrifices on Avernus shore, the great invocation to the gods of the underworld and the spirits of the silent dead, all form a noble introduction to the mysterious journey underground, in the dim light as of faint moonbeams "when Jupiter has veiled the heaven with shadow and taken colour from the world."

If the lower world itself is confused for those who desire a region as carefully mapped out and organised as Dante's Inferno, there can be no doubt as to the effectiveness of each successive scene, nor of the grimness of the monsters and goblins that haunt the gates and portals of Hell. Mythology is never an encumbrance; the figures of legend are well chosen, and the poet is at his best in the brief descriptions which he gives of their pains or of their crimes. Above all, the meeting with Dido stands out for its dramatic power, and the figure of the Queen of Carthage standing with "sick and scornful looks averse" spurning the excuses offered by her faithless lover was never surpassed even by Vergil.

Until we reach Elysium there broods over the whole description of the dead an infinite melancholy. Suffering for sin there is, but that is dealt with but briefly. *"Non ragionam di lor, ma guarda e passa."* But the sadness of death is over all, whether Vergil writes of the ghosts, streaming like autumn leaves or migratory birds to the banks of Styx and stretching their hands in yearning for the further shore, or of the crying of dead children, or of the haters of the light, the slayers of themselves who would gladly live their life again, of the sad lovers in the Fields of Grief or of the dead warriors, old friends and old enemies, who press round the hero or fly before him as they fled in life. It is a blend of popular superstition and literary mythology coloured and influenced by Platonic or Orphic eschatology.[13] That there is at times a certain confusion and lack of clearness in the description of this twilight world may be admitted;[14] but there can be no question as to the picturesqueness, the romance and pathos which suffuses the whole.

When Elysium is reached, the poet's grasp of his theme tightens. After an exquisite description of the Elysian fields, full of its happy warriors, its stainless priests, the creators of civilisation and the masters of song, dancing to the music of Orpheus in a land of light, with its own sun and stars, the poet brings us to Anchises watching the spirits of the great unborn. In response to the enquiries of his son Anchises sets forth the doctrines of the fiery World-soul that permeates all creation and of the wheel of rebirth: how the earth-stained soul must be purified of its sins ere it can come to Elysium, and how thence, all, save a happy few, when they have rolled the wheel of a thousand years, return to live on earth anew. Here still the atmosphere is Greek, be the sources, to which we shall return, what they will. And Vergil rises to the height of his beautiful theme and for the first time gives a definite picture of the life after death, though even here there are difficulties and obscurities, which, in the opinion of some, still await solution. But of the nobility of the picture as a whole none have doubted. For pure poetry and exquisite diction it ranks with the very best of Vergil's work.

To ask "How far is it to be taken seriously?" may seem an irreverent question. But it is a real question as to whether Vergil is preaching a doctrine in which he believes or whether he regards it as a *gennaion yendos*. The question admits of no definite answer. It is suggested by Servius that he was an Epicurean,[15] and for that we may compare his panegyric of Lucretius in the Georgics.[16] We are told too that he intended on the completion of the *Aeneid* to devote himself to philosophy.[17] But of his leanings we have no real indication. The teaching of Pythagoras and the Mysteries could not but appeal to him as a poet, and for one who designed to give anything more than a purely mythological description of the underworld, the doctrine of metempsychosis imposed itself as a necessity. And for the poet who, like Vergil, designed to reveal the future in a vision of the unborn heroes of Rome, its adoption became doubly imperative. It is a subject on which it were ill to dogmatise. But the primary purpose of Vergil's Pythagoreanism may well have been artistic rather than religious. That the theologian in Vergil is sunk in the artist there can be little doubt; and it is even possible that his artistic design is the *raison d'être* pure and simple of his eschatology. To some this may seem little short of blasphemy. But it is a possibility which ought not to be ignored.

It is late in the day to belaud the Sixth *Aeneid*. Its beauties are familiar, its praise a commonplace. But it is not faultless. The conception of the underworld is not clear. A certain vagueness in the treatment of such a theme has no doubt some romantic advantages; and that in the present case Vergil maintains a consistent level of romantic beauty is not to be denied. With minor blemishes and inconsistencies we need not concern ourselves here. All great works of fiction are liable to such, even when, unlike the *Aeneid*, they have received the final revision of their authors. But there are certain questions of a more serious nature which inevitably present themselves and require some mention here, although they are discussed in greater detail in the commentary. In the earlier portion of the book there is nothing that calls for serious criticism. There are, it is true, certain indications that the episode of the death and burial of Misenus did not form part of the original draft of the poem, but it has been so skilfully inserted that there can be no certainty on this point.[18] Again, the prophecy of the Sibyl is of a perfunctory nature, telling Aeneas but little that he does not already know, and in any case failing entirely to correspond with the prediction of Helenus that the Sibyl will tell him all that shall befall him in Italy.[19] This is partly to be explained by the fact that the function assigned by Helenus to the Sibyl is actually performed by Anchises, and partly by the fact that a certain vagueness and obscurity is a regular characteristic of ancient oracles, while, further, there is some evidence that the prophecy in its present form is incomplete. But there can be no doubt that the figure of the Sibyl occupies a far less important place in the picture than was designed by Vergil when he wrote the Third Book.

It is, however, when we reach the underworld that the real difficulties begin. The first problem presents itself immediately after the passage of the Styx. What is the position of the spirits who dwell on the further shore, but have no part either in the pains of Tartarus or the joys of Elysium? The souls of young children, of men unjustly condemned to death, of suicides, of hapless lovers and warriors fallen in battle, all dwell in a kind of Limbo, of whose nature and purpose Vergil gives no hint. Recent research has thrown some light upon the matter. Norden[20] proves conclusively that this grouping of spirits was traditional, that the principle underlying this grouping is that all are the souls of those who died untimely, and that there are traces of an eschatological doctrine that such spirits were condemned to wander aimlessly until the term of their natural life was fulfilled. On the other hand, he has failed to provide a key to the passage as it stands. For not merely does Vergil ignore this doctrine, but he is also unsystematic in his grouping, since among his dead lovers and warriors he has placed not a few who, if strict mythological chronology were followed, would by now have completed their term of wandering. Further, Sychæus appears among the victims of love, while Dido might as appropriately have appeared among the suicides. These criticisms may perhaps seem carping. But they are not without their importance when taken into conjunction with Vergil's silence on the cardinal point—namely, the reason for the presence of these spirits in the outer Limbo. It has long been felt by critics that this portion of Vergil's Nekyia was confusing and lacked significance, nor can it be said that the difficulty is removed by Norden's statement of the case. There is but one theory that will clear Vergil of the charge of carelessness and incoherence. We must assume that this portion of the Sixth Book gives the poet's rough draft, and that he had intended to add the necessary explanations which would have rendered the position of these spirits intelligible. It is no defence to say that Vergil, like Plato,[21] may have regarded this doctrine as trivial and unworthy of mention. For Plato its suppression made no difference, since he virtually ignores this group of spirits. But Vergil has not so ignored them; he has described them with some detail and left his reader perplexed as to the reason for their appearance at this point of his story. That there must have been some reason for this grouping is obvious, that the explanation given by Norden is true is highly probable, and that Vergil was aware merely of the traditional location of these spirits, but unaware of the reason, is extremely unlikely. The deep pathos of the lines in which he describes their fate does not excuse or explain away the blemish. The introduction of the spirits of those who died for love or fell in war has obvious advantages of which Vergil makes noble use in the scenes where Aeneas meets Dido and his old friends and comrades of Troy. But that is no reason why we should be left in darkness as to the reason of his meeting them where he does. Nor yet again can the difficulty be met by the plea that he omitted to explain, because he was speaking to those that understood. Roman familiarity with Greek eschatology was not such as to justify the omission to provide a key to the mystery.

So, too, we are perplexed by the introduction of Minos as judging in this mysterious Limbo.[22] There is no question of punishment or reward: the functions of the judge seem to be confined merely to the allotment of a dwelling-place to the souls that come before him. The judgment of the great sinners is left to Rhadamanthus.[23] It will, it is true, involve no inconsistency, if we suppose that Minos merely allots a dwelling-place, while Rhadamanthus assigns punishment for sin. But why is the description of the court of Minos embedded between two groups of those who died untimely? It is no doubt suggested by the mention of those who were unjustly condemned on earth, upon which it follows immediately. The judge of the dead may be conceived as rectifying the miscarriage of justice in the world above. But we should expect Minos to appear as the judge of all the dead, and not to be associated merely with the spirits of those who dwell in Limbo. Plead as we may, the whole situation is left obscure by the position of the passage, the lack of explanation, and the unsystematic development of the subject. We are once more driven to the theory that the passage as it stands is in the rough. It may even be doubted whether the lines dealing with Minos are in the actual position which the poet designed them ultimately to occupy. But no remedy is possible. The mischief was done by Vergil's own untimely death, and there is no reason to suppose that any blame attaches to his editors, Varius and Tucca.

Nor is this the only sign of such lack of completion. It is hard to believe that Vergil's description of the sinners in Tartarus has come down to us in what he intended to be its final form. The passage begins with a description of some of the more striking examples of punishment for great sin.[24] In this portion the only indication of lack of completion is the attribution to Ixion and Pirithous of punishments quite other than those usually assigned to them, though familiar in connexion with other sinners.[25] That this is due to textual corruption is highly improbable, while it is not likely, in view of Vergil's treatment of Ixion in the fourth Georgic, in a passage written in all probability at no very distant date from the present,[26] that he had in his mind other versions of the legend. The most probable explanation is that a line referring to Tantalus and others should have preceded the description of the penalty, but that the poet had not written the required line or lines in a form that satisfied him at the time of his death. This is, however, a less serious problem than that which follows hard upon its heels. The Sibyl proceeds to mention certain classes of criminal without any reference to mythology, those that in life hated their brethren or struck their parents, played their clients false or brooded miser-like over their gold and gave no share to their kin, adulterers slain for their sin, and those that waged impious warfare or armed slaves against their masters.[27] Then comes a short list of typical penalties,[28] which is followed once again by a short list of typical criminals—traitors who enslaved their country, corrupt politicians, and those guilty of incest.[29] Now, although there was no need for Vergil to give an exhaustive list of crimes or punishments for crime, the order seems confused and the selection of crimes somewhat casual. The text as it stands before us, is exactly what we should expect to arise if the poet had written different portions of the passage at different times[30] with a view to welding them into a compact and artistic whole. Death prevented this, and his editors did their best to give the passage a form as little unsatisfactory as possible. They did their work with skill and discretion, but there is still a lack of organisation and unity about the passage as it stands.

The remainder of the book stands on a different footing. With the exception of the fact that the vision of Cæsar of Pompey is unfinished, as the half-line, *proice tela manu, sanguis meus*,[31] shows, and not to speak of the fact that a little greater elaboration of so important a theme might seem to be desirable, there is nothing to lead us to suppose that we have not Vergil's last word. Difficulties there are, but none of them insuperable. We can form no clear idea as to what Vergil means by the "fields of air,"[32] as a description of Elysium, and the exact significance of the hero's exit by the dream-gate of ivory[33] has long been a problem to Vergilian critics. Both may be relics of some earlier design to represent the vision of the world of spirits in the form of a dream, and the spirits of the blest may in that scheme have been represented, like the heroes of the Somnium Scipionis, as dwelling in the highest heavens. But that must be a matter for conjecture and, whatever explanation we adopt, we can scarcely regard the presence of these passages as indicating lack of completion. So, too, the exquisite Marcellus episode reveals certain indications of being a later addition, but its insertion has been accomplished with such skill that the voice of criticism must be silent. More serious is the well-known difficulty presented by the poet's account of the doctrine of metempsychosis. But here Norden[34] has provided a reasonable solution of the difficulty. The great bulk of the spirits of Elysium return to earth after they "have rolled the wheel of a *thousand* years." The "few who abide in the happy fields" are those who for their virtue are spared the travail of rebirth: they dwell in bliss, each year removing the stains of earth until the "orb of time" is complete, and after the passage of *ten thousand* years are restored to the pure ethereal being that once was theirs, before they taught themselves to

> fashion aught
> But a pure celestial thought.

Of the ultimate destiny of the happy spirit, become "all fire, all air," Vergil says nothing, whether it remains in perfection of bliss in the paradise where it now dwells, or is caught up into the empyrean and reabsorbed into the divine fire.[35] It was not necessary that he should say more: he is poet, not mystagogue, and his main design is to write the Epic of the Roman people. Such vagueness and obscurity as there is in his exposition of the doctrine of rebirth is not of so serious a nature that it need trouble us, and if it be urged that an exact parallel for Norden's interpretation is not forthcoming, it is sufficiently near the Pythagorean doctrines as set forth by Plato and the later syncretistic school of Stoics to make but small demand upon our faith. It is always possible that the poet's final revision would have produced a clearer picture. But there is no need to postulate the necessity of such revision. For whatever view we take of Vergil's Nekyia, on one point all critics will be agreed, that there is but one other vision to be compared with it, the Divina Commedia of Dante, who, while following other methods and aiming at an accuracy of detail, topographical and otherwise, such as his predecessor never contemplated, paid the Sixth *Aeneid* the noblest of all tributes by choosing Vergil for his guide through the circles of the Inferno. Whatever its blemishes and obscurities, real or imaginary, the Sixth *Aeneid* is unique, and even although criticism may be a labour of love and a tribute of admiration, the critic cannot escape the feeling that he does it wrong, "being so majestical," by subjecting it to such analysis.

NOTES

1. Serv. ad Aen. 6. 752.
2. See notes on 69, 71.
3. See notes on 141, 204.
4. See notes on 212–232.
5. See Introd., p. 21 *ff.*
6. See notes on 431–4 and p. 13.
7. See notes on 612, 613 and 621, 622.
8. 8. 626 to end.
9. 789.
10. 785.
11. 851 *sqq.*
12. See Sabbadini, *Aeneis IV., V., VI.*, Introd. xxiii, xxiv.
13. See Introd., p. 19 *ff.*
14. See Introd., p. 12 *ff.*
15. Serv. ad Aen. 6. 264. Ecl. 6. 13.
16. 2. 490.
17. Sueton., *Vit. Verg.* 35.
18. See note on l. 149, Sabbadini, *Aeneis IV., V., VI.*, p. xvii.
19. 3. 440–462; 6. 83–97, 890–2; Introd., §3.
20. Norden, *VI. Aeneis*, Introd., pp. 10 *sqq.* See 426–547, Introductory Note.
21. Rep. 10-615 C.
22. 431 *sqq.*
23. 566.
24. 580.
25. 601–607.
26. See 305 note.
27. 608–614.
28. 615–620.
29. 621–624.
30. See Introd., §3, A.
31. 835.
32. 887.
33. 893 *sqq.*
34. Norden, pp. 16 *sqq.* See 733–751, Introductory Note.
35. But cp. Georg. 4, 223.

THE AWAKENING
(KATE CHOPIN)

❧ ❧

"Renewal and Rebirth in Kate Chopin's *The Awakening*"
by Robert C. Evans,
University of Auburn at Montgomery

As its title suggests, Kate Chopin's novel *The Awakening* is a book about renewal and rebirth. Edna Pontellier, its central character, is a young wife and mother whose life and outlook transform while she spends a summer vacation at Grand Isle, a resort off the coast of Louisiana, not far from New Orleans. During that vacation, she meets Robert Lebrun, an attractive and attentive young man whose mother owns the resort where Edna is staying with her middle-aged husband, Léonce, a staid and conventional businessman, and their two small boys. Thanks to her contact with Robert and also to the influence of her changed surroundings (including, especially, the impact of the seductively beautiful ocean), Edna begins to realize how dissatisfied she has become with her married life, which she finds increasingly predictable, constraining, and oppressive. With Robert's help she learns to swim, and as she finds herself more and more attracted to him, she also becomes more and more frustrated with—and resistant to—Léonce's influence on her existence. Just as she begins to realize that she has fallen in love with Robert, however, he departs abruptly for Mexico. He fears his own deepening feelings for her and the destructive impact that his growing closeness to Edna may have on her relations with her husband and children.

Edna's dissatisfaction with her old way of life, however, continues to grow even after Robert leaves and she returns to New Orleans with Léonce and their boys. She begins to neglect her social obligations, she devotes herself increasingly to her interest in painting, and she grows obviously distant from Léonce, both emotionally and sexually. When he departs for New York City on an extended business trip, she not only begins an affair with a notorious rake named Alcée Arobin but also moves out of the imposing home she and Léonce have shared. Establishing herself in a small cottage nearby, she enjoys her newfound independence but also keenly regrets Robert's absence. When she unexpectedly discovers him in New Orleans one day, they briefly resume their earlier emotional intimacy. When Robert once again quickly departs because he is convinced that Edna can never be his wife, Edna impulsively returns to Grand Isle, walks down to the beach, strips off her clothes, and swims into the Gulf of Mexico, from which she never emerges.

Clearly Edna, in some senses, is renewed and reborn during the course of this novel, but just as clearly her renewal and rebirth are complicated and perhaps even ironic. Edna, after all, is either a drowning victim or a woman who commits suicide; thus whatever "renewal" she undergoes leads to her physical destruction, and whatever "rebirth" she enjoys also results in her literal death. The final chapter of the book, in fact, has always been highly controversial; many of Chopin's contemporaries condemned the ending as morally scandalous, and more recent critics have often strongly disagreed about the significance of Edna's death. At the end of the book, many questions remain unanswered: Is Edna a weak-willed, deluded, and even selfish woman who ignores the real virtues of her husband while also neglecting her genuine obligations to her children in order to pursue a romantic fantasy that leads to pointless self-destruction? Is Edna a courageous individualist who refuses to be bound by society's strictures and whose death is a valuable affirmation of individual freedom? Is Edna, in short, genuinely renewed and reborn in spite of (and perhaps even through) her eventual death, or is her death merely the inevitable culmination of a life that has grown increasingly foolish, selfish, and self-deceived? Does Edna undergo a metaphorical rebirth at the end of the book, or does her watery demise abort any potential rebirth? Such difficult questions without easy answers comprise great works of art.

The book is compelling in part because it is so morally and artistically complex, and Edna's character, like the significance of the final chapter, is especially difficult to interpret. In one passage after another related to Edna's transformation, Chopin gives us language open to various understandings and makes meaning often hard to pin down. Edna can be—and has been—interpreted either as a daring seeker of existential freedom or as an increasingly self-centered romantic whose death is the predictable result of a lifelong indulgence in unrealistic and irresponsible fantasies. Chopin's subtle, frequently ambiguous language often makes it difficult to decide how, exactly, to respond to Edna's thoughts, feelings, and behavior; this sort of ambiguity helps make the novel a work of art rather than a simple propagandistic tract for either side of the moral debate the book has inspired.

One of the earliest passages showing Edna's growing dissatisfaction with her life is in Chapter 3. Léonce has just come back to their resort cottage after a night of gambling with his friends, and he awakens Edna. Annoyed that the still-drowsy Edna seems to pay him little attention, he accuses her of neglecting the health of one of their boys, who Léonce claims is suffering from a fever. After rising from bed and assuring herself that their son is fine, Edna is suddenly left alone with her thoughts and emotions (since Léonce has already fallen asleep):

> An indescribable oppression, which seemed to generate in some unfamiliar part of her consciousness, filled her whole being with a vague anguish. It was like a shadow, like a mist passing across her soul's summer day. It was strange and unfamiliar; it was a mood. She did not sit there inwardly upbraiding her husband, lamenting at Fate, which had directed her footsteps to the path which they had taken. She was just having a good cry to herself. (9)

Most readers will likely sympathize with Edna at this point in the book. Léonce's behavior *has* just been boorish and thoughtless, and few people would begrudge Edna her feelings of frustration and annoyance. Admittedly, Chopin does imply here that Edna seems to lack complete self-understanding and may be subject to shifting moods, but few people are immune to these shortcomings, and so, at this point in the text, Edna's reactions seem unobjectionable and are hardly extraordinary. Already, though, Chopin has begun to prepare us for the apparent death of Edna's old self and the birth of her new persona.

This emphasis on Edna's transformation becomes especially apparent near the close of Chapter 6, in paragraphs that are among the most important in the entire book:

> In short, Mrs. Pontellier was beginning to realize her position in the universe as a human being, and to recognize her relations as an individual to the world within and about her. This may seem like a ponderous weight of wisdom to descend upon the soul of a young woman of twenty-eight—perhaps more wisdom than the Holy Ghost is usually pleased to vouchsafe to any woman.
>
> But the beginning of things, of a world especially, is necessarily vague, tangled, chaotic, and exceedingly disturbing. How few of us ever emerge from such beginning! How many souls perish in its tumult! (16)

The effect—or, rather, the *effects*—of these paragraphs cannot easily be assessed or described. At first Chopin seems to credit Edna with insight and understanding: She begins to "realize" and "recognize" her status in life, but Chopin never makes clear what that status is or how Edna understands it. The language of realization and recognition then gives way to phrasing that suggests revelation. With words that recall the biblical annunciation, in which the Virgin Mary is told that she has become mysteriously pregnant with her own future savior, Chopin implies that Edna has been granted a special "wisdom." However, the effect of the phrasing is complicated since the narrator describes this "wisdom" as resembling a "ponderous weight." Thus, on the one hand Chopin seems to suggest that Edna has been blessed, but on the other she implies that the revelation may prove to be a crushing burden. Mary's annunciation was a joyous event, but Edna's may not be—partly (it is implied) because Edna, unlike Mary, may be incapable of bearing the weight that is descending upon her. This ominous undercurrent is then high-lighted and emphasized in the next paragraph, where each sentence becomes increasingly troublesome and literally "disturbing." These two paragraphs perfectly epitomize the method of this entire ambiguous, ambivalent novel: Realization and recognition, which at first seem like things to be celebrated, are later treated as poten-tially dangerous threats. Like childbirth itself, the process of Edna's rebirth—if that is what is indeed has begun to occur—will not be an easy one. It may produce something valuable and precious, but it will almost certainly involve pain and may result in serious risk or even death. Chopin could easily have written a more cheery, opti-mistic book, just as she could easily have written one more full of obviously heavy gloom. Instead, she chose the more difficult path of trying to portray both the promise and the risks as well as the rewards and the costs of Edna's transformation.

Chopin even implies, at various points, that Edna is not truly being reborn or renewed at all but may instead merely be repeating tired, stale patterns from her past. We discover in Chapter 7, for instance, that as a young girl and adolescent Edna had a habit of becoming infatuated with seemingly attractive but ultimately unattainable men. Once, for instance, she became "passionately enamored of a dignified and sad-eyed cavalry officer who visited her father in Kentucky," but he soon "melted imperceptibly out of her existence" (20). At another time, "her affections were deeply engaged by a young gentleman who visited a lady on a neighboring plantation," but the "realization" (an interesting word) that Edna meant "nothing, nothing, nothing to the engaged young man was a bitter affliction to her," so that "he, too, went the way of dreams" (20). The exaggerated and repetitious language ("nothing, nothing, nothing") suggests Edna's literal immaturity at that time, but Chopin notes that Edna had become:

> a grown young woman when she was overtaken by what she supposed to be the climax of her fate. It was when the face and figure of a great tragedian began to haunt her imagination and stir her senses. The persistence of the infatuation lent it an aspect of genuineness. The hopelessness of it colored it with the lofty tunes of a great passion.

Edna kept a framed picture of this actor on her desk, and when "alone she sometimes picked it up and kissed the cold glass passionately" (21). It was not long, though, "before the tragedian had gone to join the cavalry officer and the engaged young man and a few others; and Edna found herself face to face with realities" (21). By this time she had married Léonce Pontellier, partly because "his absolute devotion flattered her" (21), and partly to spite her father and elder sister, who disapproved of any alliance with a Catholic. Both in her multiple infatuations, then, as well as in her marriage, Edna had been motivated mainly by romantic impulsiveness and a desire to have her own way.

Are her growing feelings for Robert any different? Is Edna, in other words, being reborn and renewed through her increasing attachment to Robert, or is she merely reverting to earlier patterns of thought, emotion, and behavior? As usual, Chopin provides evidence that can be understood in both ways, and sometimes it is the same evidence that can thus be diversely interpreted. At one point, for instance, as Edna starts to assert her independence from Léonce in an increasingly forthright manner, the narrator notes that Edna nevertheless "began to feel like one who awakens gradually out of a dream, a delicious, grotesque, impossible dream, to feel again the realities pressing into her soul" (36). The "dream" mentioned here is, presumably, the dream of a life free from her current marital and maternal responsibilities—the dream of a life in which she might enjoy, untrammeled and unhindered, her newfound relationship with Robert. Yet that dream, however "delicious" it may momentarily appear to her, also seems "grotesque" and "impossible." Thus, while the language of awakening is often used in this novel to describe a rebirth to the possibility of a new kind of life, here that same term is used to describe an awakening to harsh and inescapable "realities." The passage is therefore typical of the way Chopin provides multiple and often conflicting perspectives on Edna's supposed rebirth and renewal through her developing relationship with Robert.

When Robert suddenly announces his intention to leave Grand Isle—and, indeed, to leave even New Orleans itself—in order to venture off to Mexico, Edna is devastated: For the first time she recognized anew the symptoms of infatuation which she had felt incipiently as a child, as a girl in her earliest teens, and later as a young woman. The recognition did not lessen the reality, the poignancy of the revelation by any suggestion or promise of instability. The past was nothing to her; offered no lesson which she was willing to heed. The future was a mystery which she never attempted to penetrate. The present alone was significant; was hers, to torture her as it was doing then with the biting conviction that she had lost that which she had held, that she had been denied that which her impassioned, newly awakened being demanded. (51)

Edna knows that at this point she may have fallen into a pattern in her relationship with Robert. This pattern merely replicates the futile infatuations of her youth; this awareness offers "no lesson which she *was willing* to heed" (italics added). She feels that her "being" has been "newly awakened," but this supposed awakening may simply be a reversion to patterns that have led nowhere (and to nothing) in the past. If genuine rebirth implies a true openness to profound change and a sincere willingness to grow and develop, this passage suggests that Edna is awakening in some ways while remaining asleep (or confined to the past) in others. Here as so often in this novel, Chopin's phrasing cuts both ways.

No wonder Léonce is confused by Edna! Interpreting her changes is at least as hard for him as it is for Chopin's readers. Thus the narrator notes that once the couple has returned to New Orleans and once Edna has begun to reject the patterns of respectable middle-class behavior that previously defined her life, it "sometimes entered Mr. Pontellier's mind to wonder if his wife were not growing a little unbalanced mentally. He could plainly see that she was not herself. That is, he could not see that she was becoming herself and daily casting aside that fictitious self which we assume like a garment with which to appear before the world" (64). At first glance this passage seems typically double-edged ("He could plainly see. . . . That is, he could not see"), but the phrasing is even more complicated, on reflection, than it appears on an initial reading. Edna is, in fact, becoming "unbalanced mentally," at least by the standards of the "normal" world of her day; yet what does it mean, precisely, to say that she is also "becoming herself"? Is she achieving a deeper and more admirable integrity? Is she undergoing the sort of rebirth, renewal, and transformation we should respect and celebrate? Or is she simply returning to the kind of immature, self-indulgent "self" she had once been before her marriage to Léonce led her to adopt her current "fictitious self?" And was that earlier "self" any more "real" or any more commendable than the self she is now "casting aside"? At first glance, this passage seems to critique Léonce's shortsightedness and to endorse Edna's transformation, but, on second or third glance, the significance of the passage is far less clear.

Few, if any, of the other characters in the novel are wholly sympathetic to the changes Edna begins to exhibit. Certainly Léonce is not, but his skepticism can partly be discounted because those changes challenge his own self-interests and his desire for control. (Even Léonce, however, is hardly a simple villain; Chopin could easily have made him a far less attractive character than he really is.) Edna's two most important women friends—Adèle Ratignolle (a conventional but intelligent "mother-woman" [10]) and Mademoiselle Reisz (an unconventional and often shrewdly perceptive artist)—both express misgivings of one sort or another about Edna's supposed rebirth. Even Robert, the man who ignites the transformation, twice turns away from the changes he has helped unleash. Practically the only character in the book who seems entirely pleased by Edna's new self is Alcée Arobin, the local playboy who obviously stands to benefit sexually from her newfound freedom from the straitlaced standards of middle-class morality. Yet even Edna realizes that Alcée does not truly love her, nor does she even truly love him; their relationship is rooted in mere physical desire, and Edna longs for something deeper—something more real, more meaningful, and more permanent.

The one character in the novel who seems truly capable of understanding, appreciating, and nurturing the sort of rebirth Edna desires, Doctor Mandelet, the elderly family physician, functions partly as a general practitioner, partly as a family psychologist or counselor, and partly—and this fact is especially significant—as an obstetrician. Mandelet supervises the delivery of Adèle Ratignolle's latest child near the end of the novel, and Mandelet first seems to intuit the profound alterations that appear to be taking place in Edna. He notes "a subtle change which had transformed her from the listless woman he had known into a being who, for the moment, seemed palpitant with the forces of life" (77). Mandelet also first suspects (accurately, as it turns out) that Edna's latest infatuation is with Alcée Arobin (79). Finally, Mandelet, as the novel draws to a close and after he has assisted in the birth of Adèle's newest baby, also offers to assist in the safe, supervised rebirth of Edna's personality:

> "It seems to me, my dear child," said the Doctor at parting, holding [Edna's] hand, "you seem to me to be in trouble. I am not going to ask for your confidence. I will only say that if ever you feel moved to give it to me, perhaps I might help you. I know I would understand, and I tell you there are not many who would—not many, my dear." (123)

He invites Edna to "come and see [him] soon," and he promises her that "We will talk of things you never dreamt of talking about before" (123–24). Edna, however, refuses both his invitation and his offer, not only then but also later. She explicitly justifies these refusals: "I don't want anything but my own way. That is wanting a good deal, of course, when you have to trample upon the lives, the hearts, the prejudices of others—but no matter" (123). Of course, Chopin immediately (and typically) complicates the impact of this apparently selfish statement by having Edna instantly add that she nonetheless doesn't "want to trample upon the little lives" (123). Yet the fact remains that Edna explicitly rejects the assistance of the one character in the book who possesses the sort of intelligence, insight, and compassion that might have helped her achieve a successful rebirth, a genuine awakening. And she rejects his offer of help because she doesn't "want anything but [her] own way." One response to this exchange with Mandelet, therefore, is to argue that Edna continues to be stuck—and indeed *wants* to be stuck—in the immature patterns of her youth. Mandelet might have been able to assist her in making a smooth transition to a new kind of life or at least to a new kind of self-understanding. Mandelet has the depth of experience, the breadth of wisdom, and the sort of tolerance and sympathy that might have made it possible for Edna to be reborn and awakened without suffering a disastrous miscarriage. Edna, though, rejects his offer of help, and, by rejecting that offer, she also rejects the one obvious and realistic possibility that she might have achieved genuine rebirth and renewal.

Without Mandelet's assistance (or, indeed, assistance from anyone, which she never seeks), Edna is unprepared to cope with the shock she discovers when she returns to her little cottage: Robert, to whom she has recently pledged undying love, has disappeared again, leaving a brief note that simply reads, "I love you. Good-by—because I love you" (124). It was only hours earlier that Edna had declared to him, "I love you . . . only you; no one but you. It was you who awoke me last summer out of a life-long stupid dream" (120). The extravagance of her language, however, suggests once more the possibility that Edna may not have truly awakened from the kind of romantic infatuation that had bedeviled her youth. Indeed, when Edna often declares herself fully awake and completely changed we must wonder most intensely if she may still be in the grip of old delusions. The same kind of paradox may be involved in Chopin's description of Edna's response to Robert's note: "She did not sleep. She did not go to bed. The lamp sputtered and went out. She was still awake in the morning" (124). Physically Edna is indeed still awake, but her restless night has probably made her less truly awake—less fully alert—than she needs to be at this crucial juncture in her life. She has stayed awake physically, but that very wakefulness has left her mentally (and perhaps morally) clouded.

Thus, when Edna shows up unexpectedly at Grand Isle the next day, the narrator reports that she "walked on down to the beach rather mechanically, not noticing anything special except that the sun was hot. She was not dwelling upon any particular train of thought. She had done all the thinking which was necessary after Robert went away, when she lay awake upon the sofa till morning" (126). Here, as so often elsewhere, however, the phrasing seems fundamentally ambiguous. Has Edna *really* done "*all* the thinking which was *necessary*" (italics added)? Alternatively, does this very phrasing invite us to consider the possibility that she has failed to engage in deep, considered thought? Perhaps she has done only the thinking that she cared to do or was capable of doing. In any case, what conclusions has "all" her "thinking" led her to? Is she planning to commit suicide? Shortly before heading to the beach, she had told Victor Lebrun (Robert's brother) that she was very hungry, and she had promised to return from her swim "before dinner" (126). Were these statements a consciously planned ruse, or does Edna not plan to kill herself? Does she, perhaps, merely succumb to physical and mental exhaustion after she has swum out too far to return to shore? Like so much else in this book, the final paragraphs seem ultimately inscrutable: Edna's death can be interpreted either as a deliberate act or as an unfortunate accident, and the very same evidence can be used to support either argument. Likewise, her death can be viewed either as a defeat (as the end of any possibility of genuine renewal and rebirth) or as a victory (as the very achievement of a symbolic renewal and rebirth through a grand assertion of metaphysical freedom). It is part of the artistic greatness of *The Awakening* that Chopin, by opening up the possibility of both of these interpretations, finally sanctions neither. The novel is at least as puzzling and provocative in its final paragraphs as it has been anywhere else, and so we can never, ultimately, be sure whether Edna, as the novel ends, is reborn or merely stillborn.

WORKS CITED OR CONSULTED

Anastasopoulou, Maria. "Rites of Passage in Kate Chopin's *The Awakening*." *Southern Literary Journal* 23.2 (1991): 19–30.

Chopin, Kate. *The Awakening and Other Stories*. Ed. Pamela Knights. Oxford: Oxford UP, 2000.

Green, Suzanne Disheroon and David J. Caudle. *Kate Chopin: An Annotated Bibliography of Critical Works*. Westport, Conn.: Greenwood, 1999.

Lippincott, Gail. "Thirty-Nine Weeks: Pregnancy and Birth Imagery in Kate Chopin's *The Awakening*." *This Giving Birth: Pregnancy and Childbirth in American Women's Writing*. Ed. Julie Tharp and Susan MacCallum-Whitcomb. Bowling Green, Ohio: Popular, 2000. 55–66.

Portales, Marco A. "The Characterization of Edna Pontellier and the Conclusion of Kate Chopin's *The Awakening*." *Southern Studies* 20.4 (1981): 427–36.

Roscher, Marina L. "The Suicide of Edna Pontellier: An Ambiguous Ending?" *Southern Studies* 23.3 (1984): 289–98.

BELOVED
(TONI MORRISON)

"Renewal and Rebirth
in Toni Morrison's *Beloved*"
by Blake G. Hobby,
the University of North Carolina at Asheville

With the lyrical lines, "RAINWATER held on to pine needles for dear life and Beloved could not take her eyes off Sethe," Beloved, a young black woman, emerges out of water, breathing heavily as would an asthmatic, bearing "new skin, lineless and smooth," and tasting the sweetness of Sethe's stories (51). She craves them, all the while saying to her: "Tell me your diamonds" (58). Beloved lives on memories, the dark, rough images of the past Sethe buries like coals. These same memories form the novel's pain and beauty, each bound together in a kind of sublime paradox. As she tells Beloved "her diamonds," Sethe unbraids her daughter Denver's hair, preparing to run her comb through it. Denver complains, "It hurts," but Sethe immediately responds, "Comb it every day, it won't" (60). Here the combing of hair is an extended metaphor, which describes a way that memory functions in Morrison's text. Although Sethe initially gives advice she herself cannot heed, this method of dealing with the past eventually leads to her renewal. She, with the help of a tortured friend of the past, Paul D, and thirty gospel-singing women, weeds out tangled, intolerable memories and reshapes them. Surrounded by a community of fellow journeyers whose pasts are equally unbearable, reconnected with their sense of the mythic past, and swallowed in their love, Sethe heals. She is reborn.

Sethe and her children escape to Cincinnati, where they live with Sethe's mother-in-law at 124 Bluestone Road, a refuge from enslavement. Yet, this way station soon becomes the site of an apocalyptic nightmare. Four men arrive, ready to claim the slave master's "property" and return Sethe and her children to "Sweet Home," a place neither sweet nor nurturing, a place of ritualistic humiliation and degradation. Sethe, in a courageous act, runs with her children to a shed behind the house of her mother-in-law and attacks her "already crawling baby," willing to kill her own children than have them return to slavery. Infanticide haunts Sethe and all the African-American community in Cincinnati. It serves as a metaphor for the unspeakable past that they have endured, the atavistic horrors experienced by "60 million and more" given in the first of the book's two epigraphs. Sethe's act pulls her out of life. It isolates her and her youngest daughter Denver; drives away her two sons, Howard and Bugler; and causes her preaching, "heart-loving" mother-in-law, Baby Suggs, to give up and go to bed, where Suggs contemplates the spectrum of life, never reaching the horrible, pain-filled "red" of the past.

Beloved focuses on the importance of memory in reconstructing the present for the African-American community living in Ohio. While they live in a free North after the Emancipation Proclamation, they still face discrimination. *Beloved* demands from the first page an openness that is much like religious faith, asking readers to believe in the supernatural and the fantastic, "suspending disbelief" as Coleridge might say. Morrison evokes a religious sense with the novel's second epigram, a quote from Paul's letter to the Romans: "I will call them my people, which were not my people; and her beloved, which was not beloved" (Romans 9:25). By using this well-known Romans passage, Morrison frames *Beloved* within the divine plan that Paul describes. According to Paul, God planned for Israel, the "beloved" that was not beloved, to undergo catastrophic trials as part of a greater plan. His plan includes being rejected and experiencing suffering, pain, and alienation. Yet, all of Israel's travail is part of a purposeful divine schema imperceptible to human beings, one that encompasses strife and struggle. Being the chosen of Yahweh means submitting to sufferings that "are not worth comparing with the glory that is to be revealed" (Romans 8:19). Not only does Yahweh call for his chosen people to submit to hardships, but also he brings into being a disordered world in which all "Creation groans in travail," a frail, weakened world helped at every turn by the spirit "in whom [human beings] live and move and have [their] being" (Acts 17:28). In this, the novel's second epigraph, Morrison provides a religious context for the work, asking the reader to make an imaginative leap that is like faith and providing a providential sense of history that embraces, much in the tradition of the literature of antiquity, the transformative power of suffering.

Sethe works to "beat back the past" (73), doing anything she can to keep Denver from knowing what the novel's epilogue refers to as "not a story to pass on" (274–275). Constantly plagued by images of Sweet Home that she cannot control, she envisions the future as "a matter of keeping the past at bay" (42). She works hard "to remember close to nothing," but unfortunately "her brain [is] devious," bringing her memories of Sweet Home "rolling, rolling, rolling out before her eyes, and although there was not a leaf on that farm that did not want to make her want to scream, it rolled itself out before her in shameless beauty" (6). Sweet Home "comes back whether [she] want[s] it to or not" (14). These mind pictures created by "rememory," as Sethe puts it, render the past real, more real than the present. Sethe knows that if she ever touches them life will never be the same. She speaks of her "rememory" with Denver:

> "I was talking about time. It's so hard for me to believe in it. Some things go. Pass on. Some things just stay. I used to think it was my rememory. You know. Some things you forget. Other things you never do. But it's not. Places, places are still there. If a house burns down, it's gone, but the place—the picture of it—stays, and not just in my rememory, but out there, in the world. What I remember is a picture floating around out there outside my head. I mean, even if I don't think it, even if I die, the picture of what I did, or knew, or saw is still out there. Right in the place where it happened." (35–6)

Sethe shuns the thought pictures that enter her mind. She knows that they are dangerous and may cause the past to be repeated; yet,

her rememory cannot be contained. Thus, although the novel presents the dangers of remembering, it also demonstrates that the past
must be addressed and the subconscious mind will not allow it to be
repressed.

The trees of Sweet Home, from which African Americans have
been lynched, make Sethe want to scream. She, therefore, banishes
from the present not only the pain brought with memory but all the
past joy she has experienced. In a vain attempt to avoid pain, Sethe
cannot acknowledge the beauty of Sweet Home. Isolated, cut off
from anyone except for Denver, and hardened by years of pain, Sethe
cannot feel. She is "the one who never looked away, who when a man
got stomped to death by a mare right in front of Sawyer's restaurant
did not look away; and when a sow began eating her own litter did not
look away then either" (12). She continues to stare wide-eyed at the
hanging, mutilated body of her dead mother. She attacks the present
with the same determination and strength that she summons when
the "baby's spirit" slams "Here Boy," the family pet, "into the wall
hard enough to break two of his legs and dislocate his eye, so hard
he went into convulsions and chewed up his tongue." Sethe responds
with her "hammer healing," knocking "the dog unconscious, wip[ing]
away the blood and saliva, push[ing] his eye back in his head, and
set[ting] his bones" (12). Sethe dares not touch what her rememory
brings her and tells Denver repeatedly, "you can't never go there" (36).
Sethe sees Denver as a seed of hope for the future that is "charmed," a
magical baby who avoids the jail rats that bite "everything in there but
her" (41). However, she still keeps the past from Denver. Sethe fails to
see that Denver's identity and growth are bound with her own story.
Sethe continues to avoid her rememory until two important events
occur: 1) Paul D arrives at 124 Bluestone Road, and 2) "Beloved"
appears—a mystical incarnation with baby-like skin and a scarred face
who craves sweets and lives on stories. Through Paul D and Beloved,
Sethe faces what she could not face before.

In many ways, Paul and Sethe are "mirror reflections." Paul D blots
out the memory of the 83 days spent in boxed torture, just as Sethe
cannot face the memory of being tortured by Schoolteacher's nephews
and the memory of killing her own child. Paul D suppresses memories
of "Alfred, Georgia, Sixo, Schoolteacher, Halle, his brothers, Sethe,
Mister, the taste of iron, the sight of butter, the smell of hickory,

notebook paper, one by one into the tobacco tin lodged in his chest" where "nothing in this world could pry it open," but, like Sethe, he also closes himself off (113). As Paul D stands behind Sethe while she cooks, he caresses the scars on her back that metaphorically represent both of their memories and past: unbearable wounds that they both cannot see and feel. He refuses, like Sethe, to "go inside" (46).

Central to Morrison's depiction of the healing of memory is the power of language, as she states in her 1993 Nobel lecture: "Language alone protects us from the scariness of things with no names" (28). Morrison speaks of language as the power to bring things into being, an influence of energy on ignorance and the unknown. Thus Amy, a poor, white runaway slave girl, looks at Sethe's back scarring and names her painful disfigurement a "chokeberry tree," a symbolic action that in the novel becomes a metaphor for reshaping the past (16). Amy names what Sethe cannot face. Amy also reshapes the past and, in an act of the imagination, enables Sethe to move back into being alive. While massaging the swollen feet of the pregnant Sethe, Amy utters a phrase that reverberates throughout the novel: "Anything dead coming back to life hurts" (35). The foot massage represents the way in which memory must be addressed. Amy's poetic renaming of Sethe's scarring and pronouncements about pain ring out Morrison's credo throughout the novel to "identify that which is useful from the past and that which ought to be discarded . . . [to] make it possible to prepare for the present and live it out . . . not by avoiding problems and contradictions but by examining them" ("Memory, Creation, and Writing"). Furthermore, Amy's healing words and actions mirror the novel's closing action, in which Paul D bathes Sethe in sections, putting the broken pieces of her pain-filled past together again.

Similarly, Sixo is another poetic presence in the novel. He turns potato cooking into an art form, working with the blandest of all foods and creating something exciting that elevates an impoverished slave meal to a dignified feast. He takes the determined, given reality and creates. Additionally, he reverences the past as he bows before the presences at "Redman Place," calling upon Native American spirits to approve his lovemaking with the Thirty-Mile Woman. A similar poetic gesture occurs at the end of Chapter 3 when Halle and Seth make love in the cornfield while all the men of Sweet Home, "erect as dogs," watch "the corn stalks dance at noon." Morrison ends this lyrical passage with sexually explicit language:

> The pulling down of the tight sheath, the ripping sound always convinced her it hurt.
>
> As soon as one strip of husk was down, the rest obeyed and the ear yielded up to him its shy rows, exposed at last. How loose the silk. How quick the jailed-up flavor ran free.
>
> No matter what all your teeth and wet fingers anticipated, there was no accounting for the way that simple joy could shake you.
>
> How loose the silk. How fine and loose and free. (27)

Morrison evokes this passage and employs sexual imagery to communicate the promise of life, the possibilities of living again after the husks of memory are carefully peeled back. She assures the reader that it will hurt but also that there is nothing like the joy that carefully comes after pulling back the layers that enshroud the bruised psyche so that, bearing pain in the light, a profound healing may break forth that is looser and freer than anything ever experienced. The Feast of New Corn is a sacred event, something apocalyptic that points beyond the present sense of isolation and fear to the possibility of feasting on life.

The novel breaks away from the fragmented world of the present, looks sorrowfully into the past, and creates a new way for the future. In that sense, Morrison possesses the vision of an epic poet standing between an old world and a new order, a visionary simultaneously charged with the responsibility of preserving the past and creating something new for tomorrow.

Baby Suggs, Sethe's mother-in-law, realizes the importance of living *now*, in the present, and gathers her people for ritual celebrations of life in the "clearing." Suggs tells her people "the only grace they [can] have [is] the grace they could imagine." Thus, she preaches a gospel of self-worth as a corrective against a cruel, white world that does not love their "flesh" but that "despises it" and wishes to "flay it" (88). At the climax of her "calling forth," in which children, men, and women laugh, dance, and cry, Baby Suggs exclaims: "Love your heart. For this is the prize" (89). Love in Morrison's novel is a "hot thing," both a constructive and destructive force that parallels memory. Love and memory are inevitable; they come no matter what, intruding into the lives of the ex-slaves when they least expect it. Much of the novel's mystery centers on what defines love, for Sethe claims that she kills her own child out of love, yet Paul D and the community think this kind of love is "too thick." Baby Suggs, the preacher of love, is herself horrified by Sethe's "act of love." After Sethe kills her own child, Baby Suggs gives up. Suggs goes to bed, where she contemplates colors. She screams when she gets to "orange" and cannot imagine ever facing the color that brings back the memory of pain and suffering that is unbearable: "red." The entire community originally brought together at Baby Suggs's place of safety is broken apart by Sethe's action, the action Paul D labels as too much, the result of a woman whose love is "too thick" (164). After he utters these words to Sethe, a forest springs up between the two of them, but then the communal action of the novel intervenes, with women who come to the porch to reconnect with Sethe and reclaim the past.

The thirty women in *Beloved* join their voices on the porch of 124 Bluestone Road and address the ghost. They search for "the right combination, the key, the code, the sound that broke the back of words" (261). In a lyrical and communal action, bound together and humming, they address the loneliness of the past, the loneliness that "can be rocked," the inner feeling of emptiness that can only be filled by another, but also "the loneliness that roams," the unspeakable memories of the past that haunt our collective consciousness (274). Thus Beloved, as the book's epilogue states, is "disremembered" (274). That is to say, she is addressed. She is memory grasped, reshaped, reformed. As the women on the porch decorate their tales, they splinter Beloved into harmless bits that can be consumed. She "erupts into her separate parts, to make it easy for the chewing laughter to swallow her all the way." The novel's last lyrical section repeats in the style of a mantra—"It was not a story to pass on"—a phrase that warns of the past's continual presence and the necessity to poetically reshape it. Sung to, caressed, brought into being and then reshaped, the horrific past no longer claims the people of 124. The past exists merely as part of "weather," as part of a cycle: pain, death, memory, forgetfulness, rememory, birth, rebirth. The past no longer clamors to be known because it has been addressed. It no longer desires to be called because it has been named "Beloved" (275).

At the novel's close Paul D comes to Sethe's room, where she lies in bed under the quilt contemplating colors, imitating Baby Suggs. Yet this time the quilt is portrayed in "carnival colors." Paul D courageously decides to unite his own unbearable past with Sethe: "He wants to put his story next to hers" (273), to move with Sethe into the horror of the past, and to confront the pain that alone is unbearable. He remembers what Sixo says about the Thirty-Mile Woman: "She is a friend of my mind. She gather me, man. The pieces I am, she gather them and give them back to me in all the right order" (272–3). Paul D and Sethe need each other. They must deal with the horror of the past together. Paul D reshapes Sethe. With love, he reassembles the fragmented pieces of Sethe's self, her bruised and battered psyche. His gesture stands as a metaphor for healing. Derek Walcott, in his 1992 Nobel lecture, speaks of love in a similar way, as a restorative force for the "broken vase" of the world:

> Break a vase, and the love that reassembles the fragments is stronger than that love which took its symmetry for granted when it was whole. The glue that fills the pieces is the sealing of its original shape. It is such a love that reassembles our African and Asiatic fragments, the cracked heirloom whose restoration shows its white scars. (262)

Paul D "gathers" Sethe and restores her to wholeness. As he rubs her feet and comforts her, Paul D says, "Me and you, we got more yesterday than anybody. We need some kind of tomorrow," two lines that understate the immensity of their pain-ridden lives. As Paul D leans over Sethe, taking her hand in one hand and touching her face with the other, he imparts to her what can only be given by another: a true vision of self, a vision with which he will be able to leave the bed and enter life again. Holding on to each other, Paul D tells her, "You your own best thing, Sethe. You are" (273). Thus Paul D challenges Sethe to go inside, to reimagine the past, and to reach out to others as she seeks restoration.

Beloved in its broadest sense depicts a way in which the tormented human psyche may heal. Sethe, with the help of thirty women and

Paul D, faces the horrors of the past and is reborn. In these communal actions, Morrison depicts memory as a means of liberation not only from an atavistic future but also from the imprisoning horrors of the past. In doing so, Morrison, embracing a Romantic aesthetic, lauds the poetic imagination as a force capable of grasping the wholeness of memory's worth, of being able to pull together those vital things that constitute meaning, while discarding what must be discarded to move on.

WORKS CITED

Morrison, Toni. *Beloved*. New York: Plume, 1988.

———. "Memory, Creation, and Writing." *Thought* 59 (December 1984): 385–390.

———. *The Nobel Lecture in Literature 1993*. New York: Knopf, 1994.

BEOWULF

"Beowulf: The Monsters and the Critics"
by J.R.R. Tolkien (1936)

INTRODUCTION

In this highly influential essay, J.R.R. Tolkien, noted scholar and author of *The Hobbit* and *The Lord of the Rings*, maintains that the *Beowulf* poem is primarily a kind of elegy for the departed hero, who, in this poetic enshrining of the past, enables a past culture both to survive and to be reborn. For Tolkien, the poem glimpses "the cosmic," standing "amid but above the petty wars of princes," and surpassing "the dates and limits of historical periods." *Beowulf* describes a culture at a pivotal moment of rebirth in human history, one in which Christianity has begun to be integrated into a civilization that has preserved its past in an epic poem filled with monsters. Not only is this article filled with keen insights about the poem, but it was also responsible for generating a renewal in *Beowulf* studies.

Tolkien, J.R.R. "Beowulf: The Monsters and the Critics." Sir Israel Gollancz Memorial Lecture, 1936.

It is of *Beowulf*, then, as a poem that I wish to speak; and though it may seem presumption that I should try with *swich a lewed mannes wit to pace the wisdom of an heep of lerned men*, in this department there is at least more chance for the *lewed man*. But there is so much that might still be said even under these limitations that I shall confine myself mainly to the *monsters*—Grendel and the Dragon, as they appear in what seems to me the best and most authoritative general criticism in English—and to certain considerations of the structure and conduct of the poem that arise from this theme.
[. . .]
Beowulf's dragon, if one wishes really to criticize, is not to be blamed for being a dragon, but rather for not being dragon enough, plain pure fairy-story dragon. There are in the poem some vivid touches of the right kind—as *pa se wyrm onwoc, wroht wæs geniwad; stonc æfter stane*, 2285—in which this dragon is real worm, with a bestial life and thought of his own, but the conception, none the less, approaches *draconitas* rather than *draco*: a personification of malice, greed, destruction (the evil side of heroic life), and of the undiscriminating cruelty of fortune that distinguishes not good or bad (the evil aspect of all life). But for *Beowulf*, the poem, that is as it should be. In this poem the balance is nice, but it is preserved. The large symbolism is near the surface, but it does not break through, nor become allegory. Something more significant than a standard hero, a man faced with a foe more evil than any human enemy of house or realm, is before us, and yet incarnate in time, walking in heroic history, and treading the named lands of the North. And this, we are told, is the radical defect of *Beowulf*, that its author, coming in a time rich in the legends of heroic men, has used them afresh in an original fashion, giving us not just one more, but something akin yet different: a measure and interpretation of them all.

We do not deny the worth of the hero by accepting Grendel and the dragon. Let us by all means esteem the old heroes: men caught in the chains of circumstance or of their own character, torn between duties equally sacred, dying with their backs to the wall. But *Beowulf*, I fancy, plays a larger part than is recognized in helping us to esteem them. Heroic lays may have dealt in their own way—we have little enough to judge by—a way more brief and vigorous, perhaps, though perhaps also more harsh and noisy (and less thoughtful), with the

actions of heroes caught in circumstances that conformed more or less
to the varied but fundamentally simple recipe for an heroic situation.
In these (if we had them) we could see the exaltation of undefeated
will, which receives doctrinal expression in the words of Byrhtwold
at the battle of Maldon.[1] But though with sympathy and patience
we might gather, from a line here or a tone there, the background of
imagination which gives to this indomitability, this paradox of defeat
inevitable yet unacknowledged, its full significance, it is in *Beowulf*
that a poet has devoted a whole poem to the theme, and has drawn
the struggle in different proportions, so that we may see man at war
with the hostile world, and his inevitable overthrow in Time.[2] The
particular is on the outer edge, the essential in the centre.
[. . .]

Beowulf is not, then, the hero of an heroic lay, precisely. He has
no enmeshed loyalties, nor hapless love. *He is a man, and that for him
and many is sufficient tragedy.* It is not an irritating accident that the
tone of the poem is so high and its theme so low. It is the theme in
its deadly seriousness that begets the dignity of tone: *lif is læne; eal
scæceð leoht and lif somod.* So deadly and ineluctable is the underlying
thought, that those who in the circle of light, within the besieged hall,
are absorbed in work or talk and do not look to the battlements, either
do not regard it or recoil. Death comes to the feast, and they say He
gibbers: He has no sense of proportion.

I would suggest, then, that the monsters are not an inexplicable
blunder of taste; they are essential, fundamentally allied to the underlying ideas of the poem, which give it its lofty tone and high seriousness. The key to the fusion-point of imagination that produced this
poem lies, therefore, in those very references to Cain which have
often been used as a stick to beat an ass—taken as an evident sign
(were any needed) of the muddled heads of early Anglo-Saxons. They
could not, it was said, keep Scandinavian bogies and the Scriptures
separate in their puzzled brains.
[. . .]

One of the most potent elements in that fusion is the Northern
courage: the theory of courage, which is the great contribution of
early Northern literature. This is not a military judgement. I am
not asserting that, if the Trojans could have employed a Northern
king and his companions, they would have driven Agamemnon and

Achilles into the sea, more decisively than the Greek hexameter routs the alliterative line—though it is not improbable. I refer rather to the central position the creed of unyielding will holds in the North. With due reserve we may turn to the tradition of pagan imagination as it survived in Icelandic. Of English pre-Christian mythology we know practically nothing. But the fundamentally similar heroic temper of ancient England and Scandinavia cannot have been founded on (or perhaps rather, cannot have generated) mythologies divergent on this essential point. 'The Northern Gods', Ker said, 'have an exultant extravagance in their warfare which makes them more like Titans than Olympians; *only they are on the right side, though it is not the side that wins. The winning side is Chaos and Unreason*'—mythologically, the monsters—'*but the gods, who are defeated, think that defeat no refutation.*'[3] And in their war men are their chosen allies, able when heroic to share in this 'absolute resistance, perfect because without hope'. At least in this vision of the final defeat of the humane (and of the divine made in its image), and in the essential hostility of the gods and heroes on the one hand and the monsters on the other, we may suppose that pagan English and Norse imagination agreed.

But in England this imagination was brought into touch with Christendom, and with the Scriptures. The process of 'conversion' was a long one, but some of its effects were doubtless immediate: an alchemy of change (producing ultimately the mediaeval) was at once at work. One does not have to wait until all the native traditions of the older world have been replaced or forgotten; for the minds which still retain them are changed, and the memories viewed in a different perspective: *at once they become more ancient and remote, and in a sense darker*. It is through such a blending that there was available to a poet who set out to *write* a poem—and in the case of *Beowulf* we may probably use this very word—on a scale and plan unlike a minstrel's lay, both new faith and new learning (or education), and also a body of native tradition (itself requiring to be learned) for the changed mind to contemplate together.[4] The native 'learning' cannot be denied in the case of *Beowulf.* Its display has grievously perturbed the critics, for the author draws upon tradition at will for his own purposes, as a poet of later times might draw upon history or the classics and expect his allusions to be understood (within a certain class of hearers). He was in fact, like Virgil, learned enough in the vernacular department to have an historical perspective, even an antiquarian curiosity. He cast his time into the long-ago, because already the long-ago had a special poetical attraction. He knew much about old days, and though his knowledge—of such things as sea-burial and the funeral pyre, for instance—was rich and poetical rather than accurate with the accuracy of modern archaeology (such as that is), one thing he knew clearly: those days were heathen—heathen, noble, and hopeless.

But if the specifically Christian was suppressed,[5] so also were the old gods. Partly because they had not really existed, and had been always, in the Christian view, only delusions or lies fabricated by the evil one, the *gastbona*, to whom the hopeless turned especially in times of need. Partly because their old names (certainly not forgotten) had been potent, and were connected in memory still, not only with mythology or such fairy-tale matter as we find, say, in *Gylfaginning*, but with active heathendom, religion and *wigweorþung*. Most of all because they were not actually essential to the theme.

The monsters had been the foes of the gods, the captains of men, and within Time the monsters would win. In the heroic siege and last defeat men and gods alike had been imagined in the same host. Now the heroic figures, the men of old, *hæleð under heofenum*, remained and still fought on until defeat. For the monsters do not depart, whether the gods go or come. A Christian was (and is) still like his forefathers a mortal hemmed in a hostile world. The monsters remained the enemies of mankind, the infantry of the old war, and became inevitably the enemies of the one God, *ece Dryhten*, the eternal Captain of the new. Even so the vision of the war changes. For it begins to dissolve, even as the contest on the fields of Time thus takes on its largest aspect. The tragedy of the great temporal defeat remains for a while poignant, but ceases to be finally important. It is no defeat, for the end of the world is part of the design of Metod, the Arbiter who is above the mortal world. Beyond there appears a possibility of eternal victory (or eternal defeat), and the real battle is between the soul and its adversaries. So the old monsters became images of the evil spirit or spirits, or rather the evil spirits entered into the monsters and took visible shape in the hideous bodies of the *þyrsas* and *sigelhearwan* of heathen imagination.

But that shift is not complete in *Beowulf*—whatever may have been true of its period in general. Its author is still concerned primarily with *man on earth*, rehandling in a new perspective an ancient theme: that man, each man and all men, and all their works shall die. A theme no Christian need despise. Yet this theme plainly would not be so treated, but for the nearness of a pagan time. The shadow of its despair, if only as a mood, as an intense emotion of regret, is still there. The worth of defeated valour in this world is deeply felt. As the poet looks back into the past, surveying the history of kings and warriors in the old traditions, he sees that all glory (or as we might say 'culture' or 'civilization') ends in night. The solution of that tragedy is not treated—it does not arise out of the material. We get in fact a poem from a pregnant moment of poise, looking back into the pit, by a man learned in old tales who was struggling, as it were, to get a general view of them all, perceiving their common tragedy of inevitable ruin, and yet feeling this more *poetically* because he was himself removed from the direct pressure of its despair. He could view from without, but still feel immediately and from within, the old dogma: despair of the event, combined with faith in the value of doomed resistance. He was still dealing with the great temporal tragedy, and not yet writing an allegorical homily in verse. Grendel inhabits the visible world and eats the flesh and blood of men; he enters their houses by the doors. The dragon wields a physical fire, and covets gold not souls; he is slain with iron in his belly. Beowulf's *byrne* was made by Weland, and the iron shield he bore against the serpent by his own smiths: it was not yet the breastplate of righteousness, nor the shield of faith for the quenching of all the fiery darts of the wicked.

Almost we might say that this poem was (in one direction) inspired by the debate that had long been held and continued after, and that it was one of the chief contributions to the controversy: shall we or shall we not consign the heathen ancestors to perdition? What good will it do posterity to read the battles of Hector? *Quid Hinieldus cum Christo?* The author of *Beowulf* showed forth the permanent value of that *pietas* which treasures the memory of man's struggles in the dark past, man fallen and not yet saved, disgraced but not dethroned. It would seem to have been part of the English temper in its strong sense of tradition, dependent doubtless on dynasties, noble houses, and their code of honour, and strengthened, it may be, by the more inquisitive and less severe Celtic learning, that it should, at least in some quarters and despite grave and Gallic voices, preserve much from the northern past to blend with southern learning, and new faith.

[. . .]

In *Beowulf* we have, then, an historical poem about the pagan past, or an attempt at one—literal historical fidelity founded on modern research was, of course, not attempted. It is a poem by a learned man writing of old times, who looking back on the heroism and sorrow feels in them something permanent and something symbolical. So far from being a confused semi-pagan—historically unlikely for a man of this sort in the period—he brought probably *first* to his task a knowledge of Christian poetry, especially that of the Cædmon school, and especially *Genesis*.[6] He makes his minstrel sing in Heorot of the Creation of the earth and the lights of Heaven. So excellent is this choice as the theme of the harp that maddened Grendel lurking joyless in the dark without that it matters little whether this is anachronistic or not.[7] *Secondly*, to his task the poet brought a considerable learning in native lays and traditions: only by learning and training could such things be acquired, they were no more born naturally into an Englishman of the seventh or eighth centuries, by simple virtue of being an 'Anglo-Saxon', than ready-made knowledge of poetry and history is inherited at birth by modern children.

It would seem that, in his attempt to depict ancient pre-Christian days, intending to emphasize their nobility, and the desire of the good for truth, he turned naturally when delineating the great King of Heorot to the Old Testament. In the *folces hyrde* of the Danes we have much of the shepherd patriarchs and kings of Israel, servants of the one God, who attribute to His mercy all the good things that come to them in this life. We have in fact a Christian English conception of the noble chief before Christianity, who could lapse (as could Israel) in times of temptation into idolatry.[8] On the other hand, the traditional matter in English, not to mention the living survival of the heroic code and temper among the noble households of ancient England, enabled him to draw differently, and in some respects much closer to the actual heathen *hæleð*, the character of Beowulf, especially as a young knight, who used his great gift of *mægen* to earn *dom* and *lof* among men and posterity.

Beowulf is not an actual picture of historic Denmark or Geatland or Sweden about A.D. 500. But it is (if with certain minor defects) on

a general view a self-consistent picture, a construction bearing clearly the marks of design and thought. The whole must have succeeded admirably in creating in the minds of the poet's contemporaries the illusion of surveying a past, pagan but noble and fraught with a deep significance—a past that itself had depth and reached backward into a dark antiquity of sorrow. This impression of depth is an effect and a justification of the use of episodes and allusions to old tales, mostly darker, more pagan, and desperate than the foreground.
[. . .]

The general structure of the poem, so viewed, is not really difficult to perceive, if we look to the main points, the strategy, and neglect the many points of minor tactics. We must dismiss, of course, from mind the notion that *Beowulf* is a 'narrative poem', that it tells a tale or intends to tell a tale sequentially. The poem 'lacks steady advance': so Klaeber heads a critical section in his edition.[9] But the poem was not meant to advance, steadily or unsteadily. It is essentially a balance, an opposition of ends and beginnings. In its simplest terms it is a contrasted description of two moments in a great life, rising and setting an elaboration of the ancient and intensely moving contrast between youth and age, first achievement and final death. It is divided in consequence into two opposed portions different in matter, manner, and length: A from 1 to 2199 (including an exordium of 52 lines); B from 2200 to 3182 (the end). There is no reason to cavil at this proportion; in any case, for the purpose and the production of the required effect, it proves in practice to be right.

This simple and *static* structure, solid and strong, is in each part much diversified, and capable of enduring this treatment. In the conduct of the presentation of Beowulf's rise to fame on the one hand, and of his kingship and death on the other, criticism can find things to question, especially if it is captious, but also much to praise, if it is attentive. But the only serious weakness, or apparent weakness, is the long recapitulation: the report of Beowulf to Hygelac. This recapitulation is well done. Without serious discrepancy[10] it retells rapidly the events in Heorot, and retouches the account; and it serves to illustrate, since he himself describes his own deeds, yet more vividly the character of a young man, singled out by destiny, as he steps suddenly forth in his full powers. Yet this is perhaps not quite sufficient to justify the repetition. The explanation, if not complete justification, is probably to be sought in different directions.

For one thing, the old tale was not first told or invented by this poet. So much is clear from investigation of the folk-tale analogues. Even the legendary association of the Scylding court with a marauding monster, and with the arrival from abroad of a champion and deliverer was probably already old. The plot was not the poet's; and though he has infused feeling and significance into its crude material, that plot was not a perfect vehicle of the theme or themes that came to hidden life in the poet's mind as he worked upon it. Not an unusual event in literature. For the contrast—youth and death—it would probably have been better, if we had no journeying. If the single nation of the *Geatas* had been the scene, we should have felt the stage not narrower, but symbolically wider. More plainly should we have perceived in one people and their hero all mankind and its heroes. This at any rate I have always myself felt in reading *Beowulf*; but I have also felt that this defect is rectified by the bringing of the tale of Grendel to Geatland. As Beowulf stands in Hygelac's hall and tells his story, he sets his feet firm again in the land of his own people, and is no longer in danger of appearing a mere *wrecca*, an errant adventurer and slayer of bogies that do not concern him.

There is in fact a double division in the poem: the fundamental one already referred to, and a secondary but important division at line 1887. After that the essentials of the previous part are taken up and compacted, so that all the tragedy of Beowulf is contained between 1888 and the end.[11] But, of course, without the first half we should miss much incidental illustration; we should miss also the dark background of the court of Heorot that loomed as large in glory and doom in ancient northern imagination as the court of Arthur: no vision of the past was complete without it. And (most important) we should lose the direct contrast of youth and age in the persons of Beowulf and Hrothgar which is one of the chief purposes of this section: it ends with the pregnant words *oþ þæt hine yldo benam mægenes wynnum, se þe oft manegum scod.*

In any case we must not view this poem as in intention an exciting narrative or a romantic tale. The very nature of Old English metre is often misjudged. In it there is no single rhythmic pattern progressing from the beginning of a line to the end, and repeated with variation in other lines. The lines do not go according to a tune. They are founded on a balance; an opposition between two halves of roughly equivalent[12] phonetic weight, and significant content, which are more often rhythmically contrasted than similar. They are more like masonry than music. In this fundamental fact of poetic expression I think there is a parallel to the total structure of *Beowulf*. *Beowulf* is indeed the most successful Old English poem because in it the elements, language, metre, theme, structure, are all most nearly in harmony. Judgement of the verse has often gone astray through listening for an accentual rhythm and pattern: and it seems to halt and stumble. Judgement of the theme goes astray through considering it as the narrative handling of a plot: and it seems to halt and stumble. Language and verse, of course, differ from stone or wood or paint, and can be only heard or read in a time-sequence; so that in any poem that deals at all with characters and events some narrative element must be present. We have none the less in *Beowulf* a method and structure that within the limits of the verse-kind approaches rather to sculpture or painting. It is a composition not a tune.

This is clear in the second half. In the struggle with Grendel one can as a reader dismiss the certainty of literary experience that the hero will not in fact perish, and allow oneself to share the hopes and fears of the Geats upon the shore. In the second part the author has no desire whatever that the issue should remain open, even according to literary convention. There is no need to hasten like the messenger, who rode to bear the lamentable news to the waiting people (2892 ff.). They may have hoped, but we are not supposed to. By now we are supposed to have grasped the plan. Disaster is foreboded. Defeat is the theme. Triumph over the foes of man's precarious fortress is over, and we approach slowly and reluctantly the inevitable victory of death.[13]

'In structure', it was said of *Beowulf*, 'it is curiously weak, in a sense preposterous,' though great merits of detail were allowed. In structure actually it is curiously strong, in a sense inevitable, though there are defects of detail. The general design of the poet is not only defensible, it is, I think, admirable. There may have previously existed stirring verse dealing in straightforward manner and even in natural sequence with the Beowulf's deeds, or with the fall of Hygelac; or again with the fluctuations of the feud between the houses of Hrethel the Geat and Ongentheow the Swede; or with the tragedy of the Heathobards,

and the treason that destroyed the Scylding dynasty. Indeed this must
be admitted to be practically certain: it was the existence of such
connected legends—connected in the mind, not necessarily dealt with
in chronicle fashion or in long semi-historical poems—that permitted
the peculiar use of them in *Beowulf*. This poem cannot be criticized
or comprehended, if its original audience is imagined in like case to
ourselves, possessing only *Beowulf* in splendid isolation. For *Beowulf*
was not designed to tell the tale of Hygelac's fall, or for that matter
to give the whole biography of Beowulf, still less to write the history
of the Geatish kingdom and its downfall. But it used knowledge of
these things for its own purpose—to give that sense of perspective, of
antiquity with a greater and yet darker antiquity behind. These things
are mainly on the outer edges or in the background because they
belong there, if they are to function in this way. But in the centre we
have an heroic figure of enlarged proportions.

Beowulf is not an 'epic', not even a magnified 'lay'. No terms
borrowed from Greek or other literatures exactly fit: there is no reason
why they should. Though if we must have a term, we should choose
rather 'elegy'. It is an heroic-elegiac poem; and in a sense all its first
3,136 lines are the prelude to a dirge: *him þa gegiredan Geata leode ad
ofer eorðan unwaclicne*: one of the most moving ever written. But for
the universal significance which is given to the fortunes of its hero it
is an enhancement and not a detraction, in fact it is necessary, that his
final foe should be not some Swedish prince, or treacherous friend,
but a dragon: a thing made by imagination for just such a purpose.
Nowhere does a dragon come in so precisely where he should. But
if the hero falls before a dragon, then certainly he should achieve his
early glory by vanquishing a foe of similar order.
[. . .]

It is just because the main foes in *Beowulf* are inhuman that the
story is larger and more significant than this imaginary poem of a
great king's fall. It glimpses the cosmic and moves with the thought
of all men concerning the fate of human life and efforts; it stands
amid but above the petty wars of princes, and surpasses the dates and
limits of historical periods, however important. At the beginning, and
during its process, and most of all at the end, we look down as if from
a visionary height upon the house of man in the valley of the world.
A light starts—*lixte se leoma ofer landa fela*—and there is a sound of

music; but the outer darkness and its hostile offspring lie ever in wait for the torches to fail and the voices to cease. Grendel is maddened by the sound of harps.

And one last point, which those will feel who to-day preserve the ancient *pietas* towards the past: *Beowulf* is not a 'primitive' poem; it is a late one, using the materials (then still plentiful) preserved from a day already changing and passing, a time that has now for ever vanished, swallowed in oblivion; using them for a new purpose, with a wider sweep of imagination, if with a less bitter and concentrated force. When new *Beowulf* was already antiquarian, in a good sense, and it now produces a singular effect. For it is now to us itself ancient; and yet its maker was telling of things already old and weighted with regret, and he expended his art in making keen that touch upon the heart which sorrows have that are both poignant and remote. If the funeral of Beowulf moved once like the echo of an ancient dirge, far-off and hopeless, it is to us as a memory brought over the hills, an echo of an echo. There is not much poetry in the world like this; and though *Beowulf* may not be among the very greatest poems of our western world and its tradition, it has its own individual character, and peculiar solemnity; it would still have power had it been written in some time or place unknown and without posterity, if it contained no name that could now be recognized or identified by research. Yet it is in fact written in a language that after many centuries has still essential kinship with our own, it was made in this land, and moves in our northern world beneath our northern sky, and for those who are native to that tongue and land, it must ever call with a profound appeal—until the dragon comes.

NOTES

1. This expression may well have been actually used by the *eald geneat*, but none the less (or perhaps rather precisely on that account), is probably to be regarded not as new-minted, but as an ancient and houred *gnome* of long descent.

2. For the words *hige sceal þe heardra, heorte þe cenre, mod sceal þe mare þe ure mægen lytlað* are not, of course, an exhortation to simple courage. They are not reminders that fortune favours the brave, or that victory may be snatched from defeat by

the stubborn. (Such thoughts were familiar, but otherwise expressed: *wyrd oft nereð unfægne eorl, ponne his Ellen deah.*) The words of Byhrtwold were made for a man's last and hopeless day.

3. *The Dark Ages*, p. 57.

4. If we consider the period as a whole. It is not, of course, necessarily true of individuals. These doubtless from the beginning showed many degrees from deep instruction and understanding to disjointed superstition, or blank ignorance.

5. Avoidance of obvious anachronisms (such as are found in *Judith*, for instance, where the heroine refers in her own speeches to Christ and the Trinity), and the absence of all definitely *Christian* names and terms, is natural and plainly intentional. It must be observed that there is a difference between the comments of the author and the things said in reported speech by characters. The two chief among these, Hrothgar and Beowulf, are again differentiated. Thus the only Scriptural references, to Abel (108) and to Cain (108, 1261), occur where the poet is speaking as commentator. The theory of Grendel's origin is not known to the actors: Hrothgar denies all knowledge of the ancestry of Grendel (1355). The giants (1688 ff.) are, it is true, represented pictorially, and in Scriptural terms. But this suggests rather that the author identified native and Scriptural accounts, and gave his picture Scriptural colour, since of the two accounts Scripture was truer. And if so it would be closer to that told in remote antiquity when the sword was made, more especially since the *wundorsmipas* who wrought it were actually giants (1558, 1562, 1679): they would know the true tale. See note 7.

6. The *Genesis* which is preserved for us is a late copy of a damaged original, but is still certainly in its older parts a poem whose composition must be referred to the early period. That *Genesis A* is actually older than *Beowulf* is generally recognized as the most probable reading of such evidence as there is.

7. Actually the poet may have known, what we can guess, that such creation-themes were also ancient in the North. *Völuspá* describes Chaos and the making of the sun and moon, and very similar language occurs in the Old High German fragment

known as the *Wessobrunner Gebet.* The song of the minstrel
Iopas, who had his knowledge from Atlas, at the end of the
first book of the *Aeneid* is also in part a song of origins; *hic
canit errantem lunam solisque labors, unde hominum genus et
pecudes, unde imber et ignes.* In any case the Anglo-Saxon poet's
view throughout was plainly that true, or truer, knowledge was
possessed in ancient days (when men were not deceived by the
Devil); at least they knew of the one God and Creator, though
not of heaven, for that was lost. See note 5.

8. It is of the Old Testament lapses rather than of any events in
England (of which he is not speaking) that the poet is thinking
in lines 175 ff., and this colours his manner of allusion to
knowledge which he may have derived from native traditions
concerning the Danes and the special heathen religious
significance of the site of Heorot (*Hleiðrar, æt hærgtrafum,* the
tabernacles)—it was possibly a matter that embittered the feud
of Danes and Heathobards. If so, this is another point where old
and new have blended . . .

9. Though only explicitly referred to here and in disagreement, this
edition is, of course, of great authority, and all who have used it
have learned much from it.

10. I am not concerned with minor discrepancies at any point of
the poem. They are no proof of composite authorship, nor even
of incompetent authorship. It is very difficult, even in a newly
invented tale of any length, to avoid such defects; more so still
in rehandling old and oft-told tales. The points that are seized
in the study, with a copy that can be indexed and turned to and
fro (even if never read straight through as it was meant to be),
are usually such as may easily escape an author and still more
easily his natural audience. Virgil certainly does not escape
such faults, even within the limits of a single book. Modern
printed tales, that have presumably had the advantage of proof-
correction, can even be observed to hesitate in the heroine's
Christian name.

11. The least satisfactory arrangement possible is thus to read only
lines 1–1887 and not the remainder. This procedure has none
the less been, from time to time, directed or encouraged by
more than one 'English syllabus.'

12. Equivalent but not necessarily equal, certainly not as such things may be measured by machines.

13. That the particular bearer of enmity, the Dragon, also dies is important chiefly to Beowulf himself. He was a great man. Not many even in dying can achieve the death of a single worm, or the temporary salvation of their kindred. Within the limits of human life Beowulf neither lived nor died in vain—brave men might say. But there is no hint, indeed there are many to the contrary, that it was a war to end war, or a dragon-flight to end dragons. It is the end of Beowulf, and of the hope of his people.

CANTERBURY TALES
(GEOFFREY CHAUCER)

❧ ❧

"The Opening of Chaucer's General Prologue to *The Canterbury Tales*: A Diptych"
by Colin Wilcockson,
in *Review of English Studies* (1999)

INTRODUCTION

Analyzing the first thirty-four-line passage in *The Canterbury Tales*, Colin Wilcockson focuses on the theme of renewal and rebirth, linking the budding spring world with the spiritual journey the pilgrims undertake. According to Wilcockson, "The thematic link between the natural description and the pilgrimage is that of death and rebirth. On the earthly level, the rebirth of springtime follows the death of winter and the drought of March. On the spiritual level, men's thoughts turn to the martyr who suffered physical death, but who now is alive in spirit and active in restoring life-forces to the sick."

❧

The opening thirty-four lines of the General Prologue set the scene, and divide into two equal halves. The first sixteen lines, commencing 'Whan that . . .', are concerned with matters general: the

Wilcockson, Colin. "The Opening of Chaucer's General Prologue to *The Canterbury Tales*: A Diptych." *Review of English Studies* Vol. 50, No. 199 (August 1999), 345–350.

renewal of nature in April with the simultaneous desire of men and women to set out on pilgrimages. The central two lines (17–18) are a *rime riche* (perfect rhymes on words that are different parts of speech). They state the object of the pilgrimage—the journey to the shrine of Thomas Becket:

> The hooly blisful martir for to seke,
> That hem hath holpen whan that they were seeke.

The remaining sixteen lines, commencing 'Bifil that . . .', home in on a specific group of pilgrims: their reception at the Tabard Inn and their plans for the next day. Then follows a paragraph (ll. 35–42) which is clearly separated from the foregoing by 'But nathelees'. In it Chaucer explains that he will present the reader with character sketches of the individual pilgrims, including their social rank and their dress.

The divisions I have indicated are reinforced by the scribe of the Ellesmere MS. He reserves illuminated capital letters for particular indication. Thus, each new pilgrim's description commences with a decorated initial letter: '**A** knyght ther was . . . **W**ith hym ther was his sone a yong squier . . . **T**her was also a nonne . . .', and so on. When the descriptions are complete and Chaucer moves on to the more general narrative (ll. 715–858), only the first capital of that entire 143-line passage is illuminated: '**N**ow have I toold you soothly . . .'. Yet at the beginning of the General Prologue we find the decorated capital at the first line: '**W**han that Aprill . . .'; so, too, directly after the *rime riche*, at line 19: '**B**ifil that in that seson . . .'; and at line 35: '**B**ut nathelees . . .'. Thus the second sixteen-line section I have mentioned is separated, and the scribe draws our attention to a new beginning after line 34.

This drawing of attention to structural configuration by coloured capitals is of a piece with the two successive uses of the device in sections XVI (last stanza) and XVII (first stanza) of *Pearl*, evidently to emphasize that section XV contains a cryptic six (rather than the usual five) stanzas. Apart from this 'extra' decorated capital in section XVI only the first capital letter of each section of *Pearl* is coloured. As each stanza has twelve lines, the 'five stanza per section' form totals sixty lines per section. Section XV contains, however, seventy-two lines (i.e. six stanzas), unbroken by a new

capital letter. But in section XVI an 'intrusive' capital letter introduces the fifth stanza, drawing attention to the fact that *there*
would have been a coloured capital there if the previous section had
contained the regular five stanzas of the other nineteen sections
of the poem. The next stanza again has a coloured capital, because
that introduces section XVII. It has often been pointed out that the
resulting number of stanzas—101—is also (and surely more than
coincidentally) the number of verse-paragraphs in another work
by the same poet, *Sir Gawain and the Green Knight*. Some editors
have, however, assumed that there was a non-authorial addition of
a stanza in section XV of *Pearl*; but, as the last word of the elon-
gated section XV is 'neuerþelese' (nevertheless), a word taken up as
the first word of section XVI, there would appear to be an allusion
to the numerology. Furthermore, 'neuer þe les' is the final phrase
of every one of the six stanzas of section XV.[1] Had the 'intrusive'
capital occurred at stanza 6 of section XV, one might argue that
the scribe, accustomed to a five-stanza section, anticipated a new
section and painted a decorated capital. But its removal till later
reinforces its cryptic significance. 'But nathelees' (But nevertheless)
is the phrase Chaucer also uses in line 35 of the General Prologue,
perhaps, like the *Pearl*-poet, to alert his readers to the preceding
number of lines.

The Chaucerian thirty-four-line passage is tightly structured. The
thematic link between the natural description and the pilgrimage is
that of death and rebirth. On the earthly level, the rebirth of springtime follows the death of winter and the drought of March. On
the spiritual level, men's thoughts turn to the martyr who suffered
physical death, but who now is alive in spirit and active in restoring
life-forces to the sick. Early in the passage, Chaucer integrates
these earthly-spiritual themes of death and resurrection by means of
semantic confusion followed by fusion:

> And bathed every veyne in swich licour
> Of which *vertu* engendred is the flour;
> Whan Zephirus eek with his sweete breeth
> *Inspired* hath in every holt and heeth
> The tendre croppes . . .
> (ll. 3–7; emphasis added)

The confusion occurs in the semantic fields of 'vertu' and 'inspired'. Both words, depending on context, could in the fourteenth century have theological or, as in the present instance, literally etymological senses (Latin *virtus*, strength; Latin *inspirare*, breathe into). The most common use of 'inspire' in the fourteenth century carries the implication 'infusion of a divine presence'.[2]

It was thought in the Middle Ages that God created the world in March.[3] The Nun's Priest remarks upon it:

> Whan that the month in which the world began
> That highte March, whan God first maked man ...
> (vii. 3187–8)

In line 2 of the General Prologue Chaucer specifically mentions the 'droghte of March' which is broken by April rain. In the Creation story the dry Earth is brought to life by water; God then breathes into the clay (*inspiravit*) to make man.[4] Though the March drought has been 'attributed to literary convention, but is a fact',[5] the rather unusual 'inspired' triggers off this whole series of connotations which connect the nature description with the Creation story.

These are not the only words Chaucer uses in the passage with the intention of indicating that there is a spiritual *significatio* in the physical world around us. Because their thoughts are on love, the birds do not sleep in April. Chaucer comically says that nature 'priketh hem ... in hir corages' (l. 11). The word 'corage' (Latin *cor*, French *cœur*) in the context means erotic love—and there may well be a sexual word-play on 'priketh'.[6] When 'corage' is next used in the passage, however, it is qualified by the adjective 'devout': 'To Caunterbury with ful devout corage' (l. 22). Its meaning has moved from the natural to the spiritual, from *eros* to *agape*.

Given this tendency, it may well be that the language used about the sun is intended to indicate a shift from the astronomical to the spiritual, through word-play. The sun is described anthropomorphically: it is young, it runs, it goes to rest. In the second half of the passage the pilgrims retire to sleep and agree 'erly for to rise'. The birth-death-resurrection permeating the passage may well contain the *adnominatio* sun/son (Son of God). The connection between sunrise and the resurrection of Christ the martyr archetype is present in the biblical accounts. In Mark 16:2 we read that it was on a Sunday that the two Marys met the risen Christ: 'Et valde mane [very early in the morning] . . . orto iam sole [at sunrise]'. In verse 9, we are told that Christ himself rose early: 'Surgens autem mane'. In English there exists the potential for word-play on sun/son not available in Latin. Use seems to be made of this potential (in precisely the same context) in *Piers Plowman*.[7] Dead men arise from their graves at the death of Christ and prophesy:

> Life and Deeth in this derknesse, hir oon fordooth hir oother
> Shal no wight wite witterly who shal have the maistrie
> Er *Son*day about *sonne risyng*. (xviii. 65–7)

Alastair Fowler discusses the importance of 'centrality' of position in medieval and Renaissance thinking. He gives as an example the placing of the throne at the centre of one side of a table, and remarks: 'In the linear form, elaborate symmetries often surround the significant middle point.'[8] He goes on to illustrate this pattern in many works of Renaissance literature. We have seen how the mirroring of semantic possibilities is a recurrent theme in the two halves of the Chaucerian passage. 'Elaborate symmetries' are indeed present in repeated words. The only rhyme-words which are repeated are centrally pivoted:

> A corages (l. 11)
> B pilgrymages (l. 12)
> C seke (l. 17)
> C seeke (l. 18)
> B pilgrimage (l. 21)
> A corage (l. 22)

If we look at all repeated nouns in the passage, we find the same pattern confirmed:

> sonne
> nyght
> corages
> pilgrymages

pilgrimage
corage
nyght
sonne

This kind of patterning in medieval literature has been observed by a number of scholars. For example, in his article 'Central and Displaced Sovereignty in Three Medieval Poems' (namely, *The Awntrys of Arthure*, Henryson's *Morall Fabillis*, and *Sir Gawain and the Green Knight*), A.C. Spearing analyses the importance of the central line of some medieval poems with the elaborate patterning reflected by each half, and aptly states: 'I suggest that its structure is comparable to that of a pictorial diptych.'[9] Spearing observes that diptych structures are common in medieval poetry, even when a numerological structure is absent (the Ceyx and Alcyone story and the Man in Black in the *Book of the Duchess*, for example). John Scattergood notes a self-enclosing, fold-over pattern in Chaucer's *ABC*, *Anelida and Arcite*, *The Complaint unto Pity*, and *Womanly Noblesse*.[10] P.M. Kean, writing on *Pearl*, states: 'The climax . . . is the great stanza on God's plenitude of grace which comes at the exact centre of the poem.'[11] Ian Bishop, also writing about *Pearl*, similarly remarks: 'the author of *Pearl*, instead of enunciating his text explicitly at the beginning of his composition, places it at the centre—which is the most important position in a poem whose external structure is nearly circular and whose internal structure is more or less symmetrical'.[12] Both Kean and Bishop also analyse that poem's use of numerology.

St Erkenwald is a classic diptych poem. It consists of 352 lines. Line 1 begins with a large capital letter, 'At London . . .'. The only other large capital occurs directly after line 176, the half-way point in the poem. Line 177 reads, 'Then he turnes to the toumbe and talkes to the corce . . .', where the word 'turnes' draws attention to the leaving of one set of considerations to 'turn' to another.[13] Clifford Peterson, in his edition of *St Erkenwald*, remarks: 'The presence of this capital . . . is almost certainly not accident. It divides the poem precisely into two halves of 176 lines and coincides with the beginning of a major portion of the poem, the dialogue between the bishop and the corpse, a dialogue which brings out the poem's main concerns, heavenly and worldly justice and the salvation of the righteous heathen.'[14]

Numerology is almost certainly at work in the Chaucerian passage. It contains thirty-four lines, and the half-way division at line 17 requires the two halves to 'share' the hinging *rime riche* couplet. Augustine, in a discussion of the number of fish in the story of the miraculous draught of fishes (John 21:11), explains that 153 is the Pythagorean triangular figure of 17, and that 17 is significant because 10 can denote the Decalogue, and 7 the gifts of the Holy Ghost which make it possible for man to fulfil the 10 laws and thus become a saint.[15] 'In this number [17] there is found, as in other numbers representing a combination of symbols, a wonderful mystery', Augustine writes. He then goes on to adduce the evidence of Psalm 17, where David praises God for delivering him from the hand of Saul: 'He in His Church, that is, His body, still endures the malice of enemies.' If Chaucer had in mind this particular passage from Augustine, the Beckett parallel would have been seen as particularly apt. Fowler notes that the dominant interpretation by the Church Fathers was that 153 represented symbolically the number of the Elect.[16] In *The City of God*, Augustine again remarks on the connotation of 10 with the Decalogue, and on the saintly connotation of the number 7: 'The theory of number is not to be lightly regarded, since it is made quite clear in many passages of the holy Scriptures, how highly it is to be valued . . . The number seven is also perfect . . . it was on the seventh day . . . that the rest of God is emphasised, and in this rest we hear the first mention of "sanctification".'[17] It is perhaps significant that line 17 of the Chaucerian passage contains the first mention of 'the holy, blisful [blessed] martyr', the saint whose shrine at Canterbury is the object of the pilgrims' quest.

The pivotal balance at the *rime riche* forms a hinge for the cunningly integrated diptych pattern of the passage, whose very form reinforces, is indeed part of, its spiritual significance.

NOTES

1. Many commentators accept that the additional stanza is authorial. The resulting 101 stanzas and 1212 lines may be numerologically significant: the poem makes constant reference to the book of Revelation, and mentions the 144,000 souls who will be saved according to that book. The 1212 lines in *Pearl*

may be intended to imply 12 x 12 = 144. Gollanz, however, in the EETS facsimile edition, remarks in reference to the coloured capital on fo. 52a, 'By an error, this verse begins a new section in the MS'.

2. The earliest occurrence recorded in *MED* of 'inspired' meaning 'to breathe into' is this General Prologue instance. In Vulgate Genesis 2: 5–7 (the Creation story) we are told that, though God had made the plants of the earth, they did not grow because He had not caused rain to fall on the ground. He therefore caused the earth to yield a mist to water the earth. He then created a man from the dust and breathed ('inspiravit') the spirit into him: 'sed fons ascendebat e terra, irrigans universam superficiem terrae. Formavit igitur Dominus Deus hominem de limo terrae, et inspiravit in faciem eius spiraculum vitae, et factus est homo in animam viventem.' The first example in *MED* of 'inspire' meaning to breathe or put life into a human body is in the Wyclif Bible (*c*.1382), Wisdom 15: 11. For the sense 'fill with religious ardour' *MED* cites a 1390 passage, and gives many 15th-cent. examples. Chaucer uses *inspire/enspire* on three further occasions: the Canon's Yeoman's Tale, G, l. 1470 (meaning 'enlighten'), and in two cases to imply that a supernatural being takes over the mind of a human: *Troilus and Criseyde*, III. 712 ('Venus, this nyght thow me enspire'), and IV. 187 ('What goost may yow enspire?').

3. See *Bede: Opera de Temporibus*, ed. C.W. Jones (Cambridge, Mass., 1943): *De ratione temporum*, VI. 6–7, 190–5.

4. See n. 2 above.

5. See L.D. Benson's note on General Prologue, l. 2, in *The Riverside Chaucer* (Boston, Mass., 1987), 799, where he also refers to critical suggestions about the 'convention'. Quotations from Chaucer in this article from that edition.

6. See T.W. Ross, *Chaucer's Bawdy* (New York, 1972), 167–9.

7. For Langland's use of this sort of word-play, see A.V.C. Schmidt, *The Clerkly Maker: Langland's Poetic Art* (Woodbridge, Suffolk, 1987), 125–8.

8. A. Fowler, *Triumphal Forms* (Cambridge, 1970), 23.

9. *RES* ns 33/131 (1982), 247–61.

10. A.J. Minnis with V.J. Scattergood and J.J. Smith (eds.), *The Shorter Poems*, Oxford Guides to Chaucer (Oxford, 1995). For discussion of the self-enclosing structure of *ABC* see p. 464; of *Anelida and Arcite*, p. 471; of *Complaint unto Pity*, pp. 471–2; and of *Womanly Noblesse*, p. 479.

11. P.M. Kean, *The Pearl* (London, 1967), 178.

12. I. Bishop, *Pearl in its Setting* (Oxford, 1968), 35 and 28.

13. There is a unique copy of the work, BL MS Harley 2250, fos. 72^v–75^v.

14. *St Erkenwald*, ed. C. Peterson (Berkeley, Calif., 1977), 26.

15. See C. Butler, *Number Symbolism* (London, 1970), 27; see also V.F. Hopper, *Medieval Number Symbolism* (New York, 1938), 80–2. *The Works of Aurelius Augustine*, trans. M. Dodds, 15 vols. (Edinburgh, 1871–6), i. 229–30: letter LV. 17. 31. Dodds supplies an illustration of the Pythagorean triangle with base 17 on p. 230. See also Fowler, *Triumphal Forms*, 184–5, and M.-S. Røstvig, 'Structure as Prophecy: The Influence of Biblical Exegesis upon Theories of Literary Structure', in A. Fowler (ed.), *Silent Poetry* (London, 1970), 32–72, esp. pp. 41–55.

16. Fowler, *Triumphal Forms*, 184–5, where there is also a drawing of the Pythagorean triangle with base 17.

17. Trans. H. Bettenson (Harmondsworth, 1972), 465–6.

CRIME AND PUNISHMENT
(FYODOR MIKHAILOVICH DOSTOEVSKY)

"Crime and Myth: The Archetypal Pattern of Rebirth in Three Novels of Dostoevsky"
by Alexandra F. Rudicina, in *PMLA* (1972)

INTRODUCTION

In her essay, Alexandra Rudicina argues that, "The salient dimension of Dostoevsky's creativity in his later phase is his obsessive esthetic and metaphysical concern with ultimate violence." According to Rudicina, Dostoevsky depicts murder "as an act generated exclusively by the rational mind of the murderer . . . a product of pure intellection, a rationally argued 'calculated' act of violence." Thus, rationality is explicitly linked with violent acts, but for Rudicina, rationality is more than a theme: It is an "underlying pattern" reflecting "the archetypal scheme of rebirth through transgression followed by suffering, or expiation, which informs the central myth of Christianity, the Fall of Man and his Redemption." In this excerpt, which deals primarily with *Crime and Punishment*, Rudicina focuses on the renewal and rebirth of the novel's protagonist, Raskolnikov.

Rudicina, Alexandra F. "Crime and Myth: The Archetypal Pattern of Rebirth in Three Novels of Dostoevsky." *PMLA* Vol. 87, No. 5 (Oct. 1972), 1,065–1,074.

> Verily, verily, I say unto you, except a corn of wheat fall into the
> ground and die, it abideth alone; but if it die, it bringeth forth
> much fruit.
>
> —John xii.24, used as a motto in *The Brothers Karamazov*

The salient dimension of Dostoevsky's creativity in his later phase is his obsessive esthetic and metaphysical concern with ultimate violence. Indeed, in his great novels, the prominence and urgency of the theme of murder become the cachet of his creative method.

Crime and Punishment, The Possessed, and *The Brothers Karamazov* embody a reassertion and an elaboration of this compelling concern in terms of both their thematic import and structural pattern. Murder is presented as an act generated exclusively by the rational mind of the murderer. It is a product of pure intellection, a rationally argued "calculated" act of violence; and as such it can be characterized as "le crime parfait" in the sense Albert Camus uses the term in his dialectics of murder—that is, "le meurtre légitimé" as distinguished from "le meurtre de fatalité," or crime of passion.[1]

The very urgency with which these works all insist that "le meurtre est la question" (Camus, p. 15) makes us pause to inquire into the dynamics of the organizing pattern around which the themes of crime appear to be structured. This underlying pattern reflects the archetypal scheme of rebirth through transgression followed by suffering, or expiation, which informs the central myth of Christianity, the Fall of Man and his Redemption. And in accordance with the metaphysical esthetics characteristic of his post-exile Weltanschauung,[2] his Pascalism—nay, his dread of man's autarkic intellect[3]—Dostoevsky constitutes the "crime of reason" as *the transgression*, but also as a potential *felix culpa* in his version of the Fall and Redemption as applied to modern man.

Despite the occasional probings of several critics into the themes of rebirth or regeneration in Dostoevsky's oeuvre, his major fiction has not been systematically explored for the thematic and structural relevance of the archetypal pattern of rebirth. My purpose is to isolate and follow the movement of this pattern in terms of its individuation in each of the three novels under study. I will consider the characters' existential role only in terms of their involvement in the metaphysical scheme of rebirth.

In the significantly entitled *Crime and Punishment*, Dostoevsky gives his first imaginative statement of what Allen Tate would call "a cosmic extension of the moral predicament."[4] It is a Russian intellectual and, by extension, "man under the aspect of modernity,"[5] a "superman," whom Dostoevsky features as a supreme aggressor in terms of human law and as a metaphysical transgressor against divine and universal order. His act of aggression is presented as "sanctioned" by the "rational" imperative of his intellect, his transgression as an experiment in "uttermost and final freedom."[6] Seeking, thus, to establish his protagonist in his "relationship to God,"[7] Dostoevsky will resort to the archetypal scheme.

In his proud and solitary intellection, Raskolnikov contemplates a venture that he presumes will say *"a new word."*[8] Impelled by a rational "idea," an "excrescence" of his intellect, he conceives a "logical" crime, claiming the right of an "extraordinary" man (pp. 248–49; Pt. III, Ch. v) to establish his own ethical norms and values. Specifically he asserts that this extraordinary man "may in all conscience authorize himself" to commit crime "if it is necessary . . . for the fulfillment of his ideas" (p. 250).

Raskolnikov's rational mind breaking loose from the common bonds of humanity, a mind driven by *concupiscentia invincibilis*—that concupiscence of reason that Lev Shestov deems the very cause of the Fall of Man[9]—will prompt him "to dare" (p. 401; Pt. v, Ch. iv) and "to permit his conscience to overstep . . . certain obstacles" (p. 249; Pt. III, Ch. v). He proceeds to *"remove"* (p. 249) what he calls a "louse, . . . a useless, vile, pernicious louse" (p. 399; Pt. v, Ch. iv), the old pawnbroker Alena Ivanovna.

The principle of rebirth is set in motion as soon as Raskolnikov assays his "freedom and power" (p. 317; Pt. IV, Ch. iv) by "stepping over the barriers" (p. 402; Pt. v, Ch. iv) and murdering the old moneylender and her half-witted sister, Lizaveta. Perverting the very principle of life, he thus signals his implication in an act of metaphysical transgression. This act is *the* step of ultimate gravity through which participation in the scheme of rebirth via suffering and expiation will be held out to him.

The crime merges with the punishment. As Blackmur has observed, Raskolnikov himself "becomes the very product of his crime" (p. 122).[10] The same intellection that has supplied the rationale for his project has also furnished the subtlest, most refined tools for his punishment. The hideousness of his act is essentially brought home to Raskolnikov in esthetic terms.[11] Soon enough after the deed Raskolnikov perceives the ironic discrepancy between the regal sang-froid and poise of a Napoleon marching over corpses (p. 250; Pt. III, Ch. v) and his own messy cowering procedures in the squashing of an old usurer. Recalling how he crawled under the moneylender's bed for his booty, he pictures Porfiry, the examining magistrate, asking sarcastically: "Does a Napoleon crawl under an old hag's bed?"[12]

There is unmistakably lurking in the heart of Raskolnikov a rankling sense of an extreme impropriety of his "private" murderous act. Characteristically he himself acknowledged that he was nothing but an "esthetic louse" (p. 264; Pt. III, Ch. vi). Here Dostoevsky skirts a Shakespearean projection of the "impulse to formal propriety" discerned by Robert B. Heilman in Othello, who conceived of Desdemona's murder not as an act of private revenge but as a rite of justice. It is that very propriety—which, in Heilman's terms, "puts a good face on murder"—that Raskolnikov agonizingly perceives was lacking in his own deed.[13]

Another aspect of the punishment is his "disease," which represents, ironically, an unforeseen consequence of his "calculated" act. It will be remembered that in his article dealing with the "right to commit crime" (p. 248; Pt. III, Ch. v), Raskolnikov made the point that a criminal act is almost invariably accompanied by "a collapse of willpower and reason." Such disease, he claimed, was the cause of the criminal's "extraordinary childish heedlessness" that would inevitably lead to his detection. Raskolnikov considered himself immune from such distressing consequences simply because "what he contemplated was no crime" (p. 68; Pt. I, Ch. vi).

But following the deed he collapses into a stupor from which he awakens only to discover in terror his own childish heedlessness, his carelessness in concealing the traces of his murderous deed. Assailed by the suspicion that "everything, even memory, even the simple power of reflection, was deserting him," he ascribes a punitive, retributive significance to what he apprehends as the onset of madness: "What if it is beginning already? Can this really be the beginning of my punishment?" (pp. 84–86; Pt. II, Ch. i). As his punishment grows, we follow an increasingly harrowing spectacle of humiliation and gradual disintegration of the hero's pride—that same pride that had conceived the deed and had incited him to take the dare and overstep the limits.

René Girard in his *Dostoïevskÿ: du double à l'unité* speaks of "une passion de l'orgueil moderne" that he sees inherent in the Napoleonic Prometheism underlying the model of "la sur-humanité" for Raskolnikov.[14] In his words, "Raskolnikov tue, et il tue délibérément afin d'asseoir son orgueil sur des bases inébranlables" (p. 71). Yet not once does his consciousness of the enacted "deed" stir in Raskolnikov a proud vision of himself as the "real ruler," as that Napoleon in whom, as Girard says, Hegel saw "l'incarnation vivante de la divinité" (p. 97). The man who, obsessed with his own "deification,"[15] engaged in a daring experiment—which he deemed emblematic of "freedom and power, but above all power" (p. 317; Pt. IV, Ch. iv)—finds himself unable to make good his claim and pass his test. Trapped in what he calls his cowardice, unnerved by the humiliating realization of the failure of his project, his pride disintegrating, Raskolnikov submits to Sonya's Christly mediation and gives himself up to the police.

We have dealt with the growth and multiplication of the punishment in which the protagonist has involved himself in his quest for "rebellious" freedom[16] and his arrogation of the right over the life and death of the "Other." Yet there is no expiatory aspect, no redeeming suffering at this point in his pluridimensional punishment. The awakening of the impulse to rebirth is retarded by his obdurate commitment to his "idea." Even as he has reached the decision to make a clean breast of his crime to the authorities, he vehemently protests to Sonya that his "deed" was no crime. "Crime? What crime?" he asks. "Killing a foul, noxious louse . . . who sucked the life-blood of the poor, so vile that killing her ought to bring absolution for forty sins—was that a crime?" (p. 498; Pt. VI, Ch. vii).

One of the most controversial issues in Dostoevsky criticism is the so-called "epilogue conversion": in the last two pages of the novel Dostoevsky tells us that Raskolnikov and Sonya are "raised from the dead" through the epiphany of their love, "the dawn of a new future and a perfect resurrection into a new life" glowing in their "white sick faces." The usual critical objection to this late conversion is to its "suddenness": it has been charged that the protagonist's change of heart is neither psychologically nor artistically prepared for in the earlier stages of the novel. More particularly, Ernest Simmons charges that Raskolnikov's regeneration "under the influence of the Christian humility and love of Sonya" is "neither artistically palatable nor psychologically sound" (p. 153).

In defense of the conversion I must point out that one cannot fail to discern the slow and tortuous but unmistakable rhythm of rebirth that involves in its momentum the half-resisting, half-willing protagonist who vacillates between the polarities of perdition and salvation, embodied respectively by Svidrigailov and Sonya Marmeladova. Significantly it is the famous scene in which "the murderer and the harlot . . . had come together so strangely to read the eternal book" that most compellingly foreshadows Raskolnikov's resurrection. Raskolnikov asks the saintly prostitute, "Where is that about the raising of Lazarus? Find it for me." And Sonya, reading to him from the Gospel of Saint John about the "blind, unbelieving Jews who were so soon, in an instant, to fall to the ground . . . believing" in Lazarus' resurrection, intuits that "*he, he* who is also blind and unbelieving, he also will hear in a moment, he also will believe." As she reads further—"*And he that was dead came forth*"—she exults in anticipation of Raskolnikov also rising from the dead (pp. 312–15; Pt. IV, Ch. iv).

Philip Rahv expresses impatience with "such intimations" at the close of the novel as promise that Raskolnikov's "ultimate reconcilement and salvation" will come to pass "in a new story" (Rahv, pp. 22–23). Yet it may be plausibly argued that in activating the archetype of rebirth as crystallized in the Christian myth of Fall and Redemption, Dostoevsky was conceptually as well as artistically bound to stay within his particular frame of reference. Deferring to an indefinite future Raskolnikov's emergence into "perfect resurrection" and limiting himself to mere intimations of an "undreamed-of reality," Dostoevsky fundamentally follows the Christian myth, with its promise of man's redemption.[17]

NOTES

1. See Ernest J. Simmons, *Dostoevsky: The Making of a Novelist* (New York: Knopf, 1962), pp. 155–56; Martin Kanes, "Zola's *La Bête humaine: A Study in Literary Creation*," Univ. of California Publications in Modern Philology, No. 68 (Berkeley and Los

Angeles: Univ. of California Press, 1962), pp. 31–33; and Albert Camus, *L'Homme révolté* (Paris: Gallimard, 1951), Introd., pp. 13, 17.

2. Vyacheslav Ivanov, *Freedom and the Tragic Life: A Study in Dostoevsky*, trans. Norman Cameron, ed. S. Konovalov (New York: Noonday, 1960), pp. 15–17; D.A. Traversi, "Dostoevsky," *Criterion*, 16 (1937), rpt. in *Dostoevsky: A Collection of Critical Essays*, Twentieth Century Views, ed. René Wellek (Englewood Cliffs, N. J.: Prentice-Hall, 1961), pp. 160–62.

3. Irving Howe, "Dostoevsky: The Politics of Salvation," *Politics and the Novel* (New York: Horizon Press, 1957), rpt. in *Dostoevsky: A Collection of Critical Essays*, pp. 56–57.

4. Allen Tate, "Our Cousin, Mr. Poe," *Collected Essays* (Denver, Colo.: Swallow, 1959), rpt. in *Modern Literary Criticism: An Anthology*, ed. Irving Howe (New York: Grove, 1961), p. 263.

5. Philip Rahv, "Dostoevsky in *Crime and Punishment*," *Partisan Review*, 27 (1960), rpt. in *Dostoevsky: A Collection of Critical Essays*, p. 21.

6. Nicholas Berdyaev, *Dostoevsky*, trans. Donald Attwater (Cleveland, Ohio: World, 1964), p. 68.

7. R.P. Blackmur, "Crime and Punishment," *Chimera*, 1, No. 3 (1943), rpt. as "Crime and Punishment: Murder in Your Own Room," in *Eleven Essays in the European Novel* (New York: Harcourt, 1964), p. 139.

8. *Crime and Punishment*, The Coulson Translation, ed. George Gibian (New York: Norton, 1964), p. 2 (Pt. i, Ch. i). Subsequent references are to this edition and are placed in the text, except when stated otherwise.

9. *Kierkegaard and the Existential Philosophy*, trans. Elinor Hewitt (Athens: Ohio Univ. Press, 1969), p. 304.

10. See also Paul Evdokimov, *Dostoevsky et le problème du mal* (Valence: Imprimeries Réunies, 1942), p. 135.

11. Yanko Lavrin, *Dostoevsky: A Study* (New York: Macmillan, 1947), p. 80.

12. F.M. Dostoevskij, *Prestuplenie i nakazanie: Roman v sesti castjax s epilogom. Polnoe sobranie socinenij* (Moskva: Gosudarstvennoe Izdatel'stvo Xudozestvennoj Literatury, 1956), v, 285; my translation.

13. *Magic in the Web* (Lexington: Univ. of Kentucky Press, 1956), p. 159. Quoted and commented upon by Honor Matthews in *The Primal Curse: The Myth of Cain and Abel* (New York: Schocken, 1967), pp. 46–47.

14. (Paris: Plon, 1963), p. 73.

15. See Berdyaev, *Dostoevsky*, p. 99.

16. See Berdyaev, p. 77.

17. *Crime and Punishment*, Epilogue, Ch. ii, pp. 526–27. See also Evdokimov, *Dostoevsky et le problème du mal*, p. 25.

DIVINE COMEDY
(DANTE ALIGHIERI)

"To Can Grande della Scala"
by Dante Alighieri, in *Dantis Alagherii Epistolae: The Letters of Dante* (1920)

INTRODUCTION

In this letter to Can Grande della Scala, Dante Alighieri's leading patron, Dante provides a famous overview to the ways of interpreting his *Divine Comedy*. He details how his work is "polysemous," "having several meanings," often citing Aristotle to support his claims. Focusing on renewal and rebirth, especially the soul's existence after death, Dante outlines his work's subject and the principal ways of reading his text: "For if the subject of the whole work taken in the literal sense is the state of souls after death, pure and simple, without limitation, it is evident that in this part the same state is the subject, but with a limitation, namely the state of blessed souls after death." Thus, Dante's epic poem deals with the rebirth and renewal of those who have lived a just earthly life, a rebirth that is paralleled in Dante the Pilgrim's journey and in those seeking to understand *Divine Comedy*.

Alighieri, Dante. "To Can Grande della Scala." *Dantis Alagherii Epistolae: The Letters of Dante*. Trans. Paget Toynbee. Oxford: Clarendon Press, 1966 (First published 1920). 160–211.

§5. As the Philosopher says in the second book of the *Metaphysics*, 'as a thing is in respect of being, so is it in respect of truth'; the reason of which is, that the truth concerning a thing, which consists in the truth as in its subject, is the perfect likeness of the thing as it is. Now of things which exist, some are such as to have absolute being in themselves; while others are such as to have their being dependent upon something else, by virtue of a certain relation, as being in existence at the same time, or having respect to some other thing, as in the case of correlatives, such as father and son, master and servant, double and half, the whole and part, and other similar things, in so far as they are related. Inasmuch, then, as the being of such things depends upon something else, it follows that the truth of these things likewise depends upon something else; for if the half is unknown, its double cannot be known; and so of the rest.

§6. If any one, therefore, is desirous of offering any sort of introduction to part of a work, it behoves him to furnish some notion of the whole of which it is a part. Wherefore I, too, being desirous of offering something by way of introduction to the above-mentioned part of the whole *Comedy*, thought it incumbent on me in the first place to say something concerning the work as a whole, in order that access to the part might be the easier and the more perfect. There are six points, then, as to which inquiry must be made at the beginning of every didactic work; namely, the subject, the author, the form, the aim, the title of the book, and the branch of philosophy to which it belongs. Now of these six points there are three in respect of which the part which I have had in mind to address to you differs from the whole work; namely, the subject, the form, and the title; whereas in respect of the others there is no difference, as is obvious to any one who considers the matter. Consequently, in an examination of the whole, these three points must be made the subject of a separate inquiry; which being done, the way will be sufficiently clear for the introduction to the part. Later we will examine the other three points, not only with reference to the whole work, but also with reference to the particular part which is offered to you.

§7. For the elucidation, therefore, of what we have to say, it must be understood that the meaning of this work is not of one kind only; rather the work may be described as 'polysemous', that is, having several meanings; for the first meaning is that which is conveyed by the letter, and the next is that which is conveyed by what the letter signifies; the former of which is called literal, while the latter is called allegorical, or mystical. And for the better illustration of this method of exposition we may apply it to the following verses: 'When Israel went out of Egypt, the house of Jacob from a people of strange language; Judah was his sanctuary, and Israel his dominion'. For if we consider the letter alone, the thing signified to us is the going out of the children of Israel from Egypt in the time of Moses; if the allegory, our redemption through Christ is signified; if the moral sense, the conversion of the soul from the sorrow and misery of sin to a state of grace is signified; if the anagogical, the passing of the sanctified soul from the bondage of the corruption of this world to the liberty of everlasting glory is signified. And although these mystical meanings are called by various names, they may one and all in a general sense be termed allegorical, inasmuch as they are different (*diversi*) from the literal or historical; for the word 'allegory' is so called from the Greek *alleon*, which in Latin is *alienum* (strange) or *diversum* (different).

§8. This being understood, it is clear that the subject, with regard to which the alternative meanings are brought into play, must be twofold. And therefore the subject of this work must be considered in the first place from the point of view of the literal meaning, and next from that of the allegorical interpretation. The subject, then, of the whole work, taken in the literal sense only, is the state of souls after death, pure and simple. For on and about that the argument of the whole work turns. If, however, the work be regarded from the allegorical point of view, the subject is man according as by his merits or demerits in the exercise of his free will he is deserving of reward or punishment by justice.

§9. And the form is twofold—the form of the treatise, and the form of the treatment. The form of the treatise is threefold, according to the threefold division. The first division is that whereby the whole work is divided into three cantiche; the second, whereby each cantica is divided into cantos; and the third, whereby each canto is divided into rhymed lines. The form or manner of treatment is poetic, fictive, descriptive, digressive, and figurative; and further, it is definitive, analytical, probative, refutative, and exemplificative.

§10. The title of the book is 'Here begins the *Comedy* of Dante Alighieri, a Florentine by birth, not by disposition'. For the understanding of which it must be noted that 'comedy' is so called from *comos*, a village, and *oda*, a song; whence comedy is as it were a 'rustic song'. Now comedy is a certain kind of poetical narration which differs from all others. It differs, then, from tragedy in its subject-matter, in that tragedy at the beginning is admirable and placid, but at the end or issue is foul and horrible. And tragedy is so called from *tragos*, a goat, and *oda*; as it were a 'goat-song', that is to say foul like a goat, as appears from the tragedies of Seneca. Whereas comedy begins with sundry adverse conditions, but ends happily, as appears from the comedies of Terence. And for this reason it is the custom of some writers in their salutation to say by way of greeting: 'a tragic beginning and a comic ending to you!' Tragedy and comedy differ likewise in their style of language; for that of tragedy is high-flown and sublime, while that of comedy is unstudied and lowly. And this is implied by Horace in the *Art of Poetry*, where he grants that the comedian may on occasion use the language of tragedy, and vice versa:

> Yet sometimes comedy her voice will raise,
> And angry Chremes scold with swelling phrase;
> And prosy periods oft our ears assail
> When Telephus and Peleus tell their tragic tale.

And from this it is clear that the present work is to be described as a comedy. For if we consider the subject-matter, at the beginning it is horrible and foul, as being *Hell*; but at the close it is happy, desirable, and pleasing, as being *Paradise*. As regards the style of language, the style is unstudied and lowly, as being in the vulgar tongue, in which even women-folk hold their talk. And hence it is evident why the work is called a comedy. And there are other kinds of poetical narration, such as the pastoral poem, the elegy, the satire, and the votive song, as may also be gathered from Horace in the *Art of Poetry*; but of these we need say nothing at present.

§11. It can now be shown in what manner the subject of the part offered to you is to be determined. For if the subject of the whole work taken in the literal sense is the state of souls after death, pure and simple, without limitation, it is evident that in this part the same state is the subject, but with a limitation, namely the state of blessed

souls after death. And if the subject of the whole work from the allegorical point of view is man according as by his merits or demerits in
the exercise of his free will he is deserving of reward or punishment
by justice, it is evident that in this part this subject has a limitation,
and that it is man according as by his merits he is deserving of reward
by justice.

§12. In like manner the form of the part is determined by that of
the whole work. For if the form of the treatise as a whole is threefold,
in this part it is twofold only, the division being that of the cantica
and of the cantos. The first division (into cantiche) cannot be appli-
cable to the form of the part, since the cantica is itself a part under
the first division.

§13. The title of the book also is clear. For the title of the whole
book is 'Here begins the *Comedy*', &c., as above; but the title of the
part is 'Here begins the third cantica of the *Comedy* of Dante, which
is called *Paradise*'.

§14. These three points, in which the part differs from the whole,
having been examined, we may now turn our attention to the other
three, in respect of which there is no difference between the part and
the whole. The author, then, of the whole and of the part is the person
mentioned above, who is seen to be such throughout.

§15. The aim of the whole and of the part might be manifold;
as, for instance, immediate and remote. But leaving aside any minute
examination of this question, it may be stated briefly that the aim of
the whole and of the part is to remove those living in this life from a
state of misery, and to bring them to a state of happiness.

§16. The branch of philosophy to which the work is subject, in
the whole as in the part, is that of morals or ethics; inasmuch as the
whole as well as the part was conceived, not for speculation, but with
a practical object. For if in certain parts or passages the treatment is
after the manner of speculative philosophy, that is not for the sake
of speculation, but for a practical purpose; since, as the Philosopher
says in the second book of the *Metaphysics*: 'practical men occasionally
speculate on things in their particular and temporal relations'.

§17. Having therefore premised these matters, we may now apply
ourselves to the exposition of the literal meaning, by way of sample; as
to which it must first be understood that the exposition of the letter
is in effect but a demonstration of the form of the work. The part

in question then, that is, this third cantica which is called *Paradise*,
falls by its main division into two parts, namely the prologue, and the
executive part; which second part begins:

Surge ai mortali per diverse foci.

§18. As regards the first part, it should be noted that although
in common parlance it might be termed an exordium, yet, properly
speaking, it can only be termed a prologue; as the Philosopher seems
to indicate in the third book of his *Rhetoric*, where he says that 'the
proem in a rhetorical oration answers to the prologue in poetry, and
to the prelude in flute-playing'. It must further be observed that this
preamble, which may ordinarily be termed an exordium, is one thing
in the hands of a poet, and another in those of an orator. For orators
are wont to give a forecast of what they are about to say, in order
to gain the attention of their hearers. Now poets not only do this,
but in addition they make use of some sort of invocation afterwards.
And this is fitting in their case, for they have need of invocation in a
large measure, inasmuch as they have to petition the superior beings
for something beyond the ordinary range of human powers, something almost in the nature of a divine gift. Therefore the present
prologue is divided into two parts: in the first is given a forecast of
what is to follow; in the second is an invocation to Apollo; which
second part begins

O buono Apollo, all' ultimo lavoro, &c.

§19. With reference to the first part it must be observed that to
make a good exordium three things are requisite, as Tully says in his
New Rhetoric; that the hearer, namely, should be rendered favour-
ably disposed, attentive, and willing to learn; and this is especially
needful in the case of a subject which is out of the common, as
Tully himself remarks. Inasmuch, then, as the subject dealt with in
the present work is out of the common, it is the aim of the first part
of the exordium or prologue to bring about the above-mentioned
three results with regard to this out-of-the-way subject. For the
author declares that he will relate such things as he who beheld
them in the first heaven was able to retain. In which statement all

those three things are comprised; for the profitableness of what he is about to be told begets a favourable disposition in the hearer; its being out of the common engages his attention; and its being within the range of possibility renders him willing to learn. Its profitableness he gives to be understood when he says that he shall tell of that which above all things excites the longing of mankind, namely the joys of Paradise; its uncommon nature is indicated when he promises to treat of such exalted and sublime matters as the conditions of the celestial kingdom; its being within the range of possibility is demonstrated when he says that he will tell of those things which he was able to retain in his mind—for if he was able, so will others be also. All this is indicated in the passage where he declares that he had been in the first heaven, and that he purposes to relate concerning the celestial kingdom whatsoever he was able to store up, like a treasure, in his mind. Having thus noted the excellence and perfection of the first part of the prologue, we may now proceed to the literal exposition.

§20. He says, then, that 'the glory of the First Mover', which is God, 'shines forth in every part of the universe', but in such wise that it shines 'in one part more and in another less'. That it shines in every part both reason and authority declare. Reason thus: Everything which exists has its being either from itself, or from some other thing. But it is plain that self-existence can be the attribute of one being only, namely the First or Beginning, which is God, since to have being does not argue necessary self-existence, and necessary self-existence appertains to one being only, namely the First or Beginning, which is the cause of all things; therefore everything which exists, except that One itself, has its being from some other thing. If, then, we take, not any thing whatsoever, but that thing which is the most remote in the universe, it is manifest that this has its being from something; and that from which it derives either has its being from itself, or from something else. If from itself, then it is primal; if from something else, then that again must either be self-existent, or derive from something else. But in this way we should go on to infinity in the chain of effective causes, as is shown in the second book of the *Metaphysics*. So we must come to a primal existence, which is God. Hence, mediately or immediately, everything that exists has its being from Him, because, inasmuch as[1] the second cause has its effect[2] from the first, its influence on what it acts upon[3] is like that of a body which receives and reflects a ray; since the first cause is the more effective cause. And this is stated in the book *On Causes*, namely, that 'every primary cause has influence in a greater degree on what it acts upon[3] than any second cause'. So much with regard to being.

§21. With regard to essence I argue in this wise: Every essence, except the first, is caused; otherwise there would be more than one necessarily self-existent being, which is impossible. For what is caused is the effect either of nature or of intellect; and what is of nature is, consequently, caused by intellect, inasmuch as nature is the work of intelligence. Everything, then, which is caused is the effect, mediately or immediately, of some intellect. Since, then, virtue follows the essence whose virtue it is, if the essence is of intellect, the virtue is wholly and solely of the intellectual essence whose effect it is. And so, just as we had to go back to a first cause in the case of being, so now we must do so in the case of essence and of virtue. Whence it is evident that every essence and every virtue proceeds from a primal one; and that the lower intelligences have their effect[4] as it were from a radiating body, and, after the fashion of mirrors, reflect the rays of the higher to the one below them. Which matter appears to be discussed clearly enough by Dionysius in his work *On the Celestial Hierarchy*. And therefore it is stated in the book *On Causes* that 'every intelligence is full of forms'. Reason, then, as we have seen, demonstrates that the divine light, that is to say the divine goodness, wisdom, and virtue, shines in every part.

§22. Authority likewise declares the same, but with more knowledge. For the Holy Spirit says by the mouth of Jeremiah: 'Do not I fill heaven and earth?' And in the *Psalm*: 'Whither shall I go from thy Spirit? and whither shall I flee from thy presence? If I ascend up into heaven, thou art there; if I descend into hell, thou art there also. If I take my wings,' &c. And *Wisdom* says: 'The Spirit of the Lord hath filled the whole world'. And *Ecclesiasticus*, in the forty-second chapter: 'His work is full of the glory of the Lord'. To which also the writings of the pagans bear witness; for Lucan says in his ninth book:

Jupiter is whatever thou seest, wherever thou goest.

§23. He says well, then, when he says that the divine ray, or divine glory, 'penetrates and shines through the universe'; penetrates, as to essence; shines forth, as to being. And what he adds as to 'more and less' is manifestly true, since we see that one essence exists in a more excellent degree, and another in a less; as is clearly the case with regard to the heaven and the elements, the former being incorruptible, while the latter are corruptible.

§24. And having premised this truth, he next goes on to indicate Paradise by a circumlocution; and says that he was in that heaven which receives the glory of God, or his light, in most bountiful measure. As to which it must be understood that that heaven is the highest heaven, which contains all the bodies of the universe, and is contained by none, within which all bodies move (itself remaining everlastingly at rest), and which receives virtue from no corporeal substance. And it is called the Empyrean, which is as much as to say, the heaven glowing with fire or heat; not that there is material fire or heat therein, but spiritual, which is holy love, or charity.

§25. Now that this heaven receives more of the divine light than any other can be proved by two things. Firstly, by its containing all things, and being contained by none; secondly, by its state of everlasting rest or peace. As to the first the proof is as follows: The containing body stands in the same relation to the content in natural position as the formative does to the formable, as we are told in the fourth book of the *Physics*. But in the natural position of the whole universe the first heaven is the heaven which contains all things; consequently it is related to all things as the formative to the formable, which is to be in the relation of cause to effect. And since every causative force is in the nature of a ray emanating from the first cause, which is God, it is manifest that that heaven which is in the highest degree causative receives most of the divine light.

§26. As to the second the proof is this: Everything which has motion moves because of something which it has not, and which is the terminus of its motion. The heaven of the moon, for instance, moves because of some part of itself which has not attained the station towards which it is moving; and because no part whatsoever of it has attained any terminus whatsoever (as indeed it never can), it moves to another station, and thus is always in motion, and is never at rest, which is what it desires. And what I say of the heaven of the moon applies to all the other heavens, except the first. Everything, then, which has motion is in some respect defective, and has not its whole being complete. That heaven, therefore, which is subject to no movement, in itself and in every part whatsoever of itself has whatever it is capable of having in perfect measure, so that it has no need of motion for its perfection. And since every perfection is a ray of the Primal One, inasmuch as He is perfection in the highest degree, it is manifest that the first heaven receives more than any other of the light of the Primal One, which is God. This reasoning, however, has the appearance of an argument based on the denial of the antecedent, in that it is not a direct proof[5] and according to syllogistic form. But if we consider its content[6] it is a good proof, because it deals with a thing eternal, and assumes it to be capable of being eternally defective; so that, if God did not give that heaven motion, it is evident that He did not give it material in any respect defective. And on this supposition the argument holds good by reason of the content; and this form of argument is much the same as though we should reason: 'if he is man, he is able to laugh'; for in every convertible proposition a like reasoning holds good by virtue of the content. Hence it is clear that when the author says 'in that heaven which receives more of the light of God', he intends by a circumlocution to indicate Paradise, or the heaven of the Empyrean.[7]

§27. And in agreement with the foregoing is what the Philosopher says in the first book *On Heaven*, namely that 'a heaven has so much the more honourable material than those below it as it is the further removed from terrestrial things'. In addition to which might be adduced what the Apostle says to the Ephesians of Christ: 'Who ascended up far above all heavens, that He might fill all things'. This is the heaven of the delights of the Lord; of which delights it is said by Ezekiel against Lucifer: 'Thou, the seal of similitude,[8] full of wisdom, beautiful in perfection,[9] wast in the delights of the Paradise of God'.[10]

§28. And after he has said that he was in that place of Paradise which he describes by circumlocution, he goes on to say that he saw certain things which he who descends therefrom is powerless to relate. And he gives the reason, saying that 'the intellect plunges itself to such depth' in its very longing, which is for God, 'that the memory cannot follow'. For the understanding of which it must be noted that the human intellect in this life, by reason of its connaturality and affinity to the separate intellectual substance, when in exaltation, reaches such a height of exaltation that after its return to itself memory fails, since it has transcended the range of human faculty. And this is conveyed to us by the Apostle where he says, addressing the Corinthians: 'I know a man (whether in the body, or out of the body, I cannot tell; God knoweth) how that he was caught up to the third heaven, and heard unspeakable words, which it is not lawful for a man to utter'. Behold, after the intellect had passed beyond the bounds of human faculty in its exaltation, it could not recall what took place outside of its range. This again is conveyed to us in Matthew, where we read that the three disciples fell on their faces, and record nothing thereafter, as though memory had failed them. And in Ezekiel it is written: 'And when I saw it, I fell upon my face'. And should these not satisfy the cavillers, let them read Richard of St. Victor in his book *On Contemplation*; let them read Bernard in his book *On Consideration*; let them read Augustine in his book *On the Capacity of the Soul*; and they will cease from their cavilling. But if on account of the sinfulness of the speaker they should cry out against his claim to have reached such a height of exaltation, let them read Daniel, where they will find that even Nebuchadnezzar by divine permission beheld certain things as a warning to sinners, and straightway forgot them. For He 'who maketh his sun to shine on the good and on the evil, and sendeth rain on the just and on the unjust', sometimes in compassion for their conversion, sometimes in wrath for their chastisement, in greater or lesser measure, according as He wills, manifests his glory to evil-doers, be they never so evil.

§29. He saw, then, as he says, certain things 'which he who returns has neither knowledge nor power to relate'. Now it must be carefully noted that he says 'has neither knowledge nor power'—knowledge he has not, because he has forgotten; power he has not, because even if he remembers, and retains it thereafter, nevertheless speech fails him. For we perceive many things by the intellect for which language has no terms—a fact which Plato indicates plainly enough in his books by his employment of metaphors; for he perceived many things by the light of the intellect which his everyday language was inadequate to express.

§30. Afterwards the author says that he will relate concerning the celestial kingdom such things as he was able to retain; and he says that this is the subject of his work; the nature and extent of which things will be shown in the executive part.

§31. Then when he says: 'O buono Apollo', &c., he makes his invocation. And this part is divided into two parts—in the first, he invokes the deity and makes a petition; in the second, he inclines Apollo to the granting of his petition by the promise of a certain recompense; which second part begins: 'O divina virtù'. The first part again is divided into two parts—in the first, he prays for divine aid; in the second, he adverts to the necessity for his petition, whereby he justifies it; and this part begins:

> Infino a qui l'un giogo di Parnaso, &c.

§32. This is the general meaning of the second part of the prologue; the particular meaning I shall not expound on the present occasion; for anxiety as to my domestic affairs[11] presses so heavily upon me that I must perforce abandon this and other tasks of public utility. I trust, however, that your Magnificence may afford me the opportunity to continue this useful exposition at some other time.

§33. With regard to the executive part of the work, which was divided after the same manner as the prologue taken as a whole, I shall say nothing either as to its divisions or its interpretation at present; save only that the process of the narrative will be by ascent from heaven to heaven, and that an account will be given of the blessed spirits who are met with in each sphere; and that their true blessedness consists in the apprehension of Him who is the beginning of truth, as appears from what John says: 'This is life eternal, to know thee the true God', &c.; and from what Boëtius says in his third book *On Consolation*: 'To behold thee is the end'. Hence it is that, in order to reveal the glory of the blessedness of those spirits, many things which have great profit and delight will be asked of them, as of those who behold the fullness of truth. And since, when the Beginning or First, which is God, has been reached, there is nought to be sought for beyond, inasmuch as He is Alpha and Omega, that is, the Beginning and the End, as the *Vision* of John tells us, the work ends in God Himself, who is blessed for evermore, world without end.

NOTES

1. *Ex eo quod.*
2. *Recipit,* here used absolutely, as in §21, l. 402.
3. *Causatum.*
4. *Recipiant,* used absolutely, as in §20, l. 376.
5. *Simpliciter.*
6. *Materiam.*
7. For help in rendering some of the technical passages in this and other sections I am indebted to my friend the late Dr. C.L. Shadwell, Provost of Oriel.
8. A.V. 'Thou sealest up the sum'.
9. Vulg. 'perfectus decore'; A.V. 'perfect in beauty'.
10. A.V. 'Thou hast been in Eden the garden of God'.
11. I follow Biagi here in taking the reference to be not to 'straitened circumstances', but to the pressure of family affairs; see *Bull. Soc. Dant. Ital.,* N.S. xvi. 29.

DOCTOR FAUSTUS
(CHRISTOPHER MARLOWE)

❦

"The Damnation of Faustus"
by J.P. Brockbank,
in *Marlowe: Dr. Faustus* (1962)

INTRODUCTION

In this detailed account of the allusions in Marlowe's work, J.P. Brockbank focuses on the way *Dr. Faustus* embodies Christian philosophy. While Brockbank acknowledges that Faust is condemned at the end of the play, he notes that the title character repents, vowing to burn his books and also uttering the words of Jesus on the cross: "My God, my God, why hast thou forsaken me? Why are thou so far from helping me, and from the words of my roaring?" These words alone, according to Brockbank, do not affect Faustus's damnation, but they do indicate that a character that has lost his way has found it again in his last moments of life, proclaiming salvation for all.

❦

THE WORLD'S REGARD

Faustus's performances before the Emperor are without the bizarre and outrageous quality of the anti-papist antics. Sticking to its

Brockbank, J.P. "The Damnation of Faustus." *Marlowe: Dr. Faustus*. Woodbury, N.Y.: Barron's Educational Series, 1962. 51–60.

source, the play lapses into its uncritical allegiances to civil authority. The addition of the Bruno episode makes things worse, since we are not expected to see any irony in the patriotic piety of 'poor Faustus' when he promises to 'Both love and serve the German Emperor And lay his life at holy Bruno's feet'. After the imperial ambitions voiced early in the play, Faustus's exercise of the privileges of power is disappointing. It is, of course, appropriate that it should be; but Marlowe does not sufficiently bring home to us the nature of the disappointment and betrayal. The scenes remind us that great magicians (even Simon and Cornelius Agrippa) are at best reputable court entertainers and not masters of empire. But Marlowe was evidently not much interested in the arts they practised or the whims they satisfied, and only at one point does he turn his scepticism and indifference into calculated dramatic bathos—where the Emperor, to 'satisfy' his 'longing thoughts at full' asks to see the 'little wart or mole' on the neck of Alexander's paramour. 'Patient judgments' may here recognise a trivial appetite for 'curiosity and novelty'; but for the greater part of the act this is the only taste that the play itself tries to satisfy.

The sport at the expense of Benvolio (mainly from the Faustbook) keeps alive something of the play's concern with heroic vanity (particularly at the start of IV. iii), but the plenitude of horns hardly compensates for the emptiness of Marlowe's horn of plenitude. The low-life scenes (III. iii; IV. v, vi, vii) are likewise, as Faustus puts it, when he brings them to a crisis in the Emperor's court, 'good subject for a merriment'. Robin, Dick, the Carter, the horse-courser and the Hostess are simple people at the mercy of the *magus*; their punishments, aptly administered to 'saucy varlets' who try to get the better of supernatural power, make 'artful sport' to drive away the 'sad thoughts' of the courtiers. They try, as Mephostophilis says of Faustus, 'To overreach the devil, but all in vain'.

'Vain' is perhaps the key-word for the impression given by the fourth act. It expresses what Faustus will call 'the vain pleasure of four and twenty years'. But in the course of the act the vanity, with shoulder-shrugging good humour, is as often indulged as exposed. Were it otherwise, the last act would perhaps be less impressive in calling Faustus and the audience to final account.

THE DAMNATION OF FAUSTUS

Pico, in his *Oration*, recalls 'that it was a saying of Zoroaster that the soul is winged and that, when the wings drop off, she falls again into the body; and then, after her wings have grown again sufficiently, she flies back to heaven'. After his headlong fall into the body, Faustus's wings seem to grow again in the last act.

The Vision of Helen

When 'music sounds' and Helen passes across the stage her sanctity is mirrored in the awed calm of the scholars' judgments. Her 'heavenly beauty passeth all compare'; she is 'the pride of nature's work' and a 'blessed sight'. This vision lends intensity and compassion to the austere admonitions of the Old Man, who speaks to Faustus when the scholars have left. Marlowe anticipates Milton in finding a poetry of 'kind rebuke', a moral music, to efface the magic that charms the soul to hell. And in the Scholar's 'Too simple is my wit to tell her praise' and the Old Man's 'No mortal can express the pains of hell', he seems to set himself new tasks for language to perform.

When Faustus resumes his communion with Helen the context in the scene and the play calls for an extreme and simultaneous celebration of the rival values of the heroic and moral orders; and this is accomplished with marvellous economy. From a moral point of view Faustus's will is viciously egocentric: 'let me crave of thee To glut the longing of my heart's desire'; and his eagerness to 'extinguish clear Those thoughts that do dissuade me from my vow' is a manifest sin against the Holy Spirit. And yet it is a dedicated will, and the self seems transcended by the sanctity of its aspiration and allegiance. Thoughts that would dissuade from a vow to a seemingly unfallen Lucifer are extinguished for the sake of clearness and purity, and the 'sweet embracings' of 'heavenly Helen' suggest a divine wedding in the mode of the *Song of Solomon* rather than (for example) the whoredoms of Samaria and Jerusalem in *Ezekiel* (xxiii).

Mephostophilis performs his last trick 'in twinkling of an eye'. Is Marlowe recalling St. Paul? 'In a moment, in the twinkling of an eye, at the last trump: for the trumpet shall sound, and the dead

shall be raised incorruptible . . . this mortal must put on immortality'
(1 *Cor.* xv. 52).

When Helen comes again in pageant style 'between two
Cupids' Marlowe endows Faustus with Tamburlaine's and Dido's
passions for heroic immortality. Tamburlaine had remembered
from 'Homer's Iliads', '*Hellen*, whose beauty sommond Greece to
armes, And drew a thousand ships to *Tenedos*' (2 *Tamb.* 3054).
Dido recalls 'the thousand ships' that desolated Troy and cries that
her lover will make her 'immortall with a kisse', while Aeneas calls
waves 'topless hills' and speaks of a thousand Grecians 'in whose
sterne faces shin'd the quenchless fire, That after burnt the pride of
Asia' (*Dido*, 1612, 1329, 1162, 481). Marlowe tells Helen's praises
by recalling from the heroic past the power that moved on her
behalf and, endowing the scholar with a soldier's imagination, he
allows Faustus's resolution to renew it for the future: 'And I will
combat with weak Menelaus And wear thy colours on my plumed
crest.' We feel too that Marlowe is vindicating his time's innocent
love of tournament and chivalry.

But rival feelings are awakened also. Without alluding to the Old
Testament, Marlowe moves in the same territories of the imagination,
and feels Ezekiel's fascination for conjunctions of beauty, passion and
destruction (see *Ez.* xxiii). Unlike the Sabean harlots, Helen is divine;
but the sacking of Troy and Wittenberg for her sake is related to the
Biblical image of the refining fire purging precious metals: 'All is
dross that is not Helena.' The speech looks back not only to Valdes
on 'the queen of love', Faustus's hope to 'live in all voluptuousness'
and the Prologue's exequy to 'proud audacious deeds' but also to
Mephostophilis's Last Judgment 'when all the world dissolves And
every creature shall be purified'. The purity is characteristically evoked
by 'the evening's air', 'a thousand stars', 'flaming Jupiter' and 'wanton
Arethusa's azured arms', reconciling 'sweet pleasure' with Faustus's
delight in beholding the heavens.

When Faustus kisses Helen he reconciles present with future
satisfactions—the large Romantic cry 'I will'. Shakespeare's Cleopatra
will say 'Eternity was in our lips and eyes', and Blake that 'The Gates
of the Senses open upon Eternity'; and Marlowe here persuades us
that Gluttony and Lechery have carried Faustus through hell to a
prospect of Heaven. 'Her lips suck forth my soul' may make Faustus a

witch and Helen a succuba, but 'see where it flies!' is a Simonian cry of triumph. Marlowe will not easily over-reach his own verbal magic.

The Plight of the Man

Faustus is 'but a man condemned to die' (IV. v. 21), 'has offended like a man' (V. i. 40) and has a 'distressed soul' (V. i. 65). His plight is expressed in a scrap of soliloquy, in his dealings with the Old Man and in his last talk with the scholars.

The comedy requires that Faustus should fall asleep and lose his leg (IV. v), and the opportunity is taken to remind us that his 'fatal' time draws to a final end. His distress is intense, but its nature uncertain— we cannot tell if the 'distrust' that despair drives into his thoughts is of God or of the devil. The passions of conscience, however, are in any case salutary, and Faustus is to blame for (very humanly) trying to 'confound' them with a quiet sleep. Sleep, like sloth, can be a sin. Faustus settles down for a nap in the hope of dodging moral conflict; and his 'Tush, Christ did call the thief upon the cross' is not as Greg supposes 'a sentimental piety' but a complacent blasphemy; in the Spira story and play the same sentiment is gravely weighed.

The Old Man's compassionate censure of Faustus adds a new dimension to our sense of the human predicament: 'Yet, yet, thou hast an amiable soul If sin by custom grow not into nature.' Augustine says, 'For the law of sin is the violence of custom, whereby the mind is drawn and holden, even against its will; but deservedly, for that it willingly fell into it' (*Confessions* VIII. 12). Faustus is in this state of being 'deservedly' held against will. Yet it is a bitter irony that the will in its freedom can more readily fall than climb. In putting so strong a stress on the will, it is easy to court the Pelagian heresy, which held that the human will can win salvation without grace. Marlowe encounters some difficulty in distinguishing dramatically between repentance by an act of free will and repentance through grace. The Old Man dissuades Faustus from using the devil's dagger by telling him of a hovering angel 'with a vial full of precious grace' and pleading with him to 'call for mercy and avoid despair'. Is it that Faustus cannot repent because he is without grace, and cannot have grace because he will not repent? Or is it that he cannot receive the grace of justification from the angelic vial because he has too often denied the promptings of prevenient grace? Either way, the human relationship has its own dignity and power, and leaves us to wonder why a graceless man should be so moved by another's compassion.

As 'hell strives with grace' for conquest in Faustus's breast, the powers of light and darkness seem matched in the Manichean way. But to patient judgment it appears that Faustus's yielding to evil is voluntary, while the Old Man's resistance to it makes it assist in the perfection of virtue. Faustus is again trapped by the metaphor of Lucifer as 'sovereign lord' with Mephostophilis an emissary empowered to punish a 'traitor'. He can only conceive 'presumption' as an offence against the tyranny of Pride, and it is his own pride that commits him to 'proud Lucifer'. The same pride moves his address to Helen with its presumptions of immortality and magnificence; it would be admirable were it not a last vain bid to escape from the human condition as the Old Man represents it. In the futility of his pride Faustus commands that the 'base and aged man' should suffer the 'greatest torments that our hell Affords'.

But the Old Man triumphantly endures the torments that in this life pride inflicts on humility. 'Satan begins to sift me with his pride' recalls *Luke* xxii. 31, 'Satan hath desired to have you, that he may sift you as wheat'. It is another image of purifying ordeal, and it is suffered on earth in 'our hell'—'As in this furnace God shall try my faith' (see *Is.* xlviii. 10). The Old Man will 'fly unto God' while the scholar Faustus remains below. As Augustine has it, 'The unlearned start up and take heaven by force, and we with our learning, and without heart, lo, where we wallow in flesh and blood' (*Confessions*, VIII. 19).

When Lucifer and his henchmen take up their positions to witness Faustus's end they are like the figures of revenge-play (e.g. *The Spanish Tragedy*) who gloat upon the ironic justice they exact from men. Here, however, as Mephostophilis looks forward to a spectacle of 'desperate lunacy' as man's 'labouring brain' begets 'idle fantasies To overreach the devil', the gloating takes the form of a pitiless objectivity about the nature of evil.

But the talk with the scholars supplies no 'idle fantasies' as Faustus movingly reassumes his humanity and his fellowship with other men. Yet both are flawed by his isolation and sense of his unique doom: 'had I lived with thee, then had I lived still'. We recognise humility stirring in his courtesy, but his resolute apartness is subtly touched with pride. He blames the devils for the paralysis of his moral being: 'I would weep, but the devil draws in my tears. . . . I would lift up my hands, but see, they hold 'em, they hold 'em'; but when the scholars chorus 'Who Faustus?' we are more persuaded of the reality of the incapacities for grief and penitence than of the power of the invisible spirits. Self-assertion and self-effacement meet in, 'Talk not of me, but save yourselves and depart'; as in the will he leaves for Wagner, there is a touch of irony in his magnanimity. And there is keen pathos in his farewell as it salvages a last pretext of reassurance, 'If I live till morning I'll visit you.'

A Last Judgment

After the scholars have left, the mockery of Mephostophilis administers a last turn of the screw: ''Twas I, that when thou wert i' the way to heaven, Dammed up thy passage; when thou tookst the book To view the scriptures, then I turned the leaves And led thine eye.' Faustus weeps. It is a terrifying speech, recoiling upon our whole experience of the play. But without it the exploration of the mystery of evil would not be complete; it is the dramatic equivalent of the Gospel's equally disturbing, 'Then entered Satan into Judas' (*Luke* xxii. 3). From one point of view the play's devils are only symbols of 'aspiring pride and insolence', and it is simply Faustus's wilful pride that turned the leaves and led his eye. It is *as if* the devil were directing him. But when Christianity externalised and personalised pride in its dramatic mythology of Satan it exposed itself to the hazard it meets here: man is prey to an adversary whose power daunts even Faustus and, as we have seen, daunted even Peter in his contests with Simon. In the tragic tradition, Satan's power is like a malignant fate (man is punished for the pride he was born with); in the Morality tradition it has grown into an inexplicable challenge to the power and mercy of God.

Yet the Good Angel denies the devil's ultimate power over man: 'Hadst thou affected sweet dignity Hell or the devil had had no power on thee'; and Faustus's failure to affect divinity is manifestly voluntary and culpable. But whether we take Mephostophilis's claim literally or metaphorically, we are left to repeat Augustine's unanswerable question: 'what can cause the will's evil, the will being sole cause of all evil?'

The final angelic pronouncements are, as Greg says, a Last Judgment upon Faustus. After it Faustus's death is not the natural death of the body only, but also what Augustine calls 'the eternal, penal second death' (referred to in *Rev.* xx. 14), and his soul tumbles directly into 'confusion'. The hell-fire and the tormented glutton of the Bad Angel's description retain their traditional power (see *Luke* xvi. 24) and there is no need to attribute them to a collaborator.

Damned Perpetually

Faustus's great final soliloquy consummates the play in both its aspects—Morality and Heroic Tragedy—and each in its own way triumphs over the other. In fear we acquiesce in the littleness and powerlessness of man, and in pity we share his sufferings and endorse his protest.

The horrible prospect of a man being burnt alive, which Marlowe (like the Christianity he honours) does not spare us, accounts for little of the pathos and power. In the first lines we are much more moved by the magnificent futility of the human protest against the inexorable movement of time as it enacts an inexorable moral law. We are reminded that 'all things that move between the quiet poles' are at the command of the process Faustus would escape: the 'ever-moving spheres' cannot by definition 'stand still'. Faustus had explained the seasonal 'circles' to the Duchess, who marvelled at the winter grapes (IV. vii. 23), and he had numbered the cycles of the spheres, but now his knowledge is of a different order. The cosmic rhythms evoked by the sense of the poetry seem to hold dominion over its movement. The first equally stressed eleven words echo the striking clock—'Ah Faustus, Now hast thou but one bare hour to live'; the 'perpetually' that falls with finality at the end of the first sentence returns in the mocking oxymoron 'perpetual day'; and 'rise, rise again' invokes precisely the diurnal motion it seeks to arrest.

The irony of the quotation from Ovid has long been celebrated. In the *Amores* (I. xiii. 40) it is the plea of ecstatic love, *Clamares*, '*lente currite, noctis equi*', which Marlowe had poorly translated, 'Then wouldst thou cry, stay night and runne not thus.' But here the Latin words in their English setting sound like a last attempt to cast a spell whose vanity is betrayed by the rhythm as the horses seem to quicken pace through the line, and confessed in 'the stars move still, time runs, the clock will strike'. Were the soliloquy to end here we should feel that confinement to time is the cruellest fact of man's condition.

In the next lines, however, his ordeal is confinement to earth: 'Oh, I'll leap up to my God! Who pulls me down?' The image affirming the immensity of Christ's Testament also declares its unreachable remoteness: 'See see where Christ's blood streams in the firmament.' Marlowe may be remembering both the gulf between heaven and hell (*Luke* xvi. 26) and Tamburlaine, defiant in his mortal sickness:

> Come let us march against the powers of heaven,
> And set blacke streamers in the firmament,
> To signify the slaughter of the Gods.
> Ah friends, what shall I do? I cannot stand. (2, *Tamb.* 4441)

Christ has accomplished the triumph over mortality that Tamburlaine's labouring brain could only imagine. The imperial pageant hyperbole of the earlier play has in the later been made to express the superhuman power of Christ; but he conquers by sacrifice not by slaughter—humility has become heroic. Even without appeal to Christian symbolism, the play has made the streaming blood emblematic of eternal life. Blood refuses to flow when Faustus cuts his arm, it 'dries with grief' as his 'conscience kills it', and it gushes forth from his eyes 'instead of tears'. As Faustus pleads that 'one drop' then 'half a drop' would save his soul, he confesses his barren littleness of life in the vastness of the moral universe.

As the vision of blood fades, Faustus meets the unappeased wrath of God and cries for the mountains and hills to fall on him (see, e.g., *Luke* xxiii. 30, *Rev.* vi. 16, *Hos.* x. 8). Burial in earth becomes a privilege refused to the last paroxysms of Faustus's will. He is again re-enacting the fall of Lucifer, the figure in Isaiah who is 'brought down to hell, to the sides of the pit' and 'cast out of the grave like an abominable branch' (*Is.* xiv). When Faustus hopes for a refining ordeal of dissolution and rebirth in 'the entrails of yon labouring clouds' which might 'vomit forth' his limbs and let his soul 'ascend to heaven' his words seem haunted by Lucifer's—'I will ascend above the heights of the clouds, I will be like the Most High'; and the same chapter could supply the stretching arm of God and the smoke of the Last Day (*Is.* xiv). Marlowe has assimilated and re-created the Biblical imagery, however, and it is dramatically valid whether or not we suppose it allusive. Faustus, the damned hero as the play has fashioned him, has become the fittest witness of apocalyptic vision. No chorus could speak with such moving authority, for Faustus alone has enacted all the futilities of pride.

The first phase of the soliloquy discovers the futility of human pretensions to power in the face of overwhelming cataclysm, the second makes us feel the futility of knowledge and speculation. Faustus's plea for 'some end to my incessant pain' (recalling the Faust-book and the Spira story and play) sums up that side of the Christian tradition which, with Augustine, is 'Against those that exclude both men and devils from pain eternal' (*City of God*, XXII. xxiii). Like 'Pythagoras' metempsychosis' it is wishful thinking. *The French Academy* (II. 85) could have occasioned the allusion to Pythagoras and supplied the distinction between the souls of brutes (made of 'elements') and those of men ('created of nothing'). And it would challenge Faustus's readiness to accuse the stars that reigned at his nativity by asking, 'how should the heavens, stars and planets give that to the soul which they themselves have not?' (II. 87).

Faustus moderates his struggle to escape the pain of responsibility as he curses his parents (see *Luke* xxiii. 29) and then checks himself: 'No Faustus, curse thyself, curse Lucifer That hath deprived thee of the joys of heaven.' Again, if we read 'Lucifer' as a metaphor for Pride, the problem of responsibility recedes; but it returns when we think of the devil as a person and evil as a power outside the consciousness of man. In either case, it is fitting that the pride of knowledge should be finally purged with 'I'll burn my books!' and the fellowship of sin perpetuated with 'Ah Mephostophilis!'

In the last scene, as in Shakespeare's tragedies, normal life must resume as best it can. Marlowe (there is no need to suppose a collaborator) abstains from the grotesque nastiness of the Faust-book catastrophe, and strikes an apt balance between horror, dismay and due reverence. If the noise that the scholars report seems a concession to popular taste, we may reflect that it might be a clue to the acting of

Faustus's closing words, from 'My God, my God! Look not so fierce
on me', and remember *Psalm* xxii:

> My God, my God, why hast thou forsaken me? why art thou so
> far from helping me, and from the words of my roaring?

EPILOGUE

The Epilogue seals both the Heroic-play and the Morality. In
'Cut is the bough that might have grown full straight' we feel that
the pruning has been done to maiming purpose. Marlowe may have
remembered the image from Churchyard's *Shore's Wife*, where it
also suggests wanton destruction, 'And bent the wand that mought
have grown full streight'. But the Bible haunts the lines too, and the
branch may be dead because it has failed to take nourishment from
the tree (see *John* xv. 4–7, *Psalm* lxxx). The next fine, 'And burned is
Apollo's laurel bough' alludes perhaps to the frustration of Faustus's
pre-eminence in the hidden mysteries, but again the destruction
may be wanton. The last lines are a due and weighty warning against
emulating 'forward wits' who 'practise more than heavenly power
permits'; yet they leave the wise still to wonder at the enticing deep-
ness of unlawful things.

Faustus's ordeal is specifically that of the aspiring mind (the
'unsatiable speculator' as the Faust-book has it), of that part of
our nature which is dissatisfied with being merely human and tries
vainly to come to rest in fantasies of omnipotence and omniscience.
It is a romantic agony which oscillates across an abyss between
extremities of hope and despair. Marlowe, seeing it for what it
was, related the hope to the imperial and speculative ambitions of
his time, and the despair to that side of Christianity which brings
home to us the inescapable mortality and doom of man. Goethe,
in a self-confessedly romantic age, was independently to take up
the story again and, after many oscillations, endorse its potential of
hope. Marlowe stuck to the basic shape of the story and accepted
the damnation of his hero. But not complacently. D.H. Lawrence,
who also understood the value of extreme commitments, said that a
work of art 'must contain the essential criticism on the morality to

which it adheres. And hence the antinomy, hence the conflict necessary to every tragic conception.' *Dr. Faustus* adheres to the rich and
searching morality of Augustinian thought; but it does not allow us
to come comfortably to rest in it. In the Heroic-play the reaching
mind that is punished by hell is also the mind that apprehends
heaven, and Faustus—the playwright's figment—suffers the one and
glimpses the other on the audience's behalf.

THE GREAT GATSBY
(F. SCOTT FITZGERALD)

⁙⁙⁙

"'Boats Against the Current': Mortality and the Myth of Renewal in *The Great Gatsby*"
by Jeffrey Steinbrink,
in *Twentieth Century Literature* (1980)

INTRODUCTION

In this essay on F. Scott Fitzgerald's masterwork, Jeffrey Steinbrink focuses on the myth of renewal as it is presented in *The Great Gatsby*. For Steinbrink, Gatsby follows the illusion that he can remake things and be born anew. But though Gatsby is the victim of a tragic fate, Nick Carraway, the book's narrator, may be viewed as an observer who learns from Gatsby's mistakes. In that sense, Nick is renewed, casting off Gatsby's obsession with the past and an "orgiastic future," and instead entering a timeless present in which we must continually be reborn.

∞

Fitzgerald wrote the bulk of *The Great Gatsby* in 1924, when he was twenty-eight. It might be described as an attempt to explore the

Steinbrink, Jeffrey. "'Boats Against the Current': Mortality and the Myth of Renewal in *The Great Gatsby*." *Twentieth Century Literature*, Vol. 26, No. 2 (Summer 1980), 157–70.

relationship between the past and the present in the hope of discovering a sense of balance between giddiness and despair capable of sustaining a man without delusion as he enters life's long decline. It is many other things as well, of course, but among its main concerns is how to face "the promise of . . . loneliness . . . , a thinning briefcase of enthusiasm, thinning hair" as we drive "on toward death through the cooling twilight."[1] *The Great Gatsby* exhorts those of us who would be reconciled with the future to see the past truly, to acknowledge its irrecoverability, and to chasten our expectations in view of our slight stature in the world of time and our ever-diminishing store of vitality.

We are brought to this understanding, however, only when we realize and accept the unlikelihood of regeneration or renewal in an entropic universe. Repeatedly in *The Great Gatsby* Fitzgerald allows us (and perhaps himself as well) to entertain the hope that it is possible to make a "fresh start"—to undo the calamities of the past or to relive its quintessential moments. The geographic dislocation of all the important characters in the novel is in itself suggestive of this hope; each, like Fitzgerald himself, is a midwesterner gone east, a descendant of the pioneers trying to reverse the flow of history. Of this countermigration Robert Ornstein has remarked that "To Fitzgerald . . . the lure of the East represents a profound displacement of the American dream, a turning back upon itself of the historic pilgrimage towards the frontier which had, in fact, created and sustained that dream."[2] The journey from West to East, that is, symbolically suggests an attempt to recapture the dream by drawing nearer its sources, to make a new start by getting back to what Robert Frost calls "the beginning of beginnings" in "West-running Brook." Having undertaken that journey, each of the book's main characters is made to deal with a reality which never quite meets his expectations.[3]

The notion that the flow of history can be arrested, perhaps even reversed, recurs in *The Great Gatsby* as a consequence of the universal human capacity for regret and the concomitant tendency to wish for something better. Nick Carraway has come East not simply to learn the bond business, but because his wartime experiences have left him restless in his midwestern hometown and because he wishes to make a clean break in his relationship with a woman whom he likes but has no intention of marrying. The predominant traits of Nick's character—patience, honesty, and levelheadedness—derive from his sure senses of history and social position, and yet in the chronology of the story he is first to succumb to the idea that life is subject to continual renewal. Of his roots in time and place he tells us,

> My family have been prominent, well-to-do people in this Middle Western city for three generations. The Carraways are something of a clan, and we have a tradition that we're descended from the Dukes of Buccleuch, but the actual founder of my line was my grandfather's brother, who came here in fifty-one, sent a substitute to the Civil War, and started the wholesale hardware business that my father carries on to-day (pp. 2–3).

The fresh start Nick seeks in the East represents not so much a rejection of his heritage as a declaration of its inadequacy to satisfy the rather ambiguous yearnings of the post-war generation. Stimulated by his contact with the teeming city and the novelty of his circumstances of West Egg, Nick gives in to a most compelling illusion. "I had that familiar conviction," he says, "that life was beginning over again with the summer" (p. 4).

Tom and Daisy Buchanan, their marriage in pieces, have similarly come East, determined to settle after several years of "drift[ing] here and there unrestfully wherever people played polo and were rich together" (p. 6). "'I'd be a God damned fool to live anywhere else,'" says Tom, whose foolishness is hardly a consequence of geography. Tom is a classic manifestation of entropic theory in human form. Nick describes him as "one of those men who reach such an acute limited excellence at twenty-one that everything afterward savors of anti-climax" (p. 6). Tom's single consolation may well be his muddled perception that he is not alone in his fall. "'Civilization,'" he says, "'[is] going to pieces'" (p. 10). Daisy lives with a perpetual illusion of recreation, transparent even to herself; she supposes that the meaning of life can be restored or revived by proper superficial ministrations, as rhinestones are added to an old gown. Thus she instigates senseless and enervating trips to the city, speaks thrillingly of dismal and mundane topics, and is charmed by Jay Gatsby's devotion without fully comprehending its meaning.

Even Jordan Baker, hard, cool, and perhaps the most resolutely cynical of Fitzgerald's characters, gives lip service to the regeneration myth. To Daisy's theatrical but heartfelt question, "'What'll we do with ourselves this afternoon . . . , and the day after that, and the next thirty years?'" Jordan responds, "'Don't be morbid. . . . Life starts all over again when it gets crisp in the fall'" (p. 118). Her remark neatly complements Nick's earlier acknowledgement of a sense of rebirth with the coming of summer, but Nick discovers (as Jordan apparently does not) that while these illusions may give momentary comfort, to surrender to the myth of rejuvenation is to deny both the nature of reality and the chance for a modicum of contentment. Jordan, of course, surrenders to nothing and so is unlikely to be much affected by her misconceptions.

The same cannot be said of the Great Gatsby himself. Like Nick, Daisy, Tom, and Jordan, Gatsby has emigrated from the heart of the continent to establish himself in the East, and like them he is anxious to believe that the possibilities of life do not diminish with time; unlike them, however, he adopts the myth of regeneration as the single sustaining principle of his existence. Gatsby's past is punctuated by a series of seeming fresh starts: As a young boy he jotted Franklinesque resolutions in his copy of *Hopalong Cassidy*, proving to his father's satisfaction that he "'was bound to get ahead.'" As a seventeen-year-old combing the beaches of Lake Superior he readied himself for the future by fashioning a wholly new identity. As a protegé of Dan Cody he acquired the experience which began turning his romantic musings into hard realities. As an army officer he assumed a manner in keeping with the deference paid him by society and took Daisy Fay as a kind of emotional hostage. After the war he did what he thought necessary to become what he had let Daisy believe he was, and to ransom her back.

Gatsby's accomplishments are a credit to his energy, enthusiasm, and singlemindedness, his sheer determination at all costs to stem the flow of history's current. "There was something gorgeous about him," Nick says, "some heightened sensitivity to the promises of life . . .—it was an extraordinary gift for hope, a romantic readiness such as I have never found in any other person and which it is not likely I shall ever find again" (p. 2). His gift for hope, as it turns out, is Gatsby's curse as well as his blessing, since it insulates him from the rational and experiential restraints which might otherwise temper the intensity of his ambition. Having managed so well at apparent self-creation and recreation, he allows his sensitivity to life's promises to blur into a belief in its limitless possibilities; ultimately he longs to conquer the passage of time itself. History is a very real force to Gatsby—in fact, almost a tangible commodity—and his patient, arduous assault upon it sometimes seems likely to succeed.

The extraordinary odyssey of Jay Gatsby began in the Minnesota back-country, where a restlessness to become something other than a dirt farmer drove a rather callow James Gatz to the shores of the Great Lakes and eventually into the company of Dan Cody. Serving in the entourage of millionaire Cody, whom Nick describes as "the pioneer debauchee" (p. 101), was instrumental not so much in molding the young adventurer's character as in lending tangibility to his materialistic fantasies and in indoctrinating him to the ruthlessness which easy money generates. "The truth," says Nick, "was that Jay Gatsby of West Egg, Long Island, sprang from his platonic conception of himself. He was a son of God—a phrase which, if it means anything, means just that—and he must be about His Father's business, the service of a vast, vulgar, and meretricious beauty. So he invented just the sort of Jay Gatsby that a seventeen-year-old boy would be likely to invent, and to this conception he was faithful to the end" (p. 99).

The act of self-generation, a marvelous exercise of will in the face of the force of history, established the terms of Gatsby's life and set the tone of his subsequent behavior. He learned early that detachment, disingenuousness, chicanery, and nerve often rendered even the most imposing circumstances malleable; especially under the protective mantle of his army lieutenancy he found himself capable of taking from the world almost anything he wanted, virtually without penalty. In taking Daisy, however, he allowed his detachment to slip, and once more he entered the world of time—of human ties, memories, and decay. Gatsby had sidestepped temporality momentarily by shedding his humanity and becoming a manipulator of rather than a participator in events. The cost—and the recompense—of his loving Daisy was to surrender his Platonic dreams to a tangible, corruptible reality and to reenter the stream of history. "He knew," says Nick of Gatsby at the moment of that surrender, "that when he kissed this girl, and forever wed his unutterable visions to her perishable breath, his mind would never romp again like the mind of God" (p. 112).

His affair with Daisy becomes the definitive circumstance of Gatsby's past. In a sense it is the *only* circumstance, all others—his experiences in the war, his five-months' study at Oxford, his "gonnegtion" with Meyer Wolfsheim, his lavish Long Island parties—seeming to him significant or relevant only insofar as they related to his regaining her love. Gatsby realizes the intensity of his commitment to this past only when he returns from the war to visit Louisville, Daisy's hometown, after she has wed Tom Buchanan. He finds amid the familiar walks and houses no vestige of the happiness he had known there and he understands that his memories lie buried in time as well as space. On the train which carries him away to the East Gatsby's longing to relive a moment of that time becomes almost palpable:

> The track curved and now it was going away from the sun, which, as it sank lower, seemed to spread itself in benediction over the vanishing city where she had drawn her breath. He stretched out his hand desperately as if to snatch only a wisp of air, to save a fragment of the spot she had made lovely for him. But it was all going by too fast now for his blurred eyes and he knew that he had lost that part of it, the freshest and best, forever (p. 153).

That this longing persists, undiminished, is suggested by Gatsby's striking a similar attitude when Nick first sees him, peering across the bay toward Daisy's green light, five years later. "He stretched out his arms toward the dark water in a curious way," Nick says, "and, far as I was from him, I could have sworn he was trembling" (p. 21).

Because he believes in the myth of regeneration and misapprehends the nature of history in an entropic cosmos, Gatsby becomes a victim of his past. He tells Nick that he has drifted about since the war "'trying to forget something very sad that happened to me long ago'" (p. 66), but in truth he has not only kept alive his memory of losing Daisy but devoted all his energies to getting her back. As his sympathy for his extraordinary neighbor grows Nick comes gradually to appreciate the scope and sincerity of Gatsby's single passion. "He talked a lot about the past," Nick says, "and I gathered that he wanted to recover something, some idea of himself perhaps, that had gone into loving Daisy. His life had been confused and disordered since then, but if he could once return to a certain starting place and go over it all slowly, he could find out what that thing was . . ." (pp. 111–12). To "return to a certain starting place" is precisely Gatsby's ambition—to fight back through time and make a fresh start in order to "correct" history and suspend the steady dissipation of the universe. In a passage from an early version of Chapter VIII which was eventually deleted Gatsby exclaims to Nick, "'Why I'm only thirty-two. I might be a great man if I could forget that once I lost Daisy. But my career has got to be like this—.' He drew a slanting line from the lawn to the stars. 'It's got to keep going up.'"[4]

Gatsby's declaration explicitly demonstrates his fundamental misunderstanding of the entropic world which Fitzgerald's characters inhabit. The line he draws toward the stars for Nick perpendicularly intersects the entropic curve and indicates Gatsby's determination to bend history to his will. "'That's what I've got to do,'" he says in the same deleted passage, "'—live the past all over again. And I don't want to start by running away . . . I want to turn the whole world upside down and give people something to think about.'"[5] The statement is remarkable because in Gatsby's case turning the world upside down has the ring of literal truth; his intention is to alter reality in order to bring it in line with his dream. "What more colossal *hubris* can 'a son of God' commit," asks R.W. Stallman, "than to tinker with the temporal order of the universe! To fix time and reinstate thus the past in the present (as though the interim were unreckoned and life has passed unclocked) to wipe the slate clean and begin anew—*that* is Gatsby's illusion."[6] While each of the book's major characters betrays some small faith in the myth of regeneration or renewal, Gatsby believes in it ultimately, absolutely.

Although this truth comes to Nick slowly as the threads of the story gradually unravel in his hands he is nevertheless awestruck by the proportions of Gatsby's ambition, the quality of his hope, and the degree of his confusion. "He wanted nothing less of Daisy," Nick marvels, "than that she should go to Tom and say: 'I never loved you.' After she had obliterated four years with that sentence they could decide upon the more practical measures to be taken. One of them was that, after she was free, they were to go back to Louisville and be married from her house—just as if it were five years ago" (p. 111). The custodian of common sense and of historical consciousness, Nick urges moderation. "'I wouldn't ask too much of her,'" he says. "'You can't repeat the past.'" "'Can't repeat the past?'" Gatsby cries incredulously. "'Why of course you can . . . ! I'm going to fix everything just the way it was before. . . . She'll see'" (p. 111). Here, then, is an open acknowledgement of Gatsby's presumption—of his "greatness" and his error. He will "fix" the past just as Wolfsheim fixed the 1919 World Series, by manipulating people and circumstances to suit his necessities. Gatsby, says Noble, "would bring Daisy back to 1917. He would obliterate her marriage and her motherhood. He would restore her virginity."[7] It is the supreme test of his Platonic will and of his faith in the human capacity for renewal, a test which he can only fail.

The scene of that failure is the confrontation between Gatsby and Tom Buchanan which takes place in a Plaza Hotel suite on a hot August afternoon. There Gatsby, who assures Daisy that her unhappy relationship with Tom is "'all over now,'" insists that "'It doesn't matter any more. Tell him the truth,'" he urges, "'—that you never loved him—and it's all wiped out forever'" (p. 132). Here, however, the irreversibility of human experience asserts itself as Tom—brutish and self-indulgent and sure of his instincts—breaks Daisy's spirit of rebellion by showing that it rests on a lie. "'Oh, you want too much!'" she cries to Gatsby. "'I love you now—isn't that enough? I can't help what's past . . . I did love him once but I loved you too'" (p. 133).

That Daisy "can't help what's past" marks the end of Gatsby's hopes for the future, since it is precisely that help which he had expected of her. Nick, who is as prepared to accept Daisy's limitations as Gatsby is determined to deny them, observes that after her admission ". . . only the dead dream fought on as the afternoon slipped away, trying to touch what was no longer tangible . . ." (p. 135). During the confrontation, he says, "Jay Gatsby' had broken up like glass against Tom's hard malice, and the long secret extravaganza was played out" (p. 148). The truth is that the gorgeous illusion fashioned by James Gatz on the shores of Lake Superior and enhanced by his vision of Daisy was destined almost from its inception to break up against the hard realities of human experience. Forced by Tom's very density, his "bulking" obtuseness, to see that the past, too, is solid, fixed, and irrefutable, Gatsby senses that the certainties around which his life has been so patiently organized have deserted him altogether. As Nick puts it,

> ... he must have felt that he had lost the old warm world, paid a high price for living too long with a single dream. He must have looked up at an unfamiliar sky through frightening leaves and shivered as he found what a grotesque thing a rose is and how raw the sunlight was upon the scarcely created grass. A new world, material without being real, where poor ghosts, breathing dreams like air, drifted fortuitously about ... (p. 162).

His extravaganza played out, Gatsby's death follows quickly, almost mercifully. Even before the shooting Nick finds it virtually impossible to think of his neighbor and "close friend" dispossessed of his dream (and in the passage quoted above imagines that Gatsby himself shares this attitude). Gatsby goes to his grave a "poor son of a bitch," the victim and martyr of his romantic obsession to interrupt for a moment the course of universal decline in order that it might accommodate his splendid illusion. He is not given time to contemplate his fall or to learn very much from it; no new faith, not even despair, establishes itself before he is murdered. It remains rather for Nick Carraway, in many senses Gatsby's complement as well as his chronicler, to interpret their mutual experiences over the summer and to apply the lesson of Gatsby's life to his own.[8]

That he does so is only implicitly evident at the story's end. Having determined to return to his native Minnesota, Nick wanders onto Gatsby's deserted beach during his last night in the East, perhaps—as he had said earlier of Gatsby himself—to determine what share is to remain his of the local heavens. "Gradually," he says,

> I became aware of the old island here that flowered once for Dutch sailors' eyes—a fresh, green breast of the new world. Its vanished trees, the trees that had made way for Gatsby's house, had once pandered in whispers to the last and greatest of all human dreams; for a transitory enchanted moment man must have held his breath in the presence of this continent, compelled into an aesthetic contemplation he neither understood nor

desired, face to face for the last time in history with something
commensurate to his capacity for wonder.

And as I sat there brooding on the old, unknown world, I
thought of Gatsby's wonder when he first picked out the green
light at the end of Daisy's dock. He had come a long way to
this blue lawn, and his dream must have seemed so close that he
could hardly fail to grasp it. He did not know that it was already
behind him, somewhere back in that vast obscurity beyond the
city, where the dark fields of the republic rolled on under the
night (p. 182).

In having Nick establish these parallels between Gatsby and the
Dutch sailors Fitzgerald makes several points concerning the
outcome and significance of his story with great economy.[9] First,
Gatsby is to be admired for the scope of his vision and the sincerity
with which he devotes himself to its realization. His greatness is
earned, the appellation hardly ironic. Second, like the Dutch sailors,
Gatsby fails to comprehend fully the enormity of the task which his
wonder inspires. To fulfill the promise inherent in the virgin land
is—like Gatsby's ambition to relive the past—necessarily an impos-
sibility, given the boundlessness of human hopes and the strictures
of an entropic universe. Third, any attempt to realize the dream is
destined not only to fail but to sully the dream itself. The actual
settlement of this country, by the Dutch and others, gave rise not to
edenic bliss but to mercantile avarice, divisiveness, and war. Gatsby's
dream of Daisy is perfect only until the tangible Daisy reappears;
then he begins to sense disappointment, even before his ultimate
disillusionment.

Gatsby's dream, the exercise of his Platonic will, obscures his
vision of the world as it is and clouds his understanding of the
historical process. It becomes Nick's responsibility, in telling Gatsby's
story, to see that process truly and to reconcile to it the events of the
summer of 1922. He is, in fact, driven toward this integrative view
of past and present both by his penchant for honesty and by a sense
of the connectedness of time which is part of his inheritance as a
Carraway. Unlike Gatsby, Nick accepts the circumstance of being
rooted in space and time, acknowledging both the limitations and the
reassurances which those roots provide.[10] Speaking of his home at the

end of the book—no longer "the ragged edge of the universe" but "my Middle West"—Nick says, "I am part of that, a little solemn with the feel of those long winters, a little complacent from growing up in the Carraway house in a city where dwellings are still called through decades by a family's name" (p. 177).

Nick returns to that home after Gatsby's death, reversing the tendency toward eastern migration with which the story began and indicating an intention to take up life where he had left it—to reenter the flow of his own personal history rather than resist it. In doing so he seems to many to be admitting defeat and withdrawing from the uncertainties of the present into the security of the past. Having had his glimpse of life's futility, proponents of this reading assert, Nick shrinks from further involvement and seeks a kind of non-life near the ancestral hearth.[11] Finally to regard Nick in this way, however, seems to place him ultimately in the camp of the Buchanans, whose relationship with the world at large has deteriorated to a series of retreats, escapes, and evasions. Nick has neither the callousness nor the moral opacity to behave with the vast carelessness of Tom and Daisy, and to reduce him to their stature is to deny the genuine sympathy, even love, with which he tells Gatsby's story.

The telling of that story itself is perhaps the best evidence that Nick refuses simply to withdraw from the experiences of the summer but seeks rather to learn from them. Certainly his capacity for optimism—together with his adolescent restlessness—has been greatly diminished by his having been so privileged a witness of Gatsby's fall. He returns to Minnesota a somber, sadder, and more modest man than he left. And yet for him to retire from life altogether would amount to an ultimate repudiation of Gatsby and his fragile, fated dream. Nick is determined, rather, to demonstrate Gatsby's greatness as well as his monumental foolishness, and in telling the story to examine the interplay of vision and restraint, of timeless imagination and historical reality, in the hope of striking a proper balance between the two. He sees that it is the tension between the incessant diminution of energy in an entropic universe and the perennial thrust of human expectations which gives life meaning.

It is on this note of accommodation, of very modest dreams in light of the sobering realities of history, that *The Great Gatsby* ends. Looking simultaneously back over the story he has told and forward to the future, Nick acknowledges with gratitude man's gift for hope while he accepts with equanimity the disillusionment which that gift often precipitates:

> Gatsby believed in the green light, the orgiastic future that year by year recedes before us. It eluded us then, but that's no matter—tomorrow we will run faster, stretch our arms farther. . . . And one fine morning—
>
> So we beat on, boats against the current, borne back ceaselessly into the past (p. 182).

And so we must, apparently, for according to Fitzgerald man lives successfully only in a state of equilibrium between resistance to the current and surrender to its flow. He must accommodate the lessons of his past to his visions of the future, giving it to neither, in order to stand poised for happiness or disappointment in the present.

NOTES

1. F. Scott Fitzgerald, *The Great Gatsby* (New York: Charles Scribner's Sons, 1953; first published 1925), pp. 136–37. Future page references to this text will appear parenthetically in the body of the essay.
2. Robert Ornstein, "Scott Fitzgerald's Fable of East and West," *College English*, 18 (1956–57), 141.
3. Milton R. Stern makes a similar observation somewhat more demonstratively. "In *The Great Gatsby*," he says, "Fitzgerald made out of his life with Zelda and his dream a moral history of the gnawing and murderous disappointment attendant upon discovering that the gorgeousness of America exists not in her glittering actualities, past or present, East or West, but in the fantastic sense of possibilities that drives the imagination of the archetypal American, the eternal pioneer in search of the golden moment dreamed in the past and to be recaptured in the imagined future." *The Golden Moment: The Novels of F. Scott Fitzgerald* (Urbana: Univ. of Illinois Press, 1970), p. 165.

4. Quoted in Henry Dan Piper, *F. Scott Fitzgerald: A Critical Portrait* (Carbondale, Ill.: Southern Illinois Univ. Press, 1968), p. 149.

5. Quoted in Piper; p. 149.

6. R.W. Stallman, "Gatsby and the Hole in Time," *Modern Fiction Studies*, 1 (Nov. 1955), 4.

7. Noble, p. 158.

8. Of this complementary relationship between Gatsby and Nick, John Henry Raleigh has said, "Taken together they contain most of the essential polarities that go to make up the human mind and its existence. Allegorically considered, Nick is reason, experience, waking, reality, and history, while Gatsby is imagination, innocence, sleeping, dream, and eternity . . . Nick's mind is conservative and historical, as is his lineage; Gatsby's is radical and apocalyptic—as rootless as his heritage. Nick is too much immersed in time and in reality; Gatsby is hopelessly out of it . . . They are generically two of the best types of humanity: the moralist and the radical," "F. Scott Fitzgerald's *The Great Gatsby*: Legendary Bases and Allegorical Significances," *University of Kansas City Review*, 24 (Oct. 1957), 57.

9. The identification of Gatsby with Nick's imaginary mariners has generated much discussion. "Gatsby is the spiritual descendant of these Dutch sailors," claims Ornstein. "Like them, he set out for gold and stumbled on a dream. But he journeys in the wrong direction in time as well as space. The transitory enchanted moment has come and gone for him and for the others, making the romantic promise of the future an illusory reflection of the past" (p. 141).

    "Like the sailors," observes Charles Thomas Samuels, "Gatsby tried to return to the source of life, to imbibe wonder at its breast. But man ages, time goes on, and life is a slow dying . . . When Gatsby loved Daisy he lost his dream; when the sailors took the new world they began the degradation of America's promise; when God saw what he had incarnated he went back to Heaven leaving only a blind sign of the business he would not now open. The past is our future. We have come to the end

of possibility." "The Greatness of 'Gatsby,'" *The Massa-
chusetts Review*, 7 (Autumn 1966), 793.

10. Maintaining that "Fitzgerald represents the past both as a loss
and as a source of strength," Thomas A. Hanzo asserts that
". . . in the Carraway family tradition, it confers a discipline and
standards which, even as survivals of an old morality, may still
produce better conduct than Nick witnesses on Long Island."
"The Theme and the Narrator of 'The Great Gatsby,'" *Modern
Fiction Studies*, 2 (Winter 1956–57), 189.

11. This argument is often made with considerable enthusiasm:
"[Nick's] return [to the Middle West] is not a positive
rediscovery of the well-springs of American life," insists
Ornstein. "Instead it seems a melancholy retreat from the
ruined promise of the East, from the empty present to the
childhood memory of the past," pp. 142–143.

   Similarly, Gary J. Scrimgeour maintains that ". . . Carraway's
distinctiveness as a character is that he fails to learn anything
from his story, that he can continue to blind himself even after
his privileged overview of Gatsby's fate. The defeat evident in
his disillusionment is followed not by progress but by retreat.
He returns not only to his safe environment in the Mid-West
but also to the same attitudes from which he started. . . . He
has learned nothing." "Against 'The Great Gatsby,'" *Criticism*, 8
(Winter 1966), 83–84.

HEART OF DARKNESS
(JOSEPH CONRAD)

❧ ✥ ❧

"The Journey Within"
by Albert J. Guerard,
in *Conrad the Novelist* (1958)

INTRODUCTION

For Albert J. Guerard, *Heart of Darkness* represents the rebirth—by way of a dark interior journey—of both Marlow, the novel's narrator, and Conrad, its author. As Guerard details, "Marlow reiterates often enough that he is recounting a spiritual voyage of self-discovery." Thus, for Guerard the physical journey Marlow makes is also symbolic: It is an outward sign of inner renewal and also a dark representation of our inner world, one animated by a drive for life and an overwhelming fear of death.

∞

Heart of Darkness is the most famous of [Conrad's] personal short novels: a *Pilgrim's Progress* for our pessimistic and psychologizing age. "Before the Congo I was just a mere animal."[1] The living nightmare of 1890 seems to have affected Conrad quite as importantly as did Gide's Congo experience thirty-six years later. The autobiographical basis of

---

Guerard, Albert J., "The Journey Within." *Conrad the Novelist*. Cambridge, Mass.: Harvard UP, 1958. pp. 1–59.

the narrative is well known, and its introspective bias obvious; this is Conrad's longest journey into self. But it is well to remember that *Heart of Darkness* is also other if more superficial things: a sensitive and vivid travelogue, and a comment on "the vilest scramble for loot that ever disfigured the history of human conscience and geographical exploration."[2] The Congo was much in the public mind in 1889, when Henry Stanley's relief expedition found Emin Pasha (who like Kurtz did not want to be rescued), and it is interesting to note that Conrad was in Brussels during or immediately after Stanley's triumphant welcome there in April 1890.[3] This was just before he set out on his own Congo journey. We do not know how much the Georges Antoine Klein who died on board the *Roi des Belges* resembled the fictional Kurtz, but Stanley himself provided no mean example of a man who could gloss over the extermination of savages with pious moralisms which were very possibly "sincere."

Heart of Darkness thus has its important public side, as an angry document on absurd and brutal exploitation. Marlow is treated to the spectacle of a French man-of-war shelling an unseen "enemy" village in the bush, and presently he will wander into the grove at the first company station where the starving and sick Negroes withdraw to die. It is one of the greatest of Conrad's many moments of compassionate rendering. The compassion extends even to the cannibal crew of the *Roi des Belges*. Deprived of the rotten hippo meat they had brought along for food, and paid three nine-inch pieces of brass wire a week, they appear to subsist on "lumps of some stuff like half-cooked dough, of a dirty lavender color" which they keep wrapped in leaves. Conrad here operates through ambiguous suggestion (are the lumps human flesh?) but elsewhere he wants, like Gide after him, to make his complacent European reader *see*: see, for instance, the drunken unkempt official met on the road and three miles farther on the body of the Negro with a bullet hole in his forehead.[4] *Heart of Darkness* is a record of things seen and done. But also Conrad was reacting to the humanitarian pretenses of some of the looters precisely as the novelist today reacts to the moralisms of cold-war propaganda. Then it was ivory that poured from the heart of darkness; now it is uranium. Conrad shrewdly recognized—an intuition amply developed in *Nostromo*—that deception is most sinister when it becomes self-deception, and the propagandist takes seriously his own fictions. Kurtz "could get himself to believe anything—anything." The benevolent rhetoric of his seven-teen-page report for the International Society for the Suppression of Savage Customs was meant sincerely enough. But a deeper sincerity spoke through his scrawled postscript: "Exterminate all the brutes!" The conservative Conrad (who found Donkin fit to be a labor leader) speaks through the journalist who says that "Kurtz's proper sphere ought to have been politics 'on the popular side.'"

Conrad, again like many novelists today, was both drawn to idealism and repelled by its hypocritical abuse. "The conquest of the earth, which mostly means the taking it away from those who have a different complexion or slightly flatter noses than ourselves, is not a pretty thing when you look into it too much. What redeems it is the idea only. An idea at the back of it; not a sentimental pretence but an idea; and an unselfish belief in the idea . . ." Marlow commits himself to the yet unseen agent partly because Kurtz "had come out equipped with moral ideas of some sort." Anything would seem preferable to the demoralized greed and total cynicism of the others, "the flabby devil" of the Central Station. Later, when he discovers what has happened to Kurtz's moral ideas, he remains faithful to the "nightmare of my choice." In *Under Western Eyes* Sophia Antonovna makes a distinction between those who burn and those who rot, and remarks that it is sometimes preferable to burn. The Kurtz who had made himself literally one of the devils of the land, and who in soli-tude had kicked himself loose of the earth, burns while the others rot. Through violent not flabby evil he exists in the moral universe even before pronouncing judgment on himself with his dying breath. A little too much has been made, I think, of the redemptive value of those two words—"The horror!" But none of the company "pilgrims" could have uttered them.

The redemptive view is Catholic, of course, though no priest was in attendance; Kurtz can repent as the gunman of *The Power and the Glory* cannot. *Heart of Darkness* (still at this public and wholly conscious level) combines a Victorian ethic and late Victorian fear of the white man's deterioration with a distinctly Catholic psychology. We are protected from ourselves by society with its laws and its watchful neighbors, Marlow observes. And we are protected by work. "You wonder I didn't go ashore for a howl and a dance? Well, no—I didn't. Fine sentiments, you say? Fine sentiments, be hanged! I had no time. I had to mess about with white-lead and strips of woolen blanket helping to put bandages on those leaky steam-pipes." But when the external restraints of society and work are removed, we must meet the challenge and temptation of savage reversion with our "own inborn strength. Principles won't do." This inborn strength appears to include restraint—the restraint that Kurtz lacked and the cannibal crew of the *Roi des Belges* surprisingly possessed. The hollow man, whose evil is the evil of *vacancy*, succumbs. And in their different degrees the pilgrims and Kurtz share this hollowness. "Perhaps there was nothing within" the manager of the Central Station. "Such a suspicion made one pause—for out there there were no external checks." And there was nothing inside the brick-maker, that papier-mâché Mephistopheles, "but a little loose dirt, maybe."

As for Kurtz, the wilderness "echoed loudly within him because he was hollow at the core." Perhaps the chief contradiction of *Heart of Darkness* is that it suggests and dramatizes evil as an active energy (Kurtz and his unspeakable lusts) but defines evil as vacancy. The primitive (and here the contradiction is only verbal) is compact of passion and apathy. "I was struck by the fire of his eyes and the composed languor of his expression . . . This shadow looked satiated and calm, as though for the moment it had had its fill of all the emotions." Of the two menaces—the unspeakable desires and the apathy—apathy surely seemed the greater to Conrad. Hence we cannot quite believe the response of Marlow's heart to the beating of the tom-toms. This is, I think, the story's minor but central flaw, and the source of an unfruitful ambiguity: that it slightly overdoes the kinship with the "passionate uproar," slightly undervalues the temptation of inertia.

In any event, it is time to recognize that the story is not primarily about Kurtz or about the brutality of Belgian officials but about Marlow its narrator. To what extent it also expresses the Joseph Conrad a biographer might conceivably recover, who in 1898 still felt a debt must be paid for his Congo journey and who paid it by the writing of this story, is doubtless an insoluble question. I suspect two facts (of a possible several hundred) are important. First, that going to the Congo was the enactment of a childhood wish associated with the disapproved childhood ambition to go to sea, and that this belated enactment was itself profoundly disapproved, in 1890, by the uncle and guardian.[5] It was another gesture of a man bent on throwing his life away. But even more important may be the guilt of complicity, just such a guilt as many novelists of the Second World War have been obliged to work off. What Conrad thought of the expedition of the Katanga Company of 1890–1892 is accurately reflected in his remarks on the "Eldorado Exploring Expedition" of *Heart of Darkness*: "It was reckless without hardihood, greedy without audacity, and cruel without courage . . . with no more moral purpose at the back of it than there is in burglars breaking into a safe." Yet Conrad hoped to obtain command of the expedition's ship even after he had returned from the initiatory voyage dramatized in his novel. Thus the adventurous Conrad and Conrad the moralist may have experienced collision. But the collision, again as with so many novelists of the second war, could well have been deferred and retrospective, not felt intensely at the time.

So much for the elusive Conrad of the biographers and of the "Congo Diary." Substantially and in its central emphasis *Heart of Darkness* concerns Marlow (projection to whatever great or small degree of a more irrecoverable Conrad) and his journey toward and through certain facets or potentialities of self. F.R. Leavis seems to regard him as a narrator only, providing a "specific and concretely realized point of view."[6] But Marlow reiterates often enough that he is recounting a spiritual voyage of self-discovery. He remarks casually but crucially that he did not know himself before setting out, and that he likes work for the chance it provides to "find yourself . . . what no other man can ever know." The Inner Station "was the farthest point of navigation and the culminating point of my experience." At a material and rather superficial level, the journey is through the temptation of atavism. It is a record of "remote kinship" with the "wild and passionate uproar," of a "trace of a response" to it, of a final rejection of the "fascination of the abomination." And why should there not be the trace of a response? "The mind of man is capable of anything—because everything is in it, all the past as well as all the future." Marlow's temptation is made concrete through his exposure to Kurtz, a white man and sometime idealist who had fully responded to the wilderness: a potential and fallen self. "I had turned to the wilderness really, not to Mr. Kurtz." At the climax Marlow follows Kurtz ashore, confounds the beat of the drum with the beating of his heart, goes through the ordeal of looking into Kurtz's "mad soul," and brings him back to the ship. He returns to Europe a changed and more knowing man. Ordinary people are now "intruders whose knowledge of life was to me an irritating pretence, because I felt so sure they could not possibly know the things I knew."

On this literal plane, and when the events are so abstracted from the dream-sensation conveying them, it is hard to take Marlow's plight very seriously. Will he, the busy captain and moralizing narrator, also revert to savagery, go ashore for a howl and a dance, indulge unspeakable lusts? The late Victorian reader (and possibly Conrad himself) could take this more seriously than we; could literally believe not merely in a Kurtz's deterioration through months of solitude but also in the sudden reversions to the "beast" of naturalistic fiction. Insofar as Conrad does want us to take it seriously and literally, we must admit the nominal triumph of a currently accepted but false psychology over his own truer intuitions. But the triumph is only nominal. For the personal narrative is unmistakably authentic, which means that it explores something truer, more fundamental, and distinctly less material: the night journey into the unconscious, and confrontation of an entity within the self. "I flung one shoe overboard, and became aware that that was exactly what I had been looking forward to—a talk with Kurtz." It little matters what, in terms of psychological symbolism, we call this double or say he represents: whether the Freudian id or the Jungian shadow or more vaguely the outlaw. And I am afraid it is impossible to say where Conrad's conscious understanding of his story began and ended. The important thing is that the introspective plunge and powerful dream seem true; and are therefore inevitably moving.

Certain circumstances of Marlow's voyage, looked at in these terms, take on a new importance. The true night journey can occur (except during analysis) only in sleep or in the waking dream of a profoundly intuitive mind. Marlow insists more than is necessary on the dreamlike quality of his narrative. "It seems to me I am trying to tell you a dream—making a vain attempt, because no relation of a dream can convey the dream-sensation, that commingling of absurdity, surprise, and bewilderment in a tremor of struggling revolt . . ." Even before leaving Brussels Marlow felt as though he "were about to set off for the center of the earth," not the center of a continent.[7] The introspective voyager leaves his familiar rational world, is "cut off from the comprehension" of his surroundings; his steamer toils "along slowly on the edge of a black and incomprehensible frenzy." As the crisis approaches, the dreamer and his ship move through a silence that "seemed unnatural, like a state of trance"; then enter (a few miles below the Inner Station) a deep fog. "The approach to this Kurtz grubbing for ivory in the wretched bush was beset by as many dangers as though he had been an enchanted princess sleeping in a fabulous castle."[8] Later, Marlow's task is to try "to break the spell" of the wilderness that holds Kurtz entranced.

The approach to the unconscious and primitive may be aided by a savage or half-savage guide, and may require the token removal of civilized trappings or aids; both conceptions are beautifully dramatized in Faulkner's "The Bear." In *Heart of Darkness* the token "relinquishment" and the death of the half-savage guide are connected. The helmsman falling at Marlow's feet casts blood on his shoes, which he is "morbidly anxious" to change and in fact throws overboard.[9] (The rescue of Wait in *The Nigger of the "Narcissus"* shows a similar pattern.) Here we have presumably entered an area of unconscious creation; the dream is true but the teller may have no idea why it is. So too, possibly, a psychic need as well as literary tact compelled Conrad to defer the meeting between Marlow and Kurtz for some three thousand words after announcing that it took place. We think we are about to meet Kurtz at last. But instead Marlow leaps ahead to his meeting with the "Intended"; comments on Kurtz's megalomania and assumption of his place among the devils of the land; reports on the seventeen-page pamphlet; relates his meeting and conversation with Kurtz's harlequin disciple—and only then tells of seeing through his binoculars the heads on the stakes surrounding Kurtz's house. This is the "evasive" Conrad in full play, deferring what we most want to know and see; perhaps compelled to defer climax in this way. The tactic is dramatically effective, though possibly carried to excess: we are told on the authority of completed knowledge certain things we would have found hard to believe had they been presented through a slow consecutive realistic discovery. But also it can be argued that it was psychologically impossible for Marlow to go at once to Kurtz's house with the others. The double must be brought on board the ship, and the first confrontation must occur there. We are reminded of Leggatt in the narrator's cabin, of the trapped Wait on the *Narcissus*.

The incorporation and alliance between the two becomes material, and the identification of "selves."

Hence the shock Marlow experiences when he discovers that Kurtz's cabin is empty and his secret sharer gone; a part of himself has vanished. "What made this emotion so overpowering was—how shall I define it?—the moral shock I received, as if something altogether monstrous, intolerable to thought and odious to the soul, had been thrust upon me unexpectedly." And now he must risk the ultimate confrontation in a true solitude and must do so on shore. "I was anxious to deal with this shadow by myself alone—and to this day I don't know why I was so jealous of sharing with anyone the peculiar blackness of that experience." He follows the crawling Kurtz through the grass; comes upon him "long, pale, indistinct, like a vapor exhaled by the earth." ("I had cut him off cleverly . . .") We are told very little of what Kurtz said in the moments that follow; and little of his incoherent discourses after he is brought back to the ship. "His was an impenetrable darkness. I looked at him as you peer down at a man who is lying at the bottom of a precipice where the sun never shines"—a comment less vague and rhetorical, in terms of psychic geography, than it may seem at a first reading. And then Kurtz is dead, taken off the ship, his body buried in a "muddy hole." With the confrontation over, Marlow must still emerge from environing darkness, and does so through that other deep fog of sickness. The identification is not yet completely broken. "And it is not my own extremity I remember best—a vision of grayness without form filled with physical pain, and a careless contempt for the evanescence of all things—even of this pain itself. No! It is his extremity that I seem to have lived through." Only in the atonement of his lie to Kurtz's "Intended," back in the sepulchral city, does the experience come truly to an end. "I laid the ghost of his gifts at last with a lie . . ."

Such seems to be the content of the dream. If my summary has even a partial validity it should explain and to an extent justify some of the "adjectival and worse than supererogatory insistence" to which F.R. Leavis (who sees only the travelogue and the portrait of Kurtz) objects. I am willing to grant that the unspeakable rites and unspeakable secrets become wearisome, but the fact—at once literary and psychological—is that they must remain *unspoken*. A confrontation with such a double and facet of the unconscious cannot be reported through realistic dialogue; the conversations must remain as shadowy as the narrator's conversations with Leggatt. So too when Marlow finds it hard to define the moral shock he received on seeing the empty cabin, or when he says he doesn't know why he was jealous of sharing his experience, I think we can take him literally . . . and in a sense even be thankful for his uncertainty. The greater tautness and economy of "The Secret Sharer" comes from its larger conscious awareness of the psychological process it describes; from its more deliberate use of the double as symbol. And of the two stories I happen to prefer it. But it may be the groping, fumbling *Heart of Darkness* that takes us into a deeper region of the mind. If the story is not about this deeper region, and not about Marlow himself, its length is quite indefensible. But even if one were to allow that the final section is about Kurtz (which I think simply absurd), a vivid pictorial record of his unspeakable lusts and gratifications would surely have been ludicrous. I share Mr. Leavis' admiration for the heads on the stakes. But not even Kurtz could have supported many such particulars.[10]

"I listened on the watch for the sentence, for the word, that would give me the clue to the faint uneasiness inspired by this narrative that seemed to shape itself without human lips in the heavy night air of the river." Thus one of Marlow's listeners, the original "I" who frames the story, comments on its initial effect. He has discovered how alert one must be to the ebb and flow of Marlow's narrative, and here warns the reader. But there is no single word; not even the word *trance* will do. For the shifting play of thought and feeling and image and event is very intricate. It is not vivid detail alone, the heads on stakes or the bloody shoes; nor only the dark mass of moralizing abstraction; nor the dramatized psychological intuitions apart from their context that give *Heart of Darkness* its brooding weight. The impressionist method—one cannot leave this story without subscribing to the obvious—finds here one of its great triumphs of tone. The random movement of the nightmare is also the controlled movement of a poem, in which a quality of feeling may be stated or suggested and only much later justified. But it is justified at last.

The method is in important ways different from that of *Lord Jim*, though the short novel was written during an interval in the long one, and though Marlow speaks to us in both. For we do not have here the radical obfuscations and sudden wrenchings and violent chronological ambiguities of *Lord Jim*. Nor are we, as in *Nostromo*, at the mercy of a wayward flashlight moving rapidly in a cluttered room. *Heart of Darkness* is no such true example of spatial form. Instead the narrative advances and withdraws as in a succession of long dark waves borne by an incoming tide. The waves encroach fairly evenly on the shore, and presently a few more feet of sand have been won. But an occasional wave thrusts up unexpectedly, much farther than the others: even as far, say, as Kurtz and his Inner Station. Or, to take the other figure: the flashlight is held firmly; there are no whimsical jerkings from side to side. But now and then it is raised higher, and for a brief moment in a sudden clear light we discern enigmatic matters to be explored much later. Thus the movement of the story is sinuously progressive, with much incremental repetition. The intent is not to subject the reader to multiple strains and ambiguities, but rather to throw over him a brooding gloom, such a warm pall as those two Fates in the home office might knit, back in the sepulchral city.

Yet no figure can convey *Heart of Darkness* in all its resonance and tenebrous atmosphere. The movement is not one of penetration and withdrawal only; it is also the tracing of a large grand circle of aware-ness. It begins with the friends on the yacht under the dark above Gravesend and at last returns to them, to the tranquil waterway that "leading to the uttermost ends of the earth flowed sombre under an overcast sky—seemed to lead into the heart of an immense darkness." For this also "has been one of the dark places of the earth," and Marlow employs from the first his methods of reflexive reference and casual foreshadowing. The Romans were men enough to face this darkness of the Thames running between savage shores. "Here and there a military camp lost in a wilderness, like a needle in a bundle of hay—cold, fog, tempests, disease, exile, and death—death skulking in the air, in the water, in the bush." But these Romans were "no colonists," no more than the pilgrims of the Congo nineteen hundred years later; "their administration was merely a squeeze." Thus early Marlow establishes certain political values. The French gunboat firing into a continent anticipates the blind firing of the pilgrims into the jungle when the ship has been attacked. And Marlow hears of Kurtz's first attempt to emerge from the wilderness long before he meets Kurtz in the flesh, and wrestles with his reluctance to leave. Marlow returns again and again, with increasing irony, to Kurtz's benevolent pamphlet.

The travelogue as travelogue is not to be ignored; and one of Roger Casement's consular successors in the Congo (to whom I introduced *Heart of Darkness* in 1957) remarked at once that Conrad certainly had a "feel for the country." The demoralization of the first company station is rendered by a boiler "wallowing in the grass," by a railway truck with its wheels in the air. Presently Marlow will discover a scar in the hillside into which drainage pipes for the settlement had been tumbled; then will walk into the grove where the Negroes are free to die in a "greenish gloom." The sharply visualized particulars suddenly intrude on the somber intellectual flow of Marlow's meditation: magnified, arresting. The boilermaker who "had to crawl in the mud under the bottom of the steamboat . . . would tie up that beard of his in a kind of white serviette he brought for the purpose. It had loops to go over his ears." The papier-maché Mephistopheles is as vivid, with his delicate hooked nose and glittering mica eyes. So too is Kurtz's harlequin companion and admirer, humbly dissociating himself from the master's lusts and gratifications. "I! I! I am a simple man. I have no great thoughts." And even Kurtz, shadow and symbol though he be, the man of eloquence who in this story is almost voiceless, and necessarily so—even Kurtz is sharply visualized, an "animated image of death," a skull and body emerging as from a winding sheet, "the cage of his ribs all astir, the bones of his arm waving."

This is Africa and its flabby inhabitants; Conrad did indeed have a "feel for the country." Yet the dark tonalities and final brooding impression derive as much from rhythm and rhetoric as from such visual details: derive from the high aloof ironies and from a prose that itself advances and recedes in waves. "This initiated wraith from the back of Nowhere honored me with its amazing confidence before it vanished altogether." Or, "It is strange how I accepted this unforseen partnership, this choice of nightmares forced upon me in the tenebrous land invaded by these mean and greedy phantoms." These are true Conradian rhythms, but they are also rhythms of thought. The immediate present can be rendered with great compactness and drama: the ship staggering within ten feet of the bank at the time of the attack, and Marlow's sudden glimpse of a face amongst the leaves, then of the bush "swarming with human limbs." But still more immediate and personal, it may be, are the meditative passages evoking vast tracts of time, and the "first of men taking possession of an accursed inheritance." The prose is varied, far more so than is usual in the early work, both in rhythm and in the movements from the general to the particular and back. But the shaped sentence collecting and fully expending its breath appears to be the norm. Some of the best passages begin and end with them:

> "Going up that river was like traveling back to the earliest beginnings of the world, when vegetation rioted on the earth and the big trees were kings. An empty stream, a great silence, an impenetrable forest. The air was warm, thick, heavy, sluggish. There was no joy in the brilliance of sunshine. The long stretches of the waterway ran on, deserted, into the gloom of overshadowed distances. On silvery sandbanks hippos and alligators sunned themselves side by side."[11]

The insistence on darkness, finally, and quite apart from ethical or mythical overtone, seems a right one for this extremely personal statement. There is a darkness of passivity, paralysis, immobilization; it is from the state of entranced languor rather than from the monstrous desires that the double Kurtz, this shadow, must be saved. In Freudian theory, we are told, such preoccupation may indicate fear of the feminine and passive. But may it not also be connected, through one of the spirit's multiple disguises, with a radical fear of death, that other darkness? "I had turned to the wilderness really, not to Mr. Kurtz, who, I was ready to admit, was as good as buried. And for a moment it seemed to me as if I also were buried in a vast grave full of unspeakable secrets. I felt an intolerable weight oppressing my breast, the smell of the damp earth, the unseen presence of victorious corruption, the darkness of an impenetrable night."

It would be folly to try to limit the menace of vegetation in the restless life of Conradian image and symbol. But the passage reminds us again of the story's reflexive references, and its images of deathly immobilization in grass. Most striking are the black shadows dying in the greenish gloom of the grove at the first station. But grass sprouts between the stones of the European city, a "whited sepulcher," and on the same page Marlow anticipates coming upon the remains of his predecessor: "the grass growing through his ribs was tall enough to hide his bones." The critical meeting with Kurtz occurs on a trail through the grass. Is there not perhaps an intense horror behind the casualness with which Marlow reports his discoveries, say of the Negro with the bullet in his forehead? Or: "Now and then a carrier dead in harness, at rest in the long grass near the path, with an empty water gourd and his long staff lying by his side."

All this, one must acknowledge, does not make up an ordinary light travelogue. There is no little irony in the letter of November 9, 1891, Conrad received from his guardian after returning from the Congo, and while physically disabled and seriously depressed: "I am sure that with your melancholy temperament you ought to avoid all meditations which lead to pessimistic conclusions. I advise you to lead a more active life than ever and to cultivate cheerful habits."[12] Uneven in language on certain pages, and lacking "The Secret Sharer"'s economy, *Heart of Darkness* nevertheless remains one of the great dark meditations in literature, and one of the purest expressions of a melancholy temperament.

NOTES

1. Jean-Aubry, *Life and Letters*, I, 141, and *The Sea Dreamer*, p. 175. Reportedly said to Edward Garnett. In his *Joseph Conrad in the Congo* (London, 1926), p. 73, Jean-Aubry gives a slightly different wording: "Before the Congo I was only a simple animal."

2. *Last Essays*, p. 17. In *Heart of Darkness* Conrad makes once his usual distinction between British imperialism and the imperialism of other nations. On the map in Brussels there "was a vast amount of red—good to see at any time, because one knows that some real work is done in there." His 1899 letters to E.L. Sanderson and to Mme. Angèle Zagórska on the Boer war express his position clearly. The conspiracy to oust the Briton "is ready to be hatched in other regions. It . . . is everlastingly skulking in the Far East. A war there or anywhere but in S. Africa would have been conclusive,—would have been worth the sacrifices" (Jean-Aubry, *Life and Letters*, I, 286). "That they—the Boers—are struggling in good faith for their independence cannot be doubted; but it is also a fact that

they have no idea of liberty, which can only be found under the
English flag all over the world" (*ibid.*, I, 288).

3. *Life and Letters*, I, 121, 124; *The Sea Dreamer*, pp. 154–159.
4. Compare "The Congo Diary," *Last Essays*, p. 163. Conrad did
   not use the skeleton tied to a post that he saw on Tuesday,
   July 29 (*ibid.*, p. 169). It might have seemed too blatant or
   too "literary" in a novel depending on mortuary imagery from
   beginning to end.
5. *Life and Letters*, I, 137; *The Sea Dreamer*, p. 171.
6. F.R. Leavis, *The Great Tradition* (London, 1948), p. 183.
7. Lilian Feder finds a number of parallels with the sixth book
   of the *Aeneid* in "Marlow's Descent into Hell," *Nineteenth-
   Century Fiction*, IX (March 1955) 280–292; Robert O. Evans
   finds chiefly the influence of Dante's *Inferno* in "Conrad's
   Underworld," *Modern Fiction Studies*, II (May 1956), 56–62. My
   views on literary influence differ from those of Miss Feder and
   Mr. Evans. But echoes and overtones may exist. We may apply
   to *Heart of Darkness* Thomas Mann's words on *Death in Venice*: a
   little work of "inexhaustible allusiveness."
8. The analogy of unspeakable Kurtz and enchanted princess may
   well be an intended irony. But there may be some significance
   in the fact that this once the double is imagined as an entranced
   feminine figure.
9. Like any obscure human act, this one invites several
   interpretations, beginning with the simple washing away of
   guilt. The fear of the blood may be, however, a fear of the
   primitive toward which Marlow is moving. To throw the shoes
   overboard would then mean a token rejection of the savage, not
   the civilized-rational. In any event it seems plausible to have
   blood at this stage of a true initiation story.
10. The reader irritated by the hallucinated atmosphere and
    subjective preoccupation of *Heart of Darkness* should turn
    to Robert Louis Stevenson's short novel, *The Beach of Falesá*
    (1892). A new trader, Wiltshire, takes a native mistress, and
    finds himself—thanks to a rival trader (Case)—virtually
    excommunicated. The situation distantly resembles that of
    Willems in *The Outcast of the Islands*. Later, Wiltshire goes
    inland to discover the source of Case's power over the natives;

he has heard stories that his rival worships or traffics with devils. He finds an Æolian harp in a tree (to simulate ghostly voices) and presently the place of worship:

> "Along all the top of it was a line of queer figures, idols or scarecrows, or what not. They had carved and painted faces, ugly to view, their eyes and teeth were of shell, their hair and their bright clothes blew in the wind, and some of them worked with the tugging . . .

> "Then it came in my mind that Case had let out to me the first day that he was a good forger of island curiosities, a thing by which so many traders turn an honest penny. And with that I saw the whole business, and how this display served the man a double purpose: first of all, to season his curiosities and then to frighten those that came to visit him."

Had Conrad read *The Beach of Falesá* before writing *Heart of Darkness*? The question is unimportant. The important thing is to recognize the immense distance from Case's carved faces to the skulls on Kurtz's palisade; from Case's pretended traffic with devils to Kurtz's role as one of the devils of the land; from Wiltshire's canny outwitting of a rival trader to Marlow's dark inward journey; from the inert jungle of Stevenson's South Pacific to the charged symbolic jungle of Conrad's Congo. The nighttime meeting of Case and Wiltshire is merely an exciting physical struggle. *The Beach of Falesá* is a good manly yarn totally bereft of psychological intuition.

11. "Heart of Darkness," *Youth*, pp. 92–93.

12. *Life and Letters*, I, 148. *The Sea Dreamer*, p. 183, offers a slightly different translation of these lines.

THE HOLY SONNETS
(JOHN DONNE)

"Renewal and Rebirth
in John Donne's *The Holy Sonnets*"
by Gary Ettari,
the University of North Carolina at Asheville

John Donne's *The Holy Sonnets*, written later in his life, is a series of nineteen sonnets in which Donne directly addresses God in order to become more enlightened about the difficulties of living a devout and faithful Christian life. Yet these sonnets are not, as their name might imply, calm and measured conversations with God. Rather, Donne, as in his early love poetry, speaks to God in an ardent and, some may say, irreverent voice. Readers of these poems often note that the speaker in the *Holy Sonnets* seems at times decidedly *un*holy. The uniqueness of Donne's poetic voice and his complex relationship with deity make him one of the most engaging voices of the early modern period. In his sonnets, Donne abandons the gentle and modest voice with which previous poets addressed God and instead demands God's salvation. He obsesses over his own mortality and eventual death, yet also acknowledges that death is but a path to God's grace, a way of renewal and rebirth.

To understand Donne's complex spirituality, it helps to consider his background. Donne was born in London to a Roman Catholic family in 1572. At that time, Roman Catholicism was barely tolerated in England, especially in the more populated urban areas. Queen Elizabeth I's father, Henry VIII, had made a break with the Roman

Catholic Church because it would not annul his marriage to his first wife, Catherine, in order that he could marry Anne Boleyn. Henry eventually founded the Church of England, and it was the general tendency of the English people for many decades afterward to be suspicious of, if not outright hostile toward, the Roman Catholic Church, its doctrines, and its adherents. Before Donne was born, Queen Elizabeth oversaw the passing of the Act of Uniformity (1559), which made attendance at a Sunday service in an Anglican church mandatory. By the time Donne grew into young manhood, the queen had outlawed the performance of Catholic rituals altogether.

Such religious tensions were not unique to England in the sixteenth century, but Donne, as a member of a persecuted religious minority, would have grown up in a contentious and often confusing theological atmosphere. Things were further complicated for Donne in 1593 when his brother Henry, arrested for providing sanctuary to a Catholic priest, died of a fever in prison. This event led him to question his faith, a skepticism that persisted even after he converted to the Anglican Church and eventually entered the ministry in 1615. By this time, he had written two anti-Catholic tracts, *Pseudo-Martyr* (1610) and *Ignatius his Conclave* (1611). *The Holy Sonnets*, most likely written in 1618, reflect Donne's complex relationship with God as well as the internal conflicts and self-doubt he felt as someone who had left one faith for another.

The speaker of *The Holy Sonnets* often despairs over feelings of personal unworthiness or fear of death. In most of the poems, he reaches out to God, seeking comfort in God's grace despite his own failings. Sonnet I, for example, begins

> Thou hast made me, and shall Thy work decay?
> Repair me now, for now mine end doth haste;
> I run to death and death meets me as fast,
> And all my pleasures are like yesterday. (1–4)

The question that begins the sonnet reflects both the need the speaker feels for God's presence in his life and the anxiety he feels regarding the lack of that presence. The only way he will not "decay," he realizes, is if he remembers that he is a creation of God. The three lines after the initial question indicate that the speaker indeed fears death and has a preoccupation with worldly experiences ("pleasures") that both prevents one being prepared for death and hastens death's arrival. In his request for God to "repair" him, the speaker acknowledges that he cannot earn salvation or absolution himself but must do so through God's mercy.

The preoccupation with death that appears in Sonnet I is taken up again in various sonnets, most notably Sonnet X ("Death Be Not Proud"). Here, the speaker seems momentarily relieved of his fear of death and sounds defiantly triumphant:

> Death, be not proud, though some have called thee
> Mighty and dreadful, for thou art not so;
> For those whom thou think'st thou dost overthrow
> Die not, poor death, nor yet canst thou kill me. (1–4)

The direct address to death and the speaker's almost smug attitude indicate that he has achieved, at least momentarily, a peace of mind that eluded him in the first sonnet. Death is no longer to be feared, is not "mighty" or "dreadful," but is instead "poor" because it only brings a temporary cessation of life. Later in the poem, Donne notes that "One short sleep past, we wake eternally" (13), implying that the death of the body is akin to little more than an afternoon nap in the context of the Christian notion of the body's resurrection at Judgment Day. The last line of the poem, for example, reiterates the idea that death is merely temporary: "death shall be no more; death, thou shalt die" (14). Death, seen by the unfaithful as something to be feared, is, to the speaker of the poem, simply a temporary state that, once Jesus returns to Earth and Judgment Day occurs, will no longer exist.

While Donne's preoccupation with his own mortality might seem macabre to us, it is important to understand that in the early modern period, the prospect of death was not as remote as it is in our modern age, where average human life expectancy is almost 80 years. In Donne's time, there was very little in the way of medical science as we know it now. There were no antibiotics or aspirin and only a rudimentary understanding of how diseases and viruses worked or spread. The plague was a constant worry, the literary theme of *carpe diem* ("seize the day") advised both men and women to find love and marry young, and the high infant mortality rate, combined with the lack of sanitary conditions and what we would consider to be primitive methods of treating diseases, meant that the average life span in Donne's time was somewhere in the mid-40s. The ever-present threat of death, as *The Holy Sonnets* demonstrate, also meant that, like Donne, many people at this time turned to God for comfort when faced with the prospect of their own demise. Later in his life, Donne was almost obsessed with the idea of his own death. Shortly before he died at the age of 59, he preached his own funeral sermon, *Death's Duel*, and he posed for a painting in his own death shroud. That painting was used to create an effigy for his tomb.

The prevalence of death during Donne's time should not be underestimated. Even when love was the ostensible subject of a play or poem, it was often linked with death. In Shakespeare's *Twelfth Night*, for example, the Countess Olivia, having just espied the character of Viola disguised as Cesario, says: "How now?/Even so quickly may one catch the plague?/Methinks I feel this youth's perfections/With an invisible and subtle stealth/To creep in at mine eyes" (I. v. 294–98). The striking thing about this passage is not only the association Olivia makes between erotic desire and the plague but also the symptoms of love. The "invisible and subtle stealth" with which the beloved's "perfections" enter Olivia's eyes sounds almost sinister on the one hand and like the description of the onset of a disease on the other. Such connections between love and death were common in Donne's time and help us understand that even something as delightful and joyous as love was tinged with the ever-present realization that the body, no matter its joys or sorrows, is inevitably subject to decay and death.

Donne's preoccupation with death is related to another major theme of *The Holy Sonnets*: a desire for spiritual renewal. The speaker of *The Holy Sonnets*, besides being preoccupied with death, ardently seeks spiritual renewal from God. In perhaps one of Donne's best-known poems, Holy Sonnet XIV, the speaker paradoxically desires a destruction of self in order that God may rebuild him:

> Batter my heart, three-personed God, for you
> As yet but knock, breathe, shine, and seek to mend;
> That I may rise and stand, o'erthrow me, and bend
> Your force to break, blow, burn and make me new. (1–4)

In the first quatrain of the sonnet, Donne's choice of verbs is telling. The contrast between the actions that God has so far taken in the speaker's journey of renewal, "knock, breathe, shine" as well as "mend," all imply a relatively benign deity who gently seeks to "mend" the speaker. This, as the following series of verbs indicates, is insufficient to achieve the "newness" that the speaker seeks in line 4. The actions he wants God to take are more destructive ("break, blow, burn"), which may seem initially paradoxical, but because the speaker wishes to "rise and stand," that is, be renewed and made whole through God's grace and power, he seeks first to be utterly brought low. Such an idea is common in Christian thought. In the New Testament, for example, Christ, when giving his Sermon on the Mount, states that "the meek shall inherit the earth" (Matthew 5:5) and the "poor in spirit" will possess the kingdom of heaven (Matthew 5:3), and he later says that "the last shall be first" (Matthew 19:30). The implication of both Donne's and Christ's words is that salvation and renewal in a Christian context cannot be achieved unless a believer exhibits sufficient humility and selflessness in order to obtain God's grace and, eventually, heaven.

Donne, however, does not merely appropriate the language of Christianity in his search for a spiritual center. In the last lines of Sonnet XIV, he makes startling requests of God:

> Take me to you, imprison me, for I,
> Except you enthrall me, never shall be free,
> Nor ever chaste, except you ravish me. (12–14)

In the attempt to gain spiritual "newness," Donne goes beyond even the paradoxical language mentioned previously. These final lines indicate both the intensity of the speaker's desire to be closer to God and his frustration with God. The speaker here needs God to be not fatherly and loving but rather to function as both jailer and violator of his body, wishing to be both imprisoned by God and ravished (raped) by him. Such language is violent, urgent, passionate, and, some might say, sacrilegious. However, what is clear from this sonnet and many others in the sequence, is that the intensity and zeal of Donne's language reflects his intensity and desire for God's love. The distinguishing characteristic of *The Holy Sonnets*, in other words, is not that their author sought God but rather that he sought him using such unique and unusual language.

For the sake of comparison, consider a poem written by another devotional poet, George Herbert. A contemporary of Donne's (his mother was one of Donne's patrons—in fact, Donne dedicated *The Holy Sonnets* to her) and also a poet who took holy orders in the Anglican Church, Herbert, like many writers of the day, wrestled with issues of faith. In one of his well-known poems, "The Collar," Herbert addresses God, asking, "Shall I ever sigh and pine?" (3). Herbert then asserts, "My lines and life are free" (4), presumably because he wishes them to be exempt from God's authority. Like Donne, Herbert sometimes chafed at the constraints of a Christian life, but often, in his poems, the resolution to such difficulties comes more easily to Herbert than it does to Donne. At the end of "The Collar," for example, the speaker says,

> But as I rav'd and grew more fierce and wilde
> > At every word,
> Me thoughts I heard one calling, *Childe*:
> And I reply'd, *My Lord*. (33–36)

Two things are immediately apparent in the poem's closing lines: 1) the speaker in "The Collar," like the speaker of *The Holy Sonnets*, is frustrated about his relationship with God, and 2) the speaker of "The Collar" achieves a resolution that the speaker of *The Holy Sonnets* does not. Note also that God speaks in this poem and that the speaker, in the very last line, replies to him. This does not necessarily imply that all problems the speaker has encountered vanish in the moment of his reply, but, unlike Donne's work, God speaks directly to the poem's speaker and there is in the speaker's reply at least an acknowledgment of God's presence and perhaps, in that recognition, a kind of comfort that Donne seems never to achieve.

There are, however, ways that the speaker comforts himself throughout *The Holy Sonnets* even as he seems to despair. One chief way he does this is by acknowledging his divine origins. Sonnet I begins, for example, with the question, "Thou hast made me, and shall Thy work decay?" (1), and in Sonnet II, Donne writes, "first I was made/By Thee, and for Thee, and when I was decayed/Thy blood bought that, the which before was Thine" (2–4). While the speaker struggles against his fear of death and despairs of his salvation, he also occasionally experiences solace, if not joy, in remembering that he is a creation of a loving and benevolent God. The lines in Sonnet II clearly refer to the redemptive power of Christ's blood, and both quotes show the speaker returning to his origins and seeking comfort in being one of God's creations. The same can be said for Sonnet V, where the speaker opens the poem with a declaration: "I am a little world made cunningly/Of elements and an angelic sprite" (1–2).

The speaker's attempts to connect with God via a remembrance of his origins is never, however, an easy one. For all that Donne desires a connection to deity, his paradoxical nature prevents him from achieving the very thing he seeks. At the conclusion of Sonnet XIX, the last sonnet in the sequence, the speaker appears to contradict his desire to be renewed by God:

> I durst not view heaven yesterday; and today
> In prayers and flattering speeches I court God:
> Tomorrow I quake with true fear of his rod.
> So my devout fits come and go away
> Like a fantastic ague; save that here
> Those are my best days, when I shake with feare. (9–14)

The paradox of the sonnet's closing line could describe the overarching theme of the entire sequence. The "fantastic ague" mentioned a few lines earlier echoes the fearful shaking of the last line and the corresponding contradiction that, when shaking with fear, the speaker experiences his "best days." On the surface, the speaker appears miserable, frightened of the deity he seeks so zealously. However, the description of his interactions with God a few lines earlier indicates that the seeming paradox between "best days" and "feare" are not as contradictory as we might suppose. He tells us that he "court(s)" God with "prayers" and "flattering speeches" and then quakes in fear at his "rod" or power. The relationship between calling upon God and then fearing his response establishes that the speaker is accustomed to such fear and, further, that he believes the process will lead to an enjoying of God's presence.

There is throughout Donne's work a strain of hope even while he faces the seemingly inescapable misery that sometimes accompanies mortal life. In *Meditation XVII* from *Devotions upon Emergent Occasions*, he writes:

> Tribulation is treasure in the nature of it, but it is not current money in the use of it, except we get nearer and nearer our home, heaven, by it. Another man may be sick too, and sick to death, and this affliction may lie in his bowels as gold in a mine and be of no use to him; but this bell that tells me of his affliction digs out and applies that gold to me, if by this consideration of another's dangers I take mine own into contemplation and so secure myself by making my recourse to my God, who is our only security.

According to Donne, the trials that we endure here are able, if we possess the correct frame of mind, to prepare us to meet God. Further, it is not only our own afflictions but also the afflictions of others that can perform this task. If we possess empathy ("consideration of another's dangers"), we can "secure" ourselves by turning to God and recognizing that he is the only true source of comfort.

Another point Donne makes in *The Holy Sonnets* is the importance of realizing the fleeting nature of mortality. In Sonnet VI, he calls life a "race" which is "Idly, yet quickly run" (2–3). The implicit assumption in those lines is that, because life is so brief, we must spend our time on Earth wisely and use that short space to come to the knowledge of God and eschew worldly concerns. Later in that same poem, the speaker mentions that the sins he commits with his "earth-born body" will, unless he focuses on the divine, "press" him to hell. This poem, like so many of these sonnets, ends with images of both death and rebirth: "Impute me righteous, thus purg'd of evil,/For thus I leave the world, the flesh, the devil" (13–14). The speaker actually looks forward to his time of dying, that he might leave behind not only his corrupt body but also the devil's influence over it. His desire to be "righteous," he believes, will allow him to triumph over both flesh and Satan, permitting a double victory. Indeed, in this poem as in many others in this sequence, Donne recognizes that suffering and death are necessary prerequisites to achieving a higher plane.

For Donne, then, the paradoxes and contradictions inherent in *The Holy Sonnets* and in life itself are the only way to establish a fruitful relationship with God. When thought of in that context, the association of death and joy becomes understandable. Donne can only experience joy when he feels fear of God's wrath—not because joy and fear are the same thing, but because fearing God means that God is an active presence in his life who guides his renewal and rebirth and affords at least the possibility of joy.

I KNOW WHY THE CAGED BIRD SINGS
(MAYA ANGELOU)

"Death, Rebirth, and Renewal in Maya Angelou's *I Know Why the Caged Bird Sings*"
by Robert C. Evans,
Auburn University at Montgomery

In an early and often-reprinted 1976 essay on Maya Angelou's autobiographical text *I Know Why the Caged Bird Sings*, Liliane K. Arensberg argues in passing that the work "suggests a sense of self as perpetually in the process of becoming, of dying and being reborn, in all its ramifications" (115). Later, Arensberg similarly asserts that the ending of the book is "in keeping with" its author's "death-and-rebirth fantasy," so that in at least two ways "Maya Angelou is reborn: once, into a life-affirming identity recorded within the pages of her narrative, and again, when she re-creates that life as author of her autobiography" (126).

One segment in particular of Angelou's book seems worth examining from this perspective of metaphorical death giving way to figurative life, and that is the crucial segment in which eight-year-old Maya is sexually abused, and then eventually raped, by her mother's live-in boyfriend, the ironically named Mr. Freeman, who accomplishes his deeds without the knowledge of anyone else in the household. Eventually the rape and abuse are accidentally discovered (Mr. Freeman had threatened to harm both Maya and her beloved brother, Bailey, if Maya revealed what had happened). Freeman is placed on trial; Maya, during testimony, refuses to acknowledge that there had been any contact between them before the rape itself; and then Freeman, while temporarily free, is found dead—presumably murdered by some of Maya's fearsome male relatives. Young Maya feels guilty for having been less than entirely honest during her testimony. She blames herself, in part, for Freeman's death, and she lapses into an extended silence that lasts until she is ultimately persuaded to speak again by an elderly friend of the family named Bertha Flowers. This whole episode, then, epitomizes the pattern of "dying and being reborn" that Arensberg has identified as crucial to Angelou's entire book.

In her initial descriptions of Mr. Freeman, the first-person narrator of Angelou's work describes him as a kind of pathetic creature who nonetheless possesses a certain appeal: "Mr. Freeman moved gracefully, like a big brown bear, and seldom spoke to us [i.e., to the children]. He simply waited for Mother and put his whole self into the waiting. He never read the paper or patted his foot to the radio. He waited. That was all" (69). Freeman's passivity and lack of activity will later come to seem highly ironic in light of the perverse initiative he takes later in the book, but for the moment he seems almost humiliatingly dependent on Maya's mother: "If she came home before we went to bed, we saw the man come alive. He would start out of the big chair, like a man coming out of sleep, smiling" (69). For the most part, though, he seems bored, boring, untalented ("he couldn't dance" [70]), and an object of both pity and condescension, even on the part of the eight-year-old Maya:

> I felt sorry for Mr. Freeman. I felt sorry for him as I had felt for a litter of helpless pigs born in our backyard sty in Arkansas. We fattened the pigs all year long for slaughter on the first good frost, and even as I suffered for the cute little wiggly things, I knew how much I was going to enjoy the fresh sausage and hog's headcheese they would give me only with their deaths. (70)

The phrasing in this passage seems ironic in light of later events. Maya imagines herself in a position of superiority to Freeman, but later, of course, their roles will be precisely reversed. Freeman will indeed die during the course of this text, but in another way, so will young Maya.

The difference is that Maya will be symbolically reborn. For the time being, however, Maya can assume a kind of superiority to Freeman: "His breasts," she mentions, "used to embarrass me when he walked around in his undershirt. They lay on his chest like flat titties" (67). This comment will later seem double-edged when Freeman decides to assert his masculinity in a most disgusting way.

Partly as a result of typical childhood nightmares, young Maya is allowed to share the bed in which her mother and Mr. Freeman sleep. This arrangement leads to an event far more horrific than any nightmare Maya could have imagined, for when her mother arises early one morning and leaves the young girl and Freeman in bed together, Maya awakes "to a pressure, a strange feeling on my left leg. It was too soft to be a hand, and it wasn't the touch of clothes" (70). She discovers that it is Mr. Freeman's "'thing'" on her leg (71). Ironically, then, her process of literal awakening plunges her into a strange kind of darkness—an immoral darkness engendered by Freeman and a psychological darkness, or cognitive confusion, experienced by Maya herself. She doesn't, at first, know what to think: "I wasn't afraid, a little apprehensive, maybe, but not afraid" (71).

When Freeman, now fully exposed, pulls her on top of him, she notes, "his heart was beating so hard that I was afraid that he would die. Ghost stories revealed how people who died wouldn't let go of whatever they were holding. I wondered if Mr. Freeman died holding me how I would ever get free" (71). All the imagery of death here is, of course, highly relevant to the theme of rebirth and renewal. Young Maya thinks that Freeman may presently die, but it is actually she who will experience a kind of symbolic death as a result of this whole episode and its aftermath. And yet Freeman, too, will literally die as a consequence of his actions, and Maya's guilt over his death will keep her in a kind of bondage to him—a kind of emotional and psychological death—for a long time after he is killed. He will, indeed, keep on "holding" her long after he expires; he will become a kind of "ghost" who will haunt her imagination.

For now, however, the young girl discovers that she enjoys aspects of this strange new intimacy with Mr. Freeman: "He held me so softly that I wished he wouldn't ever let me go. I felt at home." Ironically, she thinks that from "the way he was holding me I knew he'd never let me go or let anything bad ever happen to me" (71). She even fantasizes that he "was probably my real father and we had found each other at last" (71). She associates him with the source of her own being and existence, but this association is short-lived. After Mr. Freeman quickly arises from the bed and heads for the bathroom and later threatens to kill her brother if Maya tells what has happened, he becomes an obvious symbol of literal and figurative death (71–72). He will remain such a symbol, in one way or another, for the rest of his life and even beyond his death. Until then, Maya notes that there "was never any question of my disliking Mr. Freeman. I simply didn't understand him . . ." (72–73). Freeman, meanwhile, now treats her with a gruff distance, despite her desire for further contact. Her peculiar new intimacy with him seems, therefore, to have been born quickly and then to have suffered just as quick a death. It is briefly and incompletely revived (at Maya's initiative), but then it dies once more (73).

"For months," she then reports, "he stopped speaking to me again"; this foreshadows her own extended silence later in the text. Maya entertains herself by reading fantasy stories and newspaper comics—symbols of a naïve, youthful innocence that will soon end forever (74). The crucial turning point occurs one morning when Maya is summoned by Freeman, whose "pants were open" and whose "'thing' was standing out of his britches by itself" (75). This time, when Maya asserts a newfound sense of resistance and independence, Freeman "grabbed my arm and pulled me between his legs" (75). He now rapes her, threatening to kill her if she screams and to kill her young brother if she tells. Freeman's function as a symbol of death in this episode is all too clear, especially when Maya recounts the physical violence and excruciating pain of the rape. The thematic emphasis on death becomes quite explicit when she reports, "I thought I had died—I woke up in a white-walled world, and it had to be heaven. But Mr. Freeman was there and he was washing me" (76). The irony of Freeman washing the child he has just metaphorically polluted and dirtied is clear, and it also seems ironic that, to get her out of the house, he sends her to the public library, a symbol of all that is most rational and civilized in any culture.

Maya is in enormous pain, and when she returns home, her mother assumes that she must be "sick," not realizing that Freeman is the real source of illness in the house. Once again, Freeman secretly threatens to kill Maya if she reveals the truth, and after Freeman leaves the house following an argument with Maya's mother, Maya again imagines that she is dying. She notes, "I longed for death, but I didn't want to die anywhere near Mr. Freeman. I knew that even now he wouldn't have allowed death to have me unless he wished it to" (80). Maya's brother accidentally discovers the soiled panties she had hidden, and only then is the secret at last uncovered. Maya is hospitalized; the threats of death are finally revealed; Freeman is apprehended and arrested; and a trial is held. In the courtroom, Freeman's lawyers try to get Maya to confess to intimate contact long before the rape so they can make her seem partly responsible for the crime. Despite feeling guilty about lying, Maya denies any such contact, even though it did occur. Freeman is convicted and is given a sentence of "one year and one day" (83); he is briefly released and then later is "found dead on the lot behind the slaughterhouse" (a highly appropriate location that recalls the slaughtered-pig imagery from earlier in the text [83]).

Rather than feeling any joy or relief at Freeman's death, however, Maya feels some guilt: "A man was dead because I lied. Where was the balance in that? One lie surely wouldn't be worth a man's life," she notes in a sentence that nicely balances the words "lie" and "life" (84). In response to Freeman's literal, physical death, Maya comes to feel that she deserves an eternal, spiritual death: "Obviously I had forfeited my place in heaven forever. . . . Even Christ turned his back on Satan. Wouldn't he turn his back on me?" (84). Partly as a way to punish herself for her traumatic sense of guilt, Maya plunges herself into a world of isolated silence:

> I had sold myself to the Devil and there could be no escape. The only thing I could do was to stop talking to people other than Bailey. Instinctively, or somehow, I knew that because I loved him so much I'd never hurt him, but if I talked to anyone else that person might die too. Just my breath, carrying my words out, might poison people and they'd curl up and die like the black fat slugs that only pretended.
>
> I had to stop talking. (85)

That last, wonderfully brief, one-paragraph sentence mimics the very reticence it announces. Having been plunged into a kind of metaphorical death by Mr. Freeman and then having caused (at least to her own way of thinking) Freeman's death by her failure to tell the whole truth, Maya comes to consider herself an agent of death and thus commits a kind of preemptive communicative suicide.

At first her relatives are understanding, but soon they become annoyed and frustrated: "When I refused to be the child they knew and accepted me to be, I was called impudent and my muteness sullenness." Indeed, for "a while I was punished for being so uppity that I wouldn't speak; and then came the thrashings, given by any relative who felt himself offended" (85). The ironies lurking within this passage are numerous. The child who is depressed and who tries to cast herself down is accused of being "uppity"; the child who feels humiliated, guilt-ridden, and ashamed is accused of being "impudent"; the child who has descended into silence thanks to psychic trauma is then punished by physical abuse not unlike the mistreatment that ultimately led to the initial trauma. Later, having returned to the small town in Arkansas where her grandmother lives, Maya feels that she has entered a kind of "cocoon" (86); this image implies isolation, seclusion, and even protection, but it also promises rebirth.

For almost a year Maya retains her general silence—until she has a crucial encounter with a poised, intelligent, and wise old black woman named Bertha Flowers, also called "Sister Flowers" by Maya's grandmother. The various names of this woman (also called "Mrs. Flowers") seem diversely symbolic. It would probably be pushing an argument too far to suggest that her first name links her with the idea of birth, but clearly her last name links her with the imagery of springtime, beauty, and vitality. As "Sister Flowers" she is, moreover, a kind of metaphorical member of an extended family, even though she attends a different church than does Maya's grandmother. In any case, Mrs. Flowers represents to Maya all that seems worthy about human existence: "She was one of the few gentlewomen I have ever known, and has remained throughout my life the measure of what a human being can be" (91). It is largely thanks to Mrs. Flowers that Maya's human spirit—as well as the human capacity for speech—is reborn.

In contrast to the constant use of death imagery associated with Mr. Freeman, the few uses of such imagery in connection with Mrs.

Flowers are merely humorous. Thus Maya's grandmother (who is called "Momma"), to display her own skill as a dressmaker, pulls Maya's skirt up over Maya's head before the girl can resist (a comic inversion of the earlier rape). In response, Maya is mortified:

> I wouldn't look at either of them. Momma hadn't thought that taking off my dress in front of Mrs. Flowers would have killed me stone dead. . . . Mrs. Flowers had known that I would be embarrassed and that was even worse. . . . It would be fitting if I got sunstroke and died. . . . Just dropped dead on the slanting porch. (94)

All the imagery of death here, unlike the use of similar imagery in connection with Mr. Freeman, merely provokes smiles, and the adult narrator is, in retrospect, amused at her own youthful embarrassment. Mrs. Flowers symbolizes the opposite of anything associated with death; she is thus the opposite—the extreme antitype—of Mr. Freeman. She represents spiritual life, emotional renewal, and psychological rebirth, whereas he represented only physical degradation and abuse.

Mrs. Flowers, for one thing, treats Maya with the respect and concern that had been grossly violated by Mr. Freeman. She calls Maya by her formal name of "Marguerite," and instead of trying to cajole or even threaten the girl into breaking her silence, she speaks to her with kindness and reason. "'Now no one is going to make you talk—possibly no one can. But bear in mind, language is man's way of communicating with his fellow man and it is language alone which separates him from the lower animals.' That was a totally new idea to me," Maya remarks, "and I would need time to think about it" (95). Mrs. Flowers thus provokes the very kind of rationality and thoughtfulness she praises. She, the adult, does not try to force her will upon Maya, the child (as Mr. Freeman had so despicably done); instead, she treats Maya as an equal. She addresses her not as a child, nor even as a fellow female, nor even as an African American; instead, she addresses her as a fellow human being, thereby both displaying and bestowing dignity. She makes it clear to Maya that by denying her own speech, Maya is denying her own humanity; she is killing the very thing that makes her most human. To refuse to speak is to behave like an animal (as Mr. Freeman had also done, in his own perverse way). In contrast, to choose to speak is to acknowledge and affirm one's human worth. To do so is to be reborn and renewed as a fully human being.

Mrs. Flowers gives Maya her time, she shows Maya her concern, she presents Maya with books, and she encourages Maya to read those books *aloud*. "'Words mean more,'" she tells Maya, "'than what is set down on paper. It takes the human voice to infuse them with deeper shades of meaning'" (95). Whereas Mr. Freeman "seldom spoke" (69) to Maya, and then spoke mainly to cajole or threaten, Mrs. Flowers speaks eloquently and thoughtfully. Indeed, the only threat Mrs. Flower ever issues is an obviously comic one: "'I'll accept no excuse if you return a book to me that has been badly handled.'" In response, Maya's "imagination boggled at the punishment I would deserve if in fact I did abuse a book of Mrs. Flowers'. Death would be too kind and brief" (95). The mention of death here is merely an obvious, exaggerated joke, whereas with Mr. Freeman any mention of death had seemed frighteningly real.

Mrs. Flowers seems associated with life and vitality, and not only because of her intellect, her kindness, her self-respect, and her respect for others. Her house is filled with wonderful smells associated with nourishment and health: "The odors in the house surprised me. Somehow I had never connected Mrs. Flowers with food or eating or any other common experience of common people. . . . The sweet scent of vanilla had met us as she opened the door" (96). She offers Maya cookies and lemonade and also a literal and figurative seat at her table. As Maya reports, "As I ate she began the first of what we later called 'my lessons in living'" (97). Physical nutrition, then, is combined with spiritual, intellectual, and emotional sustenance, and when Mrs. Flowers reads from a Dickens novel, Maya feels as if she is hearing "poetry for the first time in my life" (97). She feels as if she is suddenly alive in a way she had not been before. In all these numerous ways, Mrs. Freeman is a powerful symbol and agent of Maya's renewal and rebirth, of her escape from darkness and silence, of her reinitiation into the human race and of her growing emergence into adulthood. Mrs. Flowers is not only the anti-type of Mr. Freeman; she is his very potent antidote as well. She is, as Maya memorably and retrospectively puts it, "the lady who threw me my first life line" (90) and thus prevented her from drowning the metaphorical death of self-imposed muteness.

Works Cited or Consulted

Angelou, Maya. *I Know Why the Caged Bird Sings*. New York: Random House, 2002.

Arensberg, Liliane K. "Death as Metaphor of Self." *Maya Angelou's* I Know Why the Caged Bird Sings*: A Casebook*. Ed. Joanne M. Braxton. New York: Oxford U P, 1999. 111–27.

Braxton, Joanne M. *Black Women Writing Autobiography: A Tradition Within a Tradition*. Philadelphia: Temple U P, 1989.

Froula, Christine. "The Daughter's Seduction: Sexual Violence and Literary History." *Signs* 11:4 (1986): 621–44.

Gilbert, Susan. "Maya Angelou's *I Know Why the Caged Bird Sings*: Paths to Escape." *Mount Olive Review* 1.1 (1987): 39–50.

Hord, Fred Lee. *Reconstructing Memory: Black Literary Criticism*. Chicago: Third World Press, 1991.

Lionnet, Françoise. *Autobiographical Voices: Race, Gender, Self-Portraiture*. Ithaca: Cornell U P, 1989.

Vermillion, Mary. "Reembodying the Self: Representations of Rape in *Incidents in the Life of a Slave Girl* and *I Know Why the Caged Bird Sings*." *Biography: An Interdisciplinary Quarterly* 15.1 (1992): 243–60.

KING LEAR
(WILLIAM SHAKESPEARE)

"Rebirth and Renewal
in Shakespeare's *King Lear*"
by Gary Ettari,
the University of North Carolina at Asheville

The subject of rebirth and renewal in *King Lear* is a complex one, in part because so much of the play focuses on disorder, confusion, and betrayal. The play begins, in fact, with both personal and political upheaval. In the first scene, we are introduced to two families, Gloucester's, consisting of Gloucester and his two sons, Edmund and Edgar, and Lear's, consisting of Lear and his three daughters, Regan, Goneril, and Cordelia. Significantly, both families lack a wife/mother figure, meaning the play begins with a vague feeling of incompleteness or absence. One of Gloucester's sons, Edmund, is illegitimate. In Elizabethan drama, bastards are generally villains. This is in part due to the cultural codes of the day: A bastard, a person who was born out of wedlock, was automatically disinherited because English laws and customs did not mandate that children born out of wedlock needed to be formally acknowledged either in one's will or, in the case of nobility, with a title. Thus, most bastards in the drama of the day were driven to achieve what they believed was rightfully theirs even though the customs of the day did not acknowledge that to be the case.

Most of the disorder in the play, in fact, results from the various members of each family trying to obtain their desires via other members of the family. For Edmund, achieving the legitimacy and fatherly attention he craves involves scheming against his "legitimate" brother, Edgar, who is highly favored by Gloucester. In one part of a well-known speech from Act I, Edmund says:

> Well then,
> Legitimate Edgar, I must have your land:
> [...]
>   if this letter speed,
> And my invention thrive, Edmund the base
> Shall top the legitimate. I grow; I prosper:
> Now, gods, stand up for bastards! (1.2. 15–16, 18–21)

By forging a letter in his brother Edgar's hand, Edmund hopes to disinherit Edgar and gain for himself the "land" held by his father. The closing lines of the quote demonstrate Edmund's frustration at his lot in life. He calls upon the gods to favor bastards in part out of frustration because he feels up to this point as if they have favored his "legitimate" brother Edgar.

Edmund's scheming is relatively straightforward when compared with the predicament of King Lear and his daughters. An old man, Lear wishes to give up his kingdom. He has divided it into thirds with the intention of giving one third of the kingdom to each of his three daughters so that Lear may, in his own words, "crawl unburthen'd towards death" (1.1.32). The only thing Lear requires of his daughters is a profession of love from each. He essentially makes these professions a contest by asking, "which of you shall we say doth love us most?" (1.1.42). Goneril and Regan, the two oldest daughters, give elaborate, hyperbolic, and insincere replies to their father. Because Lear seeks flattery and cannot discern the difference between truth and falsehood, these replies please him. When his youngest daughter, Cordelia, answers in plain, honest language ("I love your majesty/According to my bond; no more nor less"), Lear becomes outraged, disinherits Cordelia, and divides her third between Regan and Goneril (1.1.83–4). He banishes Cordelia from his kingdom, and even though Cordelia is now disinherited, the king of France, who was visiting Lear's court to seek her hand, still agrees to marry her. When Lear's faithful servant, Kent, speaks up to defend Cordelia, he, too, is banished. The decisions Lear makes in this scene have many consequences, but it is important to note another troubling aspect of Lear's character. The main reason he leaves his land to his daughters is that he does not want to continue being king. Because so much of the play's disorder results from Lear's desire to rid himself of the burdens of kingship, it is safe to presume that Shakespeare was trying to highlight the importance of taking one's political and personal responsibilities seriously. In large part, it is because Lear wants to be "unburthen'd" that he makes the foolish decisions he does.

The play therefore begins with a series of familial and political disruptions, and the last four and a half acts of the play are a close study of what people do when they confront both domestic and cosmic disorder. Edgar, Gloucester's legitimate son, for example, goes into hiding because Edmund showed his father a forged letter, purporting to be from Edgar, in which Edgar supposedly discusses murdering Gloucester for his property. Cordelia, disinherited and without property or a place to live, is shown pity by the king of France, who proposes marriage to her. Cordelia then leaves England to live in France with her new husband. Lear, too, becomes dispossessed and homeless. Having divided his kingdom in two, his plan is to stay with each of his daughters in turn. However, once Regan and Goneril gain their respective halves of the kingdom, each banishes her father from her house.

By the conclusion of Act 2, most of the play's characters are bereft of both family and shelter. Significantly, many are wandering in the wilderness. It is a familiar pattern in Shakespearean comedy to place characters from a more "civilized" world into a forest or other green space in order that they might gain a new perspective and return to civilized society changed for the better. The "green world," as critic Northrop Frye called it, has a powerful effect upon those who venture into it. While *King Lear* is a tragedy and not a comedy, the play uses the green space to begin to help characters heal themselves.

The role that nature plays in *Lear* is a multifaceted one. It is important to remember that "nature" in this play can refer to many things: to human nature, to the natural world, or to the larger, almost cosmic sense of Nature as the ordering principle of the universe. All of these manifestations of nature are at play in *King Lear*. Once Lear has been banished from the houses of both his older daughters, for example, he and his fool simply wander in the wilderness, allowing nature an opportunity to bring about change in the play's characters.

As Lear and his fool seek shelter out on the heath, a storm comes up; rather than seek shelter, Lear welcomes the storm, addressing it directly even as it rages around him:

> Rumble thy bellyful! Spit, fire! Spout, rain!
> Nor rain, wind, thunder, fire are my daughters.
> I tax not you, you elements, with unkindness;
> I never gave you kingdom, call'd you children;
> You owe me no subscription. Then let fall
> Your horrible pleasure. Here I stand your slave,
> A poor, infirm, weak, and despis'd old man (3.2. 14–20).

In this speech, Lear begins to realize the error of his ways. Although he is still bitter about his daughters banishing him, he also recognizes his own state; he is a "poor, infirm, weak and despis'd old man" and not the king he once was. He recognizes that he is at the mercy of the "horrible pleasure" of the elements, and he therefore begins to humble himself when faced with a power greater than he can command.

Many of the play's other transformations take place away from civilization as well. Edgar, the banished brother of Edmund, disguises himself as a madman named Tom O'Bedlam and inhabits the same wilderness as Lear and his fool. Ironically, Edgar meets his father, Gloucester, who has been blinded by Cornwall, Regan's husband, and joins the play's other characters in the wilderness. Failing to recognize his voice, Gloucester asks "Tom O'Bedlam" to lead him to the top of one of the Dover cliffs so he may jump and end his life. Edgar agrees to lead Gloucester up to the cliff but instead keeps him on level ground and tells him he is at the edge of the cliff. Gloucester thanks him, kneels to say a final prayer, and then jumps off what he believes to be a cliff. At this point, Edgar takes on another disguise and pretends to be someone at the bottom of the cliff who saw Gloucester float down. After being convinced that he fell from a great height, Gloucester ceases to despair and resolves to live as long as he can: "Henceforth I'll bear/Affliction till it do cry out itself/'Enough, enough,' and die" (4.4. 75–77). Gloucester, like Lear, has been humbled by his circumstances and now sees his life in a different light.

There is, however, a key difference between Gloucester and Lear. In 4.6, Lear encounters the blind Gloucester and expresses skepticism about a blind man's ability to perceive things, ironically demonstrating his own lack of vision:

> Lear: O ho, are you there with me? No eyes in your head, nor no money in your purse? Your eyes are in a heavy case, your purse in a light, yet you see how this world goes.
> Gloucester: I see it feelingly.
> Lear: What, art thou mad?

Lear's inability to understand the change that Gloucester has undergone signals that he has yet to take the final steps in the transformation from arrogance to humility, from blindness to sight. Gloucester, however, despite his blindness, has become more aware of the world around him and, even more importantly, more empathetic to the people in it. That he now sees "feelingly" indicates that he has acquired empathy and is thus able to "feel" his way through the world, not only with his hands, but with his being.

Many of the transformations undergone by the main characters are partly the result of those characters being removed from their milieu at court and at home and transported to the realm of nature. In Shakespeare's time, the view of nature was heavily influenced by classical Greek and Roman pastoral poetry, stretching as far back as the work of Theocritus, a Hellenistic Greek writer who flourished in the third century B.C.E. Most of the work produced by Theocritus and other Greek and Roman poets, such as Virgil in his *Ecologues*, offered a highly idealized version of country life, focusing mainly on the lives of shepherds who tended their flocks in fields and meadows. Most of these works described the shepherd's life as simple, easy, and full of leisure. Many writers of the English Renaissance were influenced by these earlier works and produced their own poetry, which often expressed a desire to return to a simpler life. Christopher Marlowe, in his well-known poem, "A Passionate Shepherd to His Love" writes:

> Come live with me and be my Love,
> And we will all the pleasures prove

That hills and valleys, dale and field,
And all the craggy mountains yield.

There will we sit upon the rocks
And see the shepherds feed their flocks,
By shallow rivers, to whose falls
Melodious birds sing madrigals. (1–8)

That English Renaissance writers would adopt the idealized version of nature from the classical pastoral poets is understandable. Most early modern playwrights, especially the Elizabethans, would, if they wanted to be successful, end up in London, a large and bustling city. Also, many Elizabethan writers were at court, a place that offered opportunities for advancement but that also was fraught with political intrigue and danger, making the simple, pastoral life seem at times more appealing (see, for example, Sir Thomas Wyatt's poem "Mine own John Poinz").

The natural world for Elizabethans, then, offered a respite from the cares of city and court life. In Shakespeare's plays, particularly the comedies, this desire for simplicity results in the setting of the play changing from the court to the country. In the comedies *A Midsummer Night's Dream* and *As You Like It*, for example, the difficulties faced by the characters at court are resolved after the characters spend a substantial amount of each play's time in the "green world" of the forest. It is easy to see a similar pattern in *King Lear*, especially given the role of the storm and the preponderance of the action that takes place out on the English heath, but there are also subtle differences as well. For example, nature in *Lear* is not quite as friendly or inviting as it is in the comedies. It is harsher and more dangerous, and it does not offer easy solutions. This is perhaps because in this play, Nature has more work to do than to reunite lovers or smooth over courtly quarrels; it must redeem a king, reunify two broken families, and stabilize a kingdom.

Since Gloucester is blind and Lear has begun to be humbled, the process of setting things right has begun. However, because of the play's tragic undertone, there can be neither rebirth nor renewal without loss. Many critics have argued that this recognition of loss's necessity is one of the chief features of Shakespeare's late plays, and *Lear* is no exception. In fact, one of the ironies of the play is that while Gloucester and Lear are moving from arrogance and blindness to a state of empathy and humility, other characters are descending further into the chaos of the disrupted kingdom. Cordelia, now the queen of France, is back on English soil with her husband's invading army. Edmund, who has been having romantic dalliances with both Regan and Goneril, is now the head of Regan's army and is leading that army to meet the invading French troops. Edgar, disguised now as an ordinary peasant, leads his father, Gloucester, to a safe place and joins the battle on the side of France and Lear. Just as the personal and political spheres were both disrupted at the beginning of the play, they are now brought together again.

The armies clash and Lear's side loses, with the result that Lear and Cordelia are both captured; this provides father and daughter a momentary sense of despair at the defeat of their army and their imprisonment. However, Edgar reveals to Goneril's husband, Albany, that Goneril plotted to kill him and there is a division in Regan and Goneril's army; Albany then suspects Edmund of treason and orders a trial by combat to determine Edmund's guilt or innocence. Edgar officially accuses Edmund of treason and fights him in single combat. Edgar fatally wounds Edmund, who repents; the dying Edmund tries to redeem himself by sending a messenger to stop Cordelia's execution, which he had ordered.

At this point in the final scene, deaths come rapidly. Edgar finally reveals himself to his father, Gloucester, who, caught between feelings of joy and grief, dies. Regan, poisoned by Goneril, also dies, and afterward Goneril kills herself with a dagger. In this whirlwind of action and death, we see the difference between the reordering process in Shakespeare's comedies and his late tragedies. Most of the pastoral comedies end with joyful reunions, usually including marriage, and the transition from the natural world back to the courtly one is for the most part uncomplicated. In Lear, however, the movement from the green world back to the courtly one is fraught with tragic consequences. Despite Edmund's earnest attempt to save Cordelia, she is nonetheless hanged, and in one of the most riveting scenes of the play, Lear carries her onstage in his arms and laments her death:

> No, no, no life!
> Why should a dog, a horse, a rat, have life,

And thou no breath at all? Thou'lt come no more,
Never, never, never, never, never.
Pray you undo this button. Thank you, sir.
Do you see this? Look on her! Look her lips,
Look there, look there!   *He dies.* (5.3. 306–312)

The sense of loss in Lear's words is undeniable, as is the finality. With the repetition of "never," the weight of Cordelia's death and the loss of his own sanity are palpable. Here, at the play's conclusion, we see a distinction Shakespeare is making not only between tragedy and comedy but also between loss and the possibility of redemption. At the end of the play, there seem to be almost too many losses to overcome. All three of Lear's daughters, not to mention Lear himself, are dead, as is two-thirds of Gloucester's family. The kingdom as Lear knew and ruled it has ceased to exist. When one thinks of rebirth and renewal, usually such tragic consequences do not enter the picture.

However, as Shakespeare so often insists, even in the face of such dire loss, there is the possibility of redemption and renewal. In *King Lear*, that possibility takes the shape of a new ruler. Just after Lear dies, Albany tells Edgar and Kent that they must rule the realm and "the gored state sustain." Kent declines, saying, "I have a journey, sir, shortly to go," implying that he is close to the end of his life. One other function of Kent's refusal to rule with Edgar is that Edgar will now be the sole ruler; if he is just, the kingdom divided and fractured by Lear's actions may again flourish as an organic whole. While the possibility of a reunited kingdom with Edgar at its head may seem like small comfort, perhaps what this play teaches is that rash actions have consequences not just for individuals but for kingdoms as well. This is perhaps why the rebirth and renewal in the play seem muted or incomplete when compared to the final scenes of most of the comedies. Nature has, in the case of *Lear*, still done its work, but the lack of narrative resolution at the end of the play suggests that nature can only do so much. After it corrects what flaws it can, the responsibility to create a better world ultimately rests on human shoulders.

"LITTLE GIDDING" FROM *FOUR QUARTETS* (THOMAS STEARNS ELIOT)

"The Later Quartets"
by Staffan Bergsten,
in *Time and Eternity:*
A Study in the Structure and Symbolism
of T.S. Eliot's Four Quartets (1960)

INTRODUCTION

Staffan Bergsten, in his close reading of "Little Gidding," examines the argument, imagery, and allusions of the poem. Claiming that this last of Eliot's *Quartets* is an intentional conclusion to his "poetic work as a whole," Bergsten characterizes "Little Gidding," especially its concluding section, as a "reaffirmation," one where a recognition of old age and mortality gives way to a "timeless, mystic vision." For Eliot, "the redemption of time lies, not in the negation or annihilation of time, but in the transfiguration of time in a timeless pattern." Thus "Little Gidding," with its religious and spiritually charged language, marks the end of Eliot's search for redemption through poetry. Eliot attempts to move from the "Midwinter spring" of the opening stanza to "the unimaginable Zero

Bergsten, Staffan. "The Later Quartets." *Time and Eternity: A Study in the Structure and Symbolism of T.S. Eliot's* Four Quartets. Stockholm, Sweden: Svenska Bokförlaget, 1960. pp. 206–44.

summer," a season when life is apprehended not as movement or decay but as a perpetual pattern of rebirth and renewal.

❧

The last of the *Quartets* is related to a definite place, or rather to two places. One is, as in "Burnt Norton" and "East Coker", Eliot's own surroundings in London, and the other the chapel of Little Gidding—a small village in Huntingdonshire. The First Section of "Little Gidding" is the account of a visit to that chapel. Though using the more general pronoun "you", the poet obviously draws on his own experience in visiting Little Gidding. That experience, including a host of memories and historical associations, may be taken as the "literal" meaning of the poem.

The first paragraph is symbolic throughout, and yet it is also a picture of a winter's afternoon in the English countryside as effectively impressionistic as anything Eliot has written:

> Midwinter spring is its own season
> Sempiternal though sodden towards sundown,
> Suspended in time, between pole and tropic.
> When the short day is brightest, with frost and fire,
> The brief sun flames the ice, on pond and ditches,
> In windless cold that is the heart's heat,
> Reflecting in a watery mirror
> A glare that is blindness in the early afternoon.
> And glow more intense than blaze of branch, or brazier,
> Stirs the dumb spirit: no wind, but pentecostal fire
> In the dark time of the year. Between melting and freezing
> The soul's sap quivers. There is no earth smell
> Or smell of living thing. This is the spring time
> But not in time's covenant. Now the hedgerow
> Is blanched for an hour with transitory blossom
> Of snow, a bloom more sudden
> Than that of summer, neither budding nor fading,
> Not in the scheme of generation.
> Where is the summer, the unimaginable
> Zero summer?

The winter's afternoon here described is the actual time of the poet's visit to the chapel of Little Gidding, but it also seems to stand for the afternoon and winter of his own life. Eliot here reverts to a symbolism of seasons close to that previously used in the *Quartets*. The time of the visit to the garden of Burnt Norton was late summer; in "East Coker" it is "late November"; and here in the last of the *Quartets* it is winter. In "East Coker" the poet found the hoped for serenity in the autumn of his life replaced by an upsurge of emotions rightly belonging to spring and summer, but here in "Little Gidding" there is sharp but well-balanced contrast between winter and spring. This "midwinter spring", "not in time's covenant" and "not in the scheme of genera-tion", is the forerunner of the "unimaginable / Zero summer". The psychological and spiritual implications seem clear. At a time when he might have expected sterility and drought, the aging poet feels "the soul's sap quiver"—the return of his creative powers—and this creative-ness becomes to him a "type" of the divine creativeness manifest in the Nativity of Christ in the middle of winter. But the excitement implied in the soul's quivering is also related to the "Zero summer"—it is the fear, wonder and joy of the soul contemplating the "unimaginable" summer of eternal life that comes after winter and death.

The afternoon of the poet's visit to Little Gidding is also symbolic of the afternoon of his country. In the last of the *Quartets* the theme of history achieves its final development, and the name of Little Gidding itself holds several historical associations. It is the place where Nicolas Ferrar in 1626 founded an Anglican community organized on almost monastic principles and intended to provide the opportunity for a devout life of contemplation ("You are here to kneel") in the midst of the political and religious upheaval of the time. The place is also associated with King Charles I who visited it twice, the last time in secrecy at night, shortly after his final defeat ("If you came at night like a broken king"). As already mentioned, Richard Crashaw was also one of the visitors to Little Gidding, and George Herbert was deeply influenced by the religious ideas of Nicolas Ferrar.[1] Thus Little Gidding aptly symbolizes the particular period of English history referred to in the poem. Section III, for example, contains a number of references to the time of the Civil War:

> If I think, again, of this place,
> And of people, not wholly commendable,

Of no immediate kin or kindness,
But some of peculiar genius,
All touched by a common genius,
United in the strife which divided them;
If I think of a king at nightfall,
Of three men, and more, on the scaffold
And a few who died forgotten
In other places, here and abroad,
And of one who died blind and quiet,
Why should we celebrate
These dead men more than the dying?
It is not to ring the bell backward
Nor is it an incantation
To summon the spectre of a Rose.

There is the king, again, and an allusion to his execution and to the royal emblem of the Rose—the White Rose of the Stuarts.[2] There are the members of various political and religious parties and factions, "United in the strife which divided them", together with Milton, "who died blind and quiet".

It is not difficult to see the connection between that period of distress and war and the time when "Little Gidding" was written— 1941–42. Little Gidding seems to form an instance of the "significant soil" of which Eliot speaks in the last line of "The Dry Salvages", significant both as a historical symbol and as a symbol of a tendency in Eliot's own life and personality. Eliot has always shown a tendency to revert, in his thought and reading, to the seventeenth century, its poets and playwrights, its religious and political thinkers. It was that century which witnessed the formation of the Anglican Church to which Eliot was to turn and which nurtured many of the poets and preachers who have most deeply influenced his thought and his work. It is significant also that the political thought of that period raised the very problem that Eliot raises in his essay, *The Idea of a Christian Society*—the problem of the place of the church in a secular society.

Thus the speaker's visit to Little Gidding in the midst of the war, becomes symbolic of his sense of continuity and tradition, his sense of history, but also of something else and much more important: his conviction that tradition and history, to have a real meaning, must partake of a timeless pattern. This is the theme of the First Section of "Little Gidding".

The second paragraph of the same Section resumes the theme of motion and travelling. In the previous *Quartets* motion was pictured either as circular or as progressing infinitely without a goal or destination, but here motion and travelling forward achieve dynamic purpose, not in the sense that an end or a goal is reached but because a timeless dimension is realized in time.

> And what you thought you came for
> Is only a shell, a husk of meaning
> From which the purpose breaks only when it is fulfilled
> If at all. Either you had no purpose
> Or the purpose is beyond the end you figured
> And is altered in fulfilment. There are other places
> Which also are the world's end, some at the sea jaws,
> Or over a dark lake, in a desert or a city—
> But this is the nearest, in place and time,
> Now and in England.

In prayer, the speaker goes on to say, and particularly in praying in the chapel at Little Gidding, he has experienced a moment of timeless vision similar to that in the garden of Burnt Norton. But the moment in the chapel is not only a repetition of the earlier one, it is also its fulfilment, and the experience in the garden "is altered in fulfilment" because it has become integrated with the historical and religious order of which Little Gidding is a symbol. Thus, here at the end of the First Section of "Little Gidding", the previous *Quartets* seem to realize their conclusion. The initial experience described in "Burnt Norton" has been explored and developed in its various aspects throughout the first three *Quartets*, and here it is repeated, but under completely different circumstances. Instead of the timeless moment "with no before and after" in the remote setting of the garden, the poet here connects the timeless moment with a historical tradition, and through that moment this tradition receives its meaning.

> Here, the intersection of the timeless moment
> Is England and nowhere. Never and always.

If this moment is a fulfilment of the moment in the garden, it is also altered in its fulfilment; that is to say that the meaning Eliot set out to explore appeared to be different from what he had expected at the outset. It is a meaning to be found within history, and yet it transcends history extending into the world of eternal life. This meaning, which "is beyond the end you figured", is indicated in the last two Sections of "Little Gidding".

The Second Section opens with three stanzas which, varying the Heracleitean idea of the chain of the four elements,[3] sum up the previous *Quartets* by recapitulation of significant images. There are the roses and the "Dust in the air suspended" from "Burnt Norton" I, the "wall, the wainscot and the mouse" from "East Coker" I, the images of water from "The Dry Salvages" and the "sanctuary and choir" reminiscent of the chapel at Little Gidding. This technique of recapitulating significant symbols is used already in the final Section of "Burnt Norton" and then in each of the subsequent *Quartets*. Each time the span of the speaker's recollections and the reader's associations becomes wider, and at the same time the whole set of poems is integrated into a unified symbolic structure.

However, these stanzas on the death of the elements have other implications as well. They immediately precede a scene in which the speaker is walking the streets of London just after an air raid, and some of the images in the stanzas suggest the destruction wrought by the bombs:

> Dust in the air suspended
> Marks the place where a story ended.
> Dust inbreathed was a house—
>
> — — —
>
> The parched eviscerate soil
> Gapes at the vanity of toil,
> Laughs without mirth.
>   This is the death of earth.

The scene that follows is enacted "In the uncertain hour before the morning" when the speaker encounters "some dead master", and the Section closes with the disappearance of this master "on the blowing of the horn"—the sounding of the "All Clear". The identity of the dead master seems deliberately obscured; it is not one but many, a "familiar compound ghost". The metre and tone of the passage suggest Dante, who probably forms the chief component in the "compound ghost", but there are also allusions to Virgil, Milton, Swift, Mallarmé and several others.[4]

The function of this episode seems to be partly to pay homage to all the poets of past ages, who belong to the literary tradition on which Eliot builds, and partly to bring to a conclusion all the previous passages dealing with the art of poetry. Since "Little Gidding" is concerned with connecting the private experience of the poet with a historical tradition, it seems appropriate that the expression of this experience should be connected with a literary tradition.

The theme of aging also recurs in the speech of the dead master. It is a gloomy picture he gives of old age, suggesting the fears of the aging poet himself. But like most of the themes of "Little Gidding", this one not only sums up the earlier developments of the theme of age but goes beyond them in pointing towards the final conclusion of the whole sequence of poems:

> From wrong to wrong the exasperated spirit
> Proceeds, unless restored by that refining fire
>   Where you must move in measure, like a dancer.

The symbol of the dancer is familiar, but the symbol of fire is not fully developed until the end of "Little Gidding". Earlier in the present Section it is foreshadowed in "the flickering tongue" of "the dark dove"—the fire of the bomber—which also anticipates the tongues and dove of Section IV.

The Third Section of "Little Gidding" contains perhaps the poet's clearest account of his purpose in writing the *Four Quartets*:

> This is the use of memory:
> For liberation—not less of love but expanding
> Of love beyond desire, and so liberation
> From the future as well as the past.

This is a development and explanation of the idea of personal time— of memory as first introduced in "Burnt Norton"—and in speaking of the "use of memory" Eliot seems to refer to the motive and purpose of writing the *Quartets*. The use of memory is for "liberation / From the future as well as the past". That is to say that the recollections from the poet's earlier life realized in the experience in the garden and in the subsequent meditations of the *Quartets*, had the effect of liberating him from the "enchainment of past and future", and this effect was achieved by the "expanding / Of love beyond desire". In the ecstatic vision in the rose garden the recollections of desire, of the profane ecstasy, reflected in Eliot's earlier poems, received a meaning beyond their original temporal meaning, were recognized as having a divine purpose—as, in that sense, "types" of divine love.

The idea of personal time is also bound together with the idea of history. By the "expanding / Of love beyond desire" the individual achieves liberation from time, and "Thus", the poet goes on to say,

> love of a country
> Begins as attachment to our own field of action
> And comes to find that action of little importance
> Though never indifferent. History may be servitude,
> History may be freedom. See, now they vanish,
> The faces and places, with the self which, as it could, loved them,
> To become renewed, transfigured, in another pattern.

The line of thought Eliot seems to be pursuing is that the sense of history, conceived as an extension of personal memory to include the past of the nation or even the race, may be a means of liberation. The "attachment to our own field of action" is expanded into and then beyond "love of a country". "History may be servitude"—if the temporal dimension of history is not transcended by the timeless dimension—but "History may be freedom" as well. The temporal content of memory and history must vanish, the "faces and places" referring, it seems, to the objects of desire and patriotic attachment, and also "the self which, as it could, loved them". In the line,

> To become renewed, transfigured, in another pattern,

Eliot indicates the end of the process of liberation from past and future. This is, in effect, a statement of the Dantean allegorical method used in the *Quartets*: the literal facts supplied by memory and history are renewed and transfigured in being interpreted on the various spiritual levels of meaning; and the pattern in which they are transfigured is a timeless pattern, for, as Eliot says in the last Section, "history is a pattern / Of timeless moments".

The transfiguration of human life and history in the timeless pattern must also involve a resolution of the antithesis of good and evil—this seems to be the meaning of the lines which follow, perhaps somewhat abruptly, upon the passage just considered:

> Sin is Behovely, but
> All shall be well, and
> All manner of thing shall be well.

This quotation from the *Revelations* of Julian of Norwich is the answer she received to the question how the existence of sin was to be reconciled with a good and righteous God.[5] The problem of sin and evil plays a subordinate part in the *Quartets*, and it is hardly to be expected that Eliot should really attack this problem here. But in quoting Dame Julian he indicates that in the divine order of things there is place even for that which to us appears as evil.

In the Fourth, lyric Section all the spiritual levels of meaning are set forth in symbols of great complexity. The "dark dove" of Section II is here transformed into the dove of the Holy Ghost appearing at the Baptism of Christ, and the "flickering tongue" of the aircraft's gun into the "cloven tongues like as of fire" which descended upon the Apostles on the day of Pentecost. The uniting element is fire, and the different aspects of fire relate to the different levels of meaning in "Little Gidding". The experience of "midwinter spring" at the visit to the chapel of Little Gidding was said to be "pentecostal fire / In the dark time of the year", foreshadowing the allegorical or typical meaning of the poem which is the fire of the Holy Ghost, which again is love. The literal fire of destruction is also the fire of Hell, but, on the anagogical level, it may appear as the fire of purgation:

> unless restored by that refining fire
> Where you must move in measure, like a dancer.

The moral meaning, Helen Gardner has suggested, may be defined as Charity[6]—the human reflection of divine Love.

There is a deep tone of pain and despair in "Little Gidding"—a tone most fully heard in the Fourth Section. The poem refers to a time when London seemed to be abandoned to the element of destructive fire, when Hell seemed to be realized on earth. And the only hope of liberation from despair, the poet meditates, lies in regarding the affliction as a visitation of God, in the transfiguration of the fire of destruction into the fire of purgation:

> The only hope, or else despair
>   Lies in the choice of pyre or pyre—
>   To be redeemed from fire by fire.

Here, again, the poet raises the problem of evil, and the answer is the same as in the preceding Section:

> Who then devised the torment? Love.
> Love is the unfamiliar Name
> Behind the hands that wove
> The intolerable shirt of flame
> Which human power cannot remove.
>   We only live, only suspire
>   Consumed by either fire or fire.

What the lyric seems to say, then, is that the fire which made "the soul's sap quiver" in the aging poet and the destructive fire of the war may both be transformed into the fire of purgation and ascend to union with the flames of the Spirit as a manifestation of divine Love.

The final Section of "Little Gidding" is not only a conclusion to that poem, but to the *Four Quartets* as a whole. It hardly contains a single line without an allusion to one of the earlier *Quartets*.

The Section opens with a reversion to the central idea of "East Coker":

> What we call the beginning is often the end
> And to make an end is to make a beginning.

This idea is then brought to bear on general problems of the art of poetry raised in the preceding *Quartets*. It is further connected with the theme of death and rebirth and finally it is led on to the conception of the timeless moment, the moment in the garden and that in the chapel. The symbolic and thematic development of the *Quartets* has come full circle, the poet is back where he started but the return is different from the outset because of the insight gained in the meantime:

> The moment of the rose and the moment of the yew-tree
> Are of equal duration. A people without history
> Is not redeemed from time, for history is a pattern
> Of timeless moments. So, while the light fails
> On a winter's afternoon, in a secluded chapel
> History is now and England.

The meaning of these lines may perhaps be expressed thus: The moment of mystic ecstasy occurring in temporal life and the moment of death (implied in the symbol of the yew-tree) are "of equal duration", i.e. beyond duration in the temporal sense, in the realm of timeless eternity. Since history, or rather the meaning of history, consists in a pattern of timeless moments, the absence of history, or of personal memories, does not redeem a people, or an individual, from time. The redemption of time lies, not in the negation or annihilation of time, but in the transfiguration of time in a timeless pattern. This transfiguration, however, must be achieved, for a people as well as for an individual, in time; the timeless must be apprehended in time, for "only through time time is conquered". So, while the moment in the garden seemed to be without past and future, the moment in the chapel of Little Gidding is related to time and history and to "significant soil". The timeless pattern of that moment is experienced as projected in time, and therefore the poet, in ending his long meditation on the idea of time and history in the *Quartets*, may say,

> History is now and England.

The concluding paragraph of "Little Gidding" is preceded by a line quoted from the anonymous mystical treatise, *The Cloud of Unknowing*,

> With the drawing of this Love and the voice of this Calling,

which together with the quotations from Julian of Norwich extend the spiritual tradition symbolized by the name of Little Gidding beyond the seventeenth century back to the early Christian mysticism in England.[7]

The last paragraph of the last of the *Four Quartets* is clearly devised as a "musical" finale, in which are gathered the symbols that have recurred throughout the whole sequence of poems. Here, on their final appearance, these symbols are no doubt intended to convey the whole range of meanings accumulated in them, and this wealth of meanings is in effect but another reflection of the deeply musical structure of the *Quartets*. The purely formal structure of a piece of music can often be analysed lucidly enough, but who can define the emotional effect it has? The same musical phrase, movement or composition may mean the very depth of anguish and despair to one hearer, and the height of joy to another, and still both may well be right in their interpretations. This is because music offers a good deal of freedom—what the sounds actually mean depends not a little on the hearer. But the poet is much more limited. The sounds he uses are words, and are hence tied, more or less, to particular connotations. In the *Four Quartets*, however, Eliot has attempted to use words as a musician uses sounds, so that they are sometimes capable of evoking, as we have seen, very varied interpretations. It is perhaps in this respect that the musical analogy implied in the use of the word "quartet" is most apt and most significant.

In the final paragraph of "Little Gidding" the technique of "musical" recapitulation is perhaps somewhat mechanically applied; it sometimes tends to become mere addition:

> We shall not cease from exploration
> And the end of all our exploring
> Will be to arrive where we started

And know the place for the first time.
Through the unknown, remembered gate
When the last of earth left to discover
Is that which was the beginning;
At the source of the longest river
The voice of the hidden waterfall
And the children in the apple-tree
Not known, because not looked for
But heard, half-heard, in the stillness
Between two waves of the sea.
Quick now, here, now, always—

After a variation on the theme of beginning and end from "East Coker" comes the gate leading into the rose garden, to "the last of earth left to discover" which "was the beginning"—"our first world" (BN: I). The river and the waterfall both derive from "The Dry Salvages" (I and V), and the lines that follow echo "Burnt Norton" I and V and "The Dry Salvages" II.

In the very last lines of the poem, the images of the fire and the rose recur together with the only new image in the whole paragraph— "the crowned knot of fire". This image, though perhaps derived from mystical literature,[8] seems to be prompted by the preceding images; closely bound together as these images are, they may be said in effect to crown the whole work. All the preceding images of the paragraph are in some way symbolic of the timeless, mystic vision, and together they point to the Divine Reality which is also Fire and Love and which is the ground and guarantee of the final promise and prediction:

And all shall be well and
All manner of thing shall be well
When the tongues of flame are in-folded
Into the crowned knot of fire
And the fire and the rose are one.

Thus the elaborate recapitulation of images and symbols is clearly intended, not only to bring the sequence to an artistically satisfactory close, but also to be, as it were, a benediction, a reaffirmation.

It has already been remarked that this conclusion owes a great deal to the conclusion of Dante's *Paradiso*. Eliot surely had no intention to rival Dante in writing these lines, but he seems to have aimed at a similar effect of elevation and at the same time of finality. The conclusion is a conclusion not only to "Little Gidding" and the whole sequence of the *Quartets* but, since some of the images revert to his earliest poems, a conclusion to Eliot's poetic work as a whole. Moreover, though written eighteen years ago, "Little Gidding" is the most recent poem published by Eliot and perhaps also his last.

If "Little Gidding", and the *Four Quartets* as a whole, fail to achieve the final effect the poet seems to have intended, the failure is certainly not one of poetic technique, or even of inspiration, but a failure of poetry as a medium of communication. Even the most complex poetic structure seems to fail fully to convey the meaning Eliot has tried to convey in the *Four Quartets*—a meaning not only beyond the scope of poetry but perhaps beyond communication in any medium. That Eliot himself is well aware of the limitations of poetry as a vehicle of religious truth, is evident from the meditations on the art of poetry contained in the *Quartets*. Nevertheless in completing the sequence in spite of all doubts and difficulties, Eliot reveals the depth and power of his inspiration and of the motives for persevering in the struggle to realize this inspiration. The psychological motive Eliot has indicated in describing the unwritten poem as "a burden which he [the poet] must bring to birth in order to obtain relief".[9] The moral motive may perhaps be expressed by a phrase borrowed from "East Coker": "For us there is only the trying. The rest is not our business."

NOTES

1. Vide supra, p. 60. Cf. Gardner, H., *The Art of T.S. Eliot*, London, 1949, pp. 176 ff., and Preston, p. 53, n.
2. See Stephenson, E.M., *T.S. Eliot and the Lay Reader*, 2nd ed. London, 1946, p. 91; Bradbury, J.M., "*Four Quartets*: The Structural Symbolism", *Sewanee Review*, Vol. 59, 1951, p. 268.
3. See Matthiessen, p. 190.
4. As usual, Grover Smith has discovered more allusions than any other critic: op. cit., pp. 285 ff.

5. See Gardner, H., "*Four Quartets*: A Commentary", pp. 75 f.

6. Gardner, H., *The Art of T.S. Eliot*, p. 184.

7. Gardner, H., "*Four Quartets*: A Commentary", p. 76.

8. Drew, E., *T.S. Eliot: The Design of His Poetry*, London, 1950, p. 239, n.

9. *On Poetry and Poets*, p. 98.

THE METAMORPHOSIS
(FRANZ KAFKA)

ᘦᘓ ᘗᘓ

"Realism and Unrealism:
Kafka's 'Metamorphosis'"
by Norman N. Holland,
in *Modern Fiction Studies* (1958)

INTRODUCTION

In his analysis of *The Metamorphosis*, Norman Holland traces the influence of biblical imagery and symbolism on Kafka's portrayal of Gregor Samsa's metamorphosis and death. Drawing correspondences between Kafka's work and passages from the Bible, Holland claims that *The Metamorphosis* is a kind of allegory in which Gregor's death "parallels the Biblical accounts of Christ's death." Thus, *The Metamorphosis* "satirizes Christians, who are only distressed, angry, and, ultimately, cruel when a second Christ appears." Holland points out how Kafka critiques a modern world of spiritual alienation, not unlike T.S. Eliot's *The Waste Land*, in which the poet, like Kafka, yearns for rebirth and renewal. In addition to being a satirical allegory for the Passion, Gregor's transformation, according to Holland, "dramatizes the human predicament . . . trapped between a set of dark instinctual

---

Holland, Norman N. "Realism and Unrealism: Kafka's 'Metamorphosis.'" *Modern Fiction Studies* 4.2 (Summer 1958): 143–50.

urges on one hand and an obscure drive to serve 'gods' on the other." In the end, the Samsa family does not understand or recognize the significance of Gregor's transformation; they are unwilling to accept or account for "the cause of all [their] unhappiness." According to Holland, Gregor's transformation and death force readers to a renewal of awareness, where we must confront, using Freud's terms, "the cage of the id and superego." *The Metamorphosis*, "by its very unreality," drives readers to "see the realities, Biblical and Freudian, hiding behind the ordinary reality of the story."

∽⤬∾

In allegory, symbolism, and surrealism—the three genres are in this respect, at least, indistinguishable—the writer mixes unrealistic elements into a realistic situation. Thus, Kafka, in *Metamorphosis*, puts into the realistic, prosaic environment of the Samsa household a situation that is, to put it mildly, unrealistic: "As Gregor Samsa awoke one morning from a troubled dream, he found himself changed in his bed to some monstrous kind of vermin." Kafka's strategy does not in essence differ from the techniques of Spenser and Bunyan: though they used for the unreal elements allegorical names, they, too, set them in realistic or conventional situations. Kafka's method, while rather more overpowering, works the same way: the unreal elements, be they allegorical names or human cockroaches, set up a kind of electric field; the most trite and prosaic detail brought into that field glows with extra meaning. To read allegory is simply to "probe" this field of meaning. We can probe it only if we momentarily put aside the unreality which creates the field and measure the extra values given the realistic elements. By reading them imaginatively, we can understand the nature of the field; only then can we turn back to and understand the unreal element that created the field.

If we look first at the unrealistic elements, there is a danger that we will be dazzled and see no more, as in the usual crude reading of *Metamorphosis*: Samsa is a cockroach, Samsa equals Kafka, Kafka thinks of himself as a cockroach, and so on. Reading Kafka that way is like seeing *The Faerie Queene* as a moralistic tract about Temperance or Justice without realizing the rich, plastic meanings Spenser's realism develops for his allegorical names. Looking first at the realistic elements and their extra values avoids a second danger in reading allegory: substituting abstractions for the realism of the story. Kafka's meaning, as Mr. Eliseo Vivas points out, "is something not to be better stated abstractly in terms of ideas and concepts, to be found beyond the fable, but within it, at the dramatic level, in the interrelationships . . . among the characters and between them and the universe."

If, momentarily, we put aside the unreality of Gregor Samsa's metamorphosis, we can see that the story builds on a commonplace, even a trite, situation: a man feels sick and decides to stay home from work. For fully the first sixth of the story Gregor goes through exactly the kind of internal monologue any of us might if we had caught a discomforting, but not disabling, cold. "Nothing is more degrading than always to have to rise so early." "How would it be if I go to sleep again for awhile?" "I'd like to see what my boss would say if I tried it; I should be sacked immediately." "What a job I've chosen . . . To hell with it all!" Job, employer, and employee are the core of the realism of *Metamorphosis*; not unnaturally, they form the heart of the allegory as well.

Metamorphosis has three parts, each marked by Gregor's emerging from his bedroom into the Samsa dining-room and then retreating. The first part of the story tells of Gregor's metamorphosis and of his job. In the second part, Gregor's father goes back to work for the first time since the failure of his own business five years before. In the third part, Gregor's mother and sister go to work, although Gregor had hoped to send his sister to the conservatory, and the family takes in three lodgers, employers, as it were, in the home. After Gregor's death, in the third part, the lodgers are thrown out, and the Samsas write three letters of excuse to their three employers, and take the day off. Only by reading imaginatively the passages that deal with employers, employees, and jobs, can we see the extra meaning Gregor's metamorphosis gives to these elements.

Gregor, a traveling salesman who sells cloth, says of his boss: "That's a funny thing; to sit on a desk so as to speak to one's employees from such a height, especially when one is hard of hearing and people must come close! Still, all hope is not lost; once I have got

together the money my parents owe him—that will be in about five or
six years—I shall certainly do it. Then I'll take the big step!" Gregor
muses about the firm:

> Why was Gregor, particularly, condemned to work for a firm
> where the worst was suspected at the slightest inadvertence
> of the employees? Were the employees, without exception, all
> scoundrels? Was there among their number not one devoted
> faithful servant, who, if it did so happen that by chance he
> missed a few hours work one morning might have found
> himself so numbed with remorse that he just could not leave
> his bed?

After Gregor's metamorphosis, his father goes to work for a
bank. "By some capricious obstinacy, [he] always refused to take off
his uniform even at home . . . as if to keep himself always ready to
carry out some order; even in his own home, he seemed to await his
superior's voice." Gregor's mother "was killing herself mending the
linen of strangers, the sister ran here and there behind her counter at
the customers' bidding."

The three lodgers whom the family takes in "were very earnest and
serious men; all three had thick beards . . . and they were fanatically
tidy; they insisted on order, not only in their own room, but also, now
that they were living here, throughout the whole household, and especially in the kitchen." Gregor's mother brings them a plate of meat in
the dining room. "The lodgers leaned over it to examine it, and the
one who was seated in the middle and who appeared to have some
authority over the others, cut a piece of meat as it lay on the dish to
ascertain whether it was tender or whether he should send it back to
the kitchen. He seemed satisfied, however, and the two women, who
had been anxiously watching, gave each other a smile of relief."

These descriptions are ambiguous, even cryptic—but not in themselves unrealistic; the pallor of unreality is cast by the impossible metamorphosis always present to our minds. The description of Gregor's
boss has breadth enough to apply not just to a petty office tyrant, but
even to an Old Testament God. Indeed, the reference to the high desk
echoes the Old Testament metaphor of the God "most high" who yet
can "hear" us: "Though the Lord be high, yet hath he respect unto the

lowly" (Ps. 138:6); "The Lord's hand is not shortened, that it cannot save; neither his ear heavy, that it cannot hear: But your iniquities have separated between you and your God, and your sins have hid his face from you, that he will not hear" (Is. 59:1–2). Read this way, the debt that Gregor assumed for his parents and must pay resembles original sin. Only after he has expiated the sin-debt can he "take the big step" toward freedom.

The description of the "firm," with its atmosphere of universal guilt and punishment, also hints at original sin: "A faithful man who can find?" (Prov. 20:6). Gregor and his fellow-workers are treated like the evil servant whose lord "shall come in a day when he looketh not for him, and in an hour that he is not aware of, and shall cut him asunder, and appoint him his portion with the hypocrites: there shall be weeping and gnashing of teeth" (Matt. 24:50–51). Gregor is indeed cut off from men; he gets his "portion" of garbage from his hypocritical family, and one evening when he eavesdrops on the three lodgers eating: "It seemed curious to Gregor that he could hear the gnashing of their teeth above all the clatter of cutlery." The lodgers themselves, "very earnest and serious," "fanatically tidy," resemble gods. Frau Samsa's submitting a plate of meat to them is almost like making a burnt offering to some very choosy deities: "Your burnt offerings are not acceptable, nor your sacrifices sweet unto me" (Jer. 6:20).

The fact that employers come in threes after the metamorphosis hints at a shift from Old Testament to New like that of "In the Penal Colony"; more immediately, however, it suggests that each member of the family has to take up a share of the burden of subservience that Gregor had borne alone before. Thus, Gregor had proudly brought home cash as a traveling salesman for a cloth concern. His job is now broken into its separate components. His father goes to work for a bank: he now wears the special clothes and acquires Gregor's pride in supporting the family. His mother deals with the cloth, "the linen of strangers." His sister "ran here and there." The fact that there are three lodgers suggests that there is a "god" for each member of the family. The one in the middle, the most important one, corresponds to Gregor's father.

Space does not permit a full development of all the realistic elements in *Metamorphosis* that Gregor's predicament has charged with extra, non-realistic meaning. In every case, however, the same procedure would apply: an imaginative reading of the passages dealing with a particular "realistic" detail. In the few passages I have already quoted, some of these elements emerge. Employers are like gods. Money suggests psychic resources; debts suggest psychic deficits or guilt. Traveling—not only Gregor's normal occupation, but even after his metamorphosis, he learns "to distract himself by walking"— suggests the need to serve an employer, an escape from freedom (sitting still) for *homo viator*. Cloth and clothing are the badges of subservience; it is only in states of nightdress or undress that the inner self can emerge.

Other passages would show many more realistic elements with significance beyond mere physical reality. Food, for example, suggests devotion—reverent offerings demanded by lodgers or communion with one's equals. All the family intercourse of the Samsas seems to take place in the dining room. "Breakfast was the most important meal of the day," because it was the transition from bed, one's private life, to employment. The outdoors, the place where one goes to work, where one travels and wears formal clothing, belongs to the employers. Gregor himself sees his problem as that of getting out of bed: "He would dress, and above all, he would have breakfast; then would come the time to reflect, for he felt that it was not in bed that a reasonable solution could be found. He recalled how often an unusual position adopted in bed had resulted in slight pains which proved imaginary as soon as he arose."

The trifid division of the locale into bedroom (private self), dining room (personal relationships), and outdoors (obligations) hints at that other division into id, ego, and superego. The rooms correspond to areas of experience, the whole apartment upstairs to life on earth and the outdoors downstairs to heaven, with "some unearthly deliverance . . . at the foot of the stairs." Locks and doors, then, symbolize the barriers between these areas of experience. Normally, we break down such barriers by speech, but Gregor can no longer speak intelligibly: he can, however, twist open the lock to his bedroom with his mouth. Locks also symbolize Gregor's imprisonment in the body of an insect. Thus, at first, "without differentiating between them, he hoped for great and surprising things from the locksmith and the doctor."

Once understood, Kafka's method is quite straightforward. In every case, he has charged a specific realistic element of the story with a specific non-realistic or spiritual value. Having understood the method and some of the values created in this field of meaning, one can go on to understand the non-realistic element that creates the field. If, in every case, Kafka converts a spiritual concept down to a physical fact, then the transformation of Gregor to dung-beetle, of man to animal, must stand for the transformation of god to man, and, indeed, Kafka has given Gregor a number of Christ-like attributes. At the opening of the story, Gregor had taken on the responsibility of working for the whole family—in particular, he had taken on his parents' debts (guilt or original sin). His metamorphosis takes place around Christmas; he remains a bug for three months and dies at the end of March. What finally kills Gregor is an apple thrown by his father, the apple, presumably, of Eden and mortality. "One lightly-thrown apple struck Gregor's back and fell off without doing any harm, but the next one literally pierced his flesh [sic]. He tried to drag himself a little further away, as if a change of position could relieve the shattering agony he suddenly felt, but he seemed to be nailed fast to the spot."

Gregor becomes weaker and weaker until he dies. The account of his death parallels the Biblical accounts of Christ's death:

He lay in this state of peaceful and empty meditation till the clock struck the third morning hour. He saw the landscape grow lighter through the window.	Now from the sixth hour there was darkness over all the land unto the ninth hour (Matt. 27:45).
He realized that he must go. . . . Against his will, his head fell forward and his last feeble breath streamed from his nostrils [sic].	After this, Jesus knowing that all things were accomplished that the scripture might be fulfilled . . . said, It is finished: and He bowed His head, and gave up the ghost (John 19:28–30).
The charwoman arrived early in the morning—and though she had often been forbidden to do so, she always slammed the door so loudly in her vigor and haste that once she was in the house it was impossible to get any sleep.	Behold, the veil of the temple was rent in twain from the top to the bottom; and the earth did quake, and rocks rent; and the graves were opened; and many bodies of the saints which slept arose (Matt. 27:51–52).

The Samsas arise from their beds and learn of Gregor's death; they cross themselves. "Well," says Herr Samsa, "we can thank God for that!" The charwoman, "gigantic . . . with bony features and white hair, which stood up all around her head," wearing a "little ostrich feather which stood upright on her hat," which "now waved lightly in all directions," describes Gregor as "absolutely dead as a doornail," "stone dead." "The angel of the Lord," says Matthew, "descended from heaven, and came and rolled back the stone from the door, and sat upon it. His countenance was like lightning, and his raiment white as snow." "He is not here: for he is risen," becomes another kind of divine comedy: "'Well, . . .' she replied, and she laughed so much she could hardly speak for some while. 'Well, you needn't worry about getting rid of that thing in there, I have fixed it already.'"

One question, however, remains: why a cockroach? Several critics have pointed out *Metamorphosis*'s descent from the "loathly lady" genre of medieval tales, in which, as in "Beauty and the Beast," someone is transformed into a loathsome animal and can be transformed back only by love. Love, in other words, is tested by disgust, and in *Metamorphosis*, love is found lacking. In at least one such tale which Kafka probably knew, Flaubert's "The Legend of St. Julian the Hospitaller," the loathsome creature turns out to be Christ. Kafka, however, could have used any loathsome animal, a toad, a snake, a spider: why a cockroach? The German word is *Mistkaefer*, applied to Gregor only once—by the charwoman. Technically, the word means a dung-beetle, not a cockroach, and the distinction is important. For one thing, biologically, a cockroach undergoes only a partial metamorphosis, while the beetles go through a total metamorphosis. More important, dung beetles are scarabs. "The Egyptian scarab," says the redoubtable *Britannica*, "is an image of the sacred dung-beetle . . . which was venerated as a type of the sun-god. Probably the ball of dung, which is rolled along by the beetle in order to place its eggs in it, was regarded as an image of the sun in its course across the heavens, which may have been conceived as a mighty ball rolled by a gigantic beetle." Gregor, we should remember was a traveling salesman; a collection of samples was "entrusted" to him. Samson (Samsa) means in Hebrew "the sun's man." In German, the title of the story, *Die Verwandlung*, like the hieroglyphic beetle-sign, means either an insect's metamorphosis or transformation in a general sense.

Die Verwandlung, moreover, is the normal word for transubstan-
tiation. The dung-beetle, then, was the one animal that gave Kafka
everything he needed: total metamorphosis from a wingless grub to a
hard-working, traveling-salesman-like adult plus the combination of
loathsomeness and divinity.

Samson's sacrifice is a traditional analogue to Christ's; in German
he is called a *Judenchrist.* Gregor's first name means "vigilant," and
so he was when he supported his family. When he is a dim-sighted
scarab, though, his first name makes an ironic contrast to his last:
Samson was blinded. Samsa, like Samson, rid the chosen people (his
family) of the domineering Philistines (the lodgers who didn't like
the sister's music) by his own self-destruction, his wished-for death.
Gregor, at one point, longs to climb up on his sister's shoulder and kiss
her neck; in general, Gregor has a great many incestuous impulses. In
this context, his name echoes the medieval legend of Pope Gregory,
who in expiating his incestuous birth and marriage became the holiest
man in Christendom: chained to a barren rock for seventeen years,
the legend says he became an ugly little hedgehog-like creature.

Gregory-Gregor's situation strongly resembles that prophesied by
Isaiah: "His visage was so marred more than any man, and his form
more than the sons of men . . . he hath no form nor comeliness; and
when we shall see him, there is no beauty that we should desire him.
He is despised and rejected of men; a man of sorrows, and acquainted
with grief: and we hid as it were our faces from him; he was despised,
and we esteemed him not. Surely he hath borne our griefs, and carried
our sorrows: yet we did esteem him stricken, smitten of God, and
afflicted. But he was wounded for our transgressions, he was bruised
for our iniquities" (Is. 52:14–53:5). In fact, a good deal of the incidental
imagery of *Metamorphosis* was derived from Isaiah. For example, the
statement that Gregor's sister had worn on her neck "neither collar
nor ribbon ever since she had been working in the shop," corresponds
to, "Loose thyself from the bands of thy neck, O captive daughter
of Zion" (52:2). The details of Gregor's death are taken from the
Passion, and the whole allegorical scheme of employers as gods and
money as spiritual resources probably came from the various New
Testament parables of lords, stewards, and "talents."

In a crude sense, then, *Metamorphosis* satirizes Christians, who
are only distressed, angry, and, ultimately, cruel when a second Christ

appears. They take gods in times of trouble, even into their own homes, then throw them out when the trouble ends. After Gregor's death, a butcher's boy comes up the stairs, meeting and passing the evicted lodger-gods going down the stairs. Priest-like, he brings the meat that the Samsas will eat themselves, suggesting communion, as opposed to the burnt offerings they had formerly made to the lodgers. At one level, Kafka is parodying Christ's sacrifice, but a merely theological account of the story is far from complete. It neglects the rich sexual symbolism, the double doors, for example, through which Gregor must pass (a birth image) or the phallic symbols associated with his father: indeed, at one point Herr Samsa is described in terms rather more appropriate to a phallus. Kafka is reaching for more than theological allegory.

At the risk of being trite, I would like to suggest that Gregor's transformation dramatizes the human predicament. That is, we are all blind, like Samson, trapped between a set of dark instinctual urges on one hand and an obscure drive to serve "gods" on the other. Like dung-beetles, our lives are defined by the urge to mate and the urge to labor that comes from it. Our only freedom is not to know we are imprisoned. *Metamorphosis* represents abstractions physically and charges physical realities with spiritual significance. Gregor's physical transformation, then, stands for a spiritual transformation. Gregor *is* a dung-beetle means he *is spiritually like* one. His back, "hard as armor plate," dramatizes and *substitutes for* his awareness of this human predicament. Similarly, his metamorphosis forces his family to a reluctant awareness of this imprisonment: again, the physical events of the story, taking jobs, for example, dramatize and *substitute for* the awareness itself. Finally, Gregor's metamorphosis forces the reader to an awareness of the cage of id and superego. The reader, so long as he believes in the metamorphosis, by its very unreality is driven to see the realities, Biblical and Freudian, hiding behind the ordinary reality of the story.

The first part of *Metamorphosis* forces this understanding on us, but the ending whimsically urges on us the virtues of ignorance. As Gregor's sister says, "You must get the idea out of your head that this is Gregor. We have believed that for too long, and that is the cause of all our unhappiness. How could it be Gregor?" That is, so long as we believe in Gregor's metamorphosis, the realistic details of the story are fraught with significance. If we can forget Gregor's predicament and ours, we can relapse into blissful ignorance. To read *Metamorphosis*, one must put aside the "unreal" metamorphosis momentarily; the trouble with the Samsas is that they put it aside forever.

ORLANDO
(VIRGINIA WOOLF)

"Renewal, Rebirth, and Change in Virginia Woolf's *Orlando*"
by Lorena Russell,
the University of North Carolina at Asheville

On the one hand, Virginia Woolf's *Orlando, A Biography* (1928) is an obvious candidate for considering the literary theme of renewal and rebirth. The main character of the story, after all, not only lives several centuries with little effect but also changes from a man to a woman in the middle of the tale. Yet rebirth and renewal are centrally about character transformation, and as the novel concludes, readers are left pondering not so much the forces of change and renewal as they are the persistence of the character in the face of such dramatic biological and historical flux. As Orlando moves through various epochs, maneuvering life's blows and fortunes demands a capacity for renewal. Yet at the core, Orlando's personality essentially stays the same. The tension the novel establishes between powerful social forces and a persistent yet adaptable personality arises from Woolf's imaginative and satiric treatment of social renewal and individual rebirth.

This impulse to recast literary themes is not unique within Woolf's oeuvre and points in large part to her status as a modernist writer and literary critic. Woolf's life, from 1882 to 1941, places her in a time of radical transition between the Victorian and modern eras. She was frequently preoccupied with understanding the cultural, philosophical, and aesthetic transformations that characterized this historical moment. Essays such as "Modern Fiction" and "The New Biography" exemplify her attempts at framing the changes under way in how one writes a character in fiction or a subject in biography. Her autobiographical essays, diaries, and letters further identify her attempts to carve out new literary and social spaces apart from the stifling atmosphere of her Victorian upbringing. Novels like *Mrs. Dalloway* (1925) and *The Waves* (1931) experiment with different ways of presenting lived experience. Rather than focusing on the external details that might reveal character, Woolf's approach works from the inside out, placing readers squarely inside her characters' minds as they sort through a multitude of memories and impressions.

Orlando's formal and thematic treatments of renewal and rebirth are thus part of a broader modernist impulse to define itself in the context of broad-ranging cultural and political transformations, and as such they reflect Woolf's long-standing interest in moving literature toward a new aesthetic. Woolf's interests were not confined to the realm of aesthetics alone. She was equally concerned with cultural revolutions regarding sex and gender, and these political concerns are central to understanding the broad themes of renewal and rebirth in *Orlando*. As a feminist, Woolf was persistently engaged in understanding women's evolving social status. While writing *Orlando*, she was simultaneously writing lectures to later be published under the title of *A Room of One's Own* (1929), and the feminist polemic of these lectures most certainly influenced her novel.

On a more personal level, *Orlando* reflects Woolf's intimacy with her friend and lover, the poet and writer Vita Sackville-West. Vita's son, Nigel Nicholson, famously characterized the novel as "the longest and most charming love letter in literature" (225). Woolf's own letters and diaries reveal that the novel was in large part written as a playful biography of Sackville-West, whose aristocratic lineage (like that of Orlando's life) traced back to the Elizabethan era. Vita's sexuality and masculinity find expression as well through Orlando's androgynous and bisexual character. Presenting a lesbian theme, even in fiction, was a risky thing for the time, but the fantastic conceit of a sex change helped to soften the novel's lesbian content. (Woolf was well-aware of the obscenity charges launched (and prosecuted) against Radclyffe Hall's lesbian novel, *The Well of Loneliness*. Hermione Lee notes that Woolf excised some of the more risqué references from her manuscript of *Orlando* in a likely response to the suppression of Hall's novel (517).

The use of comedy and satire lend the novel a pervasive tone of ironic deflation, enabling Woolf to further inhibit her readers' tendency to take the book too seriously. In her diary Woolf describes how the release of writing the book offers her respite from her more formal writing tasks: "I felt happier than for months . . . & abandoned myself to the pure delight of this farce: Which I enjoy as much as I've ever enjoyed anything . . . I am writing Orlando half in a mock style very clear in plain, so that people will understand every word. But the balance between truth and fantasy must be careful" (162). Many of the details of the novel were drawn directly from Vita's recently published family history as well as her private letters, and the dedication and photographs in *Orlando* make the biographical link with Sackville-West quite explicit, albeit complex. The satirical effect of the novel is heightened by the novel's intrusive "Biographer," whose voice makes explicit the challenges of writing the story of a life.

The complexity of *Orlando*'s relationship to biography thus functions on several levels, ranging from the aesthetic to the political to the personal. Each of these levels further finds expression in the story's fanciful and satirical treatment of time, rebirth, and transformation. The novel's full title, *Orlando: A Biography*, seemingly establishes the text as a work of nonfiction, a concept soon undermined by the fanciful nature of the tale. Woolf sets the concept of biography (and history) on its heels, largely by defying our expectations of how history and character interrelate in the arena of rebirth and renewal.

Character in fiction is often very much about change. In fact, change marks the difference between "round" and "flat" characters. Readers are invited on the basis of these terms to judge how well developed a character is based on how much change that character goes through. Certainly, Orlando matures through the course of the novel and learns from experience, but Woolf's treatment of time in the end means that *Orlando* is not so much about character rebirth as it is about adaptation.

For Woolf, an individual's capacity must be measured against what a particular society or historical era allows. Change becomes less about what an individual accomplishes through his or her agency, and more about how metaphorical rebirth results from cultural forces. She further offers the radical idea that the material reality of the world itself changes and that artists, being in touch with the ever-so-powerful "spirit of the age," reflect those changes in their writings and in their outlooks. The novel, for example, recounts how Orlando experiences the time of the Renaissance as one of mutability. In Elizabeth's time, "everything was different" (20). It was a time of intense transformation, when "roses fade and petals fall" (21). As he enters the Jacobean period, a certain moribund spirit seems to settle upon his character, and he takes to wandering the catacombs among the bones of his ancestors.

When the Age of Prose arrives, the Biographer notes, "perhaps the senses were a little duller and honey and cream less seductive to the palate. Also that the streets were better drained and the houses better lit had its effect upon the style, it cannot be doubted" (83). The shift from the eighteenth to the nineteenth century is marked by a pall in the sky, a growing darkness signaling not only the material soot of the industrial revolution but also the intellectual darkness that is a pervasive force in Orlando's experience: "All was dark; all was doubt; all was confusion" (165). Orlando's narrative of transformation and development is one that speaks less to universalizing values and more toward the sense of what the material reality of the various eras allows and prohibits.

For Woolf, an individual's personality is not merely influenced by those events he or she experiences in a lifetime. Rather, the personality is an accumulation of historical experience that is carried on from one's ancestors. One of the more radical features of Woolf's "new biography" as represented by *Orlando*, then, is that to tell the story of a "life" includes being able to tell the stories of one's ancestors. Orlando's longevity thus becomes another way that Woolf challenges the orthodox view of biography: "The true length of a person's life, whatever the *Dictionary of Literary Biography* says, is always a matter of dispute" (224). The emphasis on ancestry is further tied to aristocracy, dependent as it is for its claim to social superiority through its ability to trace lineage through blood relations.

This notion of an "accumulated life" holds certain implications for treating the concept of rebirth. Woolf's theory of an accumulated personality lends her characterizations a certain persistence and predictability. By writing the character Orlando as basically immune to time's ravages, the concept of transformation is set into relief against the notion of a persistent personality. The story begins in the Renaissance during the reign of Queen Elizabeth I and ends in the early twentieth century. Yet, the character of Orlando persists throughout, aging only twenty years in spite of a time frame that spans three centuries (he is sixteen when the story opens and she is thirty-six at story's end).

While Orlando's enduring personality, memories, and affections create a sense of stability, the character nevertheless passes through several moments in the text that clearly mark a kind of rebirth. In the novel's first chapter, Orlando (though publically engaged to an English lady) falls madly in love with a visiting Russian princess, Sasha. The entire episode takes place during the "Great Frost" of 1606, a fantastic time when the Thames was said to have frozen solid. The moment is made even more fantastic through Woolf's elaborations, as she describes how various levels of Elizabethan society took to the ice, performing their day-to-day business and celebrations in this new, crystalline environment.

Love becomes the impetus for Orlando's initial transformation. As he gazes on Sasha:

> the thickness of his blood melted, the ice turned to wine in his veins; he heard the waters flowing and the birds singing; spring broke over the hard wintry landscape; his manhood woke; he grasped a sword in his hand; he charged a more daring foe than Pole or Moor; he dived in deep water.... (30)

While all around him is frozen in white, Orlando seems to be undergoing a kind of internal spring awakening, and we are told that "the change in Orlando was extraordinary" (31). The powers of this romantic love fall short, however, as Orlando becomes smitten with jealousy and then is abandoned by Sasha at the moment when a sudden spring thaw violently interrupts the frozen world on the river, creating a scene of "riot and confusion" as ice blocks carry countless victims downstream (46). As he watches the Russian ship disappear over the horizon, Orlando ends the first chapter in a state of despair and heartbreak.

As the next chapter opens, we find that Orlando has fallen into social disrepute and is living a life of solitary depression at his family estate. We are told how he went to bed on the night of Friday, June 17, and, much to the consternation of his staff and physicians, stayed asleep for a week. When he awakens, he dresses as usual, seemingly unaware of his unnatural slumber. The Biographer notes a muddling of his memory, "an imperfect recollection of his past life" (50), yet the memory of Sasha is something that Orlando will retain until the twentieth century.

The Biographer, in his typically mock-evasive style, briefly entertains the notion of rebirth to explain this preternatural moment. He asks: "[h]ad Orlando, worn out by the extremity of his suffering, died for a week, and then come to life again? And if so, of what nature is death and of what nature life? Having waited well over half an hour for an answer to these questions, and none coming, let us get on with the story" (51). Woolf teases the reader with the possibility of miraculous resurrection but then denies the theme and the philosophical discourse that would necessarily follow such a reading. Our impatient narrator is not here to reveal "the secret of life" but rather to tell the story of a life. And, as it turns out, telling "the story of a life" (the story of "Vita," whose name means "life") turns out to be quite complicated enough.

Aside from challenging the reader's (and the Biographer's) conventional understanding of capturing personality through time, *Orlando* further challenges our sense of what cannot be known by human beings, using gender and sexuality to add another complication to the puzzle of rebirth and renewal. Orlando's emergence as a woman comes midway in the story and follows a deep sleep similar to what the character experienced following the loss of Sasha. While serving as the British ambassador in Istanbul, Orlando (having slept through a revolution) awakens one morning to find himself transformed into a woman.

This moment of rebirth marks the most memorable scene in the novel, memorable not only for its fantastic presentation but for the scene's careful treatment of change and stasis. The moment is marked by tension conveyed as pageant. Trumpets cheer the Biographer to tell "the Truth and nothing but the Truth" against the inhibiting forces of Purity, Chastity, and Modesty (99, 100–102). At last, Truth wins out.

Purity, Chastity, and Modesty retreat to their champions, "virgins and city men; lawyers and doctors, those who prohibit; those who deny" (101), leaving the Biographer free to describe the transformation in a tone of ironic inflation: "while the trumpets pealed Truth! Truth! Truth! We have no choice left but confess—he was a woman" (102).

But rather than stress the change implicit in this rebirth, the Biographer offers a statement assuring readers that the character they had come to know was, for all intents and purposes, the same:

> Orlando had become a woman—there is no denying it. But in every other respect, Orlando remained precisely as he had been. The change of sex, though it altered their future, did nothing whatever to alter their identity. Their faces remained . . . practically the same. His memory—but in future we must, for convention's sake, say 'her' for 'his' and 'she' for 'he'—her memory then, went back through all the events of her past life without encountering any obstacle. . . . It is enough for us to state the simple fact; Orlando was a man till the age of thirty; when he became a woman and has remained so ever since. (103)

By allowing the character this consistent memory, the novel affords Orlando the ability to comment on how life as a woman differs from that as a man. Gender difference, we come to learn, has as much to do with clothing as anything else. Orlando lives for an interim period with gypsies, wearing "those Turkish coats and trousers which can be worn indifferently by either sex" (103). It is only when she dons a dress and boards a ship for England "that she realized, with a start the penalties and the privileges of her position" (113). While the dress shows off her (ever handsome) legs to advantage, she realizes she is at the same time vulnerable, dependent on the men around her for rescue should she end up in the water.

Later, in the eighteenth century, Orlando learns of the freedom she acquires by wearing men's clothing at night, leading a double life as lord and lady: "She had, it seems, no difficulty in sustaining the different parts, for her sex changed far more frequently than those who have worn only one set of clothing can conceive" (161). Just as Orlando despairs the masculine bias of the Augustan Age, the option of cross-dressing becomes a force of renewal, one that enables her to enjoy some of the freedom and respect she had enjoyed as a man. This gender fluidity further enabled Orlando (much like Vita Sackville-West) to benefit from what we could characterize as bisexuality: "From the probity of breeches she turned to the seductiveness of petticoats and enjoyed the love of both sexes equally" (161). By writing a character that effectively contains both sexes, Woolf defuses the potentially explosive concept of same-sex desire.

Orlando's memory of her life as a man gives her special insight into gender bias:

> She remembered how, as a young man, she had insisted that women must be obedient, chaste, scented, and exquisitely appareled. "Now I shall have to pay in my own person for those desires," she reflected; "for women are not (judging from my own short experience of the sex) obedient, chaste, scented, and exquisitely appareled by nature. They can only attain these graces, without which they may enjoy none of the delights of life, by the most tedious discipline." (116)

Historical change further highlights gender disparity in the novel. Orlando finds herself quite restrained and belittled by the gender expectations of the Augustan and Romantic eras. She is excluded from the salons of the Enlightenment, where "wit" becomes defined as a masculine pastime. Her greatest challenge comes with the Victorian era, where "the spirit of the nineteenth century was antipathetic to her in the extreme, and thus it took her and broke her, and she was aware of her defeat at its hands as she had never been before" (178). Literally a "child of the Renaissance," Orlando's free spirit is severely challenged by the sexual prudery of the nineteenth century.

Yet, once again, through a symbolic rebirth, Orlando adapts and survives. Her writing style degrades into "the most insipid verse she had ever read in her life" (174) and she is beset with "an extraordinary tingling and vibration all over her" that came to be concentrated onto the second finger of her left hand" (175). For as a woman in the Victorian era, Orlando needed to be married, and the tingling that besets her body signals the necessity of her marriage. In a scene strongly recalling *Jane Eyre*, she breaks her ankle and embraces the "spongy turf" of the moors, declaring, "I am nature's bride" (182). When a dark man on horseback nearly runs her over, the following interchange occurs: "He started. The horse stopped. 'Madam,' the man cried, leaping to the ground, 'you're hurt!' 'I'm dead, Sir!' she replied. A few minutes later, they became engaged" (183). Once again, we are presented with a scene that seemingly signals rebirth, only to have the potential solemnity of the moment ironically undercut.

In the end, *Orlando* comments more on social prejudice than the dramatic potential of human renewal and rebirth. Still, the story requires at least the thematic possibility of rebirth, as though Orlando's adaptation to the variable epochs and cultures can only be expressed through symbolic death and renewal. In the end, Woolf's ironic deflation of the theme leaves us with a very broad and expansive concept of character and personality, one that contains generations of history and, as such, multiple possibilities of sex and gender. By challenging common-sense notions of time, Woolf has also found a way to challenge the conventions and expectations of traditional biography. Her fanciful portrait of her friend Vita Sackville-West thus invites us to imaginatively reconsider subjectivity, gender, sexuality, and time by considering the everyday possibilities of rebirth and renewal.

WORKS CITED

Briggs, Julia. *Virginia Woolf: An Inner Life*. New York: Harcourt, 2005.

DeSalvo, Louise A. "Lighting the Cave: The Relationship between Vita Sackville-West and Virginia Woolf." *Signs* 8.2 (1982): 195–214. JSTOR. Ramsey Library, UNC Asheville 16 January 2008 <http://links.jstor.org/>

Lee, Hermione. *Virginia Woolf*. New York: Knopf, 1996.

Nicholson, Nigel. *Portrait of a Marriage*. New York: Antheneum, 1973.

Sproles, Karyn Z. *Desiring Women: The Partnership of Virginia Woolf and Vita Sackville-West*. Toronto: U of Toronto P, 2006.

Swinton, Tilda. Interview: "Actress Swinton Moves from Art House to Hollywood." *All Things Considered*, National Public Radio. 17 January 2008.

Woolf, Virginia. *The Diary of Virginia Woolf. Vol. 3, 1925–1930*. Eds. Anne
    Olivier Bell with Andrew McNeillie. New York: Harcourt Brace, 1980.
———. *Orlando: A Biography*. Ed. Mark Hussey. Annotated Ed. Orlando, Fla.:
    Harcourt, 2006.

THE SCARLET LETTER
(NATHANIEL HAWTHORNE)

❧ ☙

"Hester's Bewitched Triangle:
Within the Spell of the 'A'"
by Blake Hobby,
the University of North Carolina at Asheville

[...The] SCARLET LETTER, so fantastically embroidered
and illuminated upon her bosom ... had the effect of a spell,
taking her out of ordinary relations with humanity, and
enclosing her in a sphere by herself. (58)

As the eyes of puritanical Boston gaze at Hester Prynne, babe in
arms, embroidered "A" on her breast, Hester bears the scrutiny of
a guilt-ridden society in search of the nearest scapegoat. The scarlet
letter "A," rich in symbolism and key to the allegory of redemption
Hawthorne weaves, casts a seductive spell over the novel that envelops
its characters, governs its actions, and forms an archetypal pattern of
renewal and rebirth. For Hawthorne, the "A" is both an object of and
catalyst for desire: an outward, visible sign that inspires Hester, keeps
her moving, and ultimately leads her to understand her fate. But to
arrive where she does, she must perform a penitent role in a triangular
relationship that rivals the best of passion plays, one filled with tragic
decisions, raging jealousies, and woeful suffering.

   In his work *Deceit, Desire, and the Novel*, René Girard describes
how literary characters often act out of jealousy and envy and how
novelists from Cervantes to Stendhal to Flaubert to Dostoevsky

to Proust have enshrined characters whose desires dictate not only the action of the novel but also their fate. With Girard's theory in mind, the "A" is an object that governs what Hester Prynne, Arthur Dimmesdale, Roger Chillingworth, and the Boston townsfolk desire. Once chosen, the "A" determines the actions of those captivated by it, only relinquishing its hold when the novel's characters seek humility, self-understanding, and renewal.

Atop the infamous scaffold to enact a rite of communal penance, Hester has a panoramic vision in which, as her memory's "picture-gallery" rolls, she contemplates her relationship to the world:

> ... the scaffold of the pillory was a point of view that revealed
> to Hester Prynne the entire track along which she had been
> treading, since her happy infancy. Standing on that miserable
> eminence, she saw again her native village, in Old England, and
> her paternal home; a decayed house of gray stone, obliterated
> shield of arms over the portal, in token of antique gentility. She
> saw her father's face with its bald brow, and reverend white
> beard, that flowed over the old-fashioned Elizabethan ruff; her
> mother's too, with the look of heedful and anxious love which
> it always wore in her remembrance, and which, even since her
> remonstrance in her death, had so often laid the impediment
> of a gentle remonstrance in her daughter's pathway. She saw
> her own face, glowing with girlish beauty, and illuminating all
> the interior of the musky mirror in which she had been wont
> to gaze at it. (63)

Hester remembers the ways of her native village and her own experience of poverty. She ruminates on the memory of her parents who, although long dead, still govern her thoughts, actions, and sensibilities. She focuses on her beauty as a young girl, which seems to have disappeared from the mirror into which she used to gaze.

Filled with remorse for the way she has lived, lamenting the losses she has experienced, the innocence she no longer can claim, and the love she has never known, she confronts Roger Chillingworth for the first time. His sight jars another series of images:

Next rose before her, in memory's picture-gallery, the intricate and narrow thoroughfares, the tall, gray houses, the huge cathedrals, and the public edifices, ancient in date and quaint in architecture, of a Continental city; where a new life had awaited her, still in connection with the misshapen scholar; a new life, but feeding itself on time-worn materials, like a tuft of green moss on a crumbling wall. (63)

Hester remembers how her marriage with Chillingworth was to be a "new life," a fresh start, and yet she feels it was based on "time-worn" materials, something diseased that grows on a dead structure, devoid of the possibility of new life. As she comes back from the "memory portrait," she again views herself and all of the townspeople who level "their stern regards" at her (64). Overwhelmed by the present moment of shame, and clutching baby Pearl, she is overcome, and her vision fades:

> Could it be true? She clutched the child so fiercely to her breast, that it sent forth a cry; she turned her eyes downward at the scarlet letter, and even touched it with her finger, to assure herself that the infant and the shame were real. Yes!—these were her realities,—and all else had vanished! (64)

Hester's first visit to the scaffold offers a moment of illumination, a dream-like vision in which she sees the distance between her reality and her ideal. Hester is unable to hold onto the "memory portrait." Her vision fades; she no longer understands the distance between the present suffering she knows and the ideal that her imagination supplies.

Poised for catharsis in the first scaffold scene, Hester becomes possessed. She negates the experience and becomes the victim of what Girard calls "mimetic desire." She follows "an other": the "A" itself. As Harold Bloom notes, "even as Hester devotes herself to the sufferings of other women, she has yielded to Puritan society's initial judgment upon her. In doing so, she certainly has abandoned much of value in her own personal stance". Hester firmly resolves during this first visit to the scaffold to suffer and to be a martyr. She resigns herself to suffer for Dimmesdale, for Pearl, for Chillingworth, and for the community. In so doing, she dooms herself to a hellish life of illusions, in which she vainly imagines that "she might be the destined prophetess" who would "establish the whole relation between man and woman on a surer ground of mutual happiness" (287). In this opening scene Hester undergoes what Girard calls a "mimetic crisis":

> Desire is the mimetic crisis in itself; it is the acute mimetic rivalry with the other that occurs in all the circumstances we call "private," ranging from eroticism to professional or intellectual ambition. The crisis can be stabilized at different levels according to the individuals concerned, but it always lacks the resources of catharsis and expulsion. (Girard, *Things Hidden* 288)

Like other novel protagonists, Hester suffers paralyzed judgment the moment the mediator (the letter "A") is felt (Girard 4). She loses the ability to judge and discern and comes under the spell of the "A." She becomes, as does Don Quixote, a victim of triangular desire. Don Quixote desires to be like Amadis de Gaul and therefore leads a life of illusions and adventures while imitating the great knight-errant. So Hester also, under the spell of the "A," desires to be the great martyr, bearing the mark of sin for all to see, and in so doing, she becomes a victim of triangular desire: The "A" dictates every movement she makes.

The opening scene of *The Scarlet Letter* dramatically describes the power of the "A," but it also reveals the complicated triangle consisting of Hester, Dimmesdale, and Chillingworth that forms the tension and conflict of the novel. Similarly, Edith Wharton's *The Age of Innocence* opens with a view of the opera in which the triangular relationship among May, Newland, and the Countess Olenska is established. Wharton's novel also focuses on an external mediator: social convention. Like the letter "A," social conventions motivate the novel's characters and lead them to follow mediated desires.

Both scapegoat and martyr, Hester believes she knows how to create an ideal world. She holds fast to an idealized vision of a martyr, of Dimmesdale, and of the perfect mother. She believes she can hold on to any ideal by boldly confronting the world on her own. Hester never sees the distance, however, between the ideal and reality. She sees herself as capable of transforming the world. Hester cuts herself off from society. On the edge of the community and by the sea, she creates a self-contained world. Isolated from the community, she suffers at her own hand and becomes sick and blind. Her conviction and her self-imposed isolation cause her to miss opportunities for happiness. Her desire to be the great martyr places her in a kind of "dream universe" wherein she is bewitched. Following the mediated desire of the "A," she sees illusions as real. She follows a blinding desire that removes her from the normal sphere of human relations. She, like other Romantic novel protagonists, sees herself as the source of the ideal reality. Lukács speaks of the exalted self of the Romantic protagonist:

> . . . the self, cut off from transcendence, recognizes itself as the source of the ideal reality, and, as necessary consequence, as the only material worthy of self-realization. . . . [M]an becomes the author of his own life and at the same time the observer of that life as a created work of art. (118)

Hester, cut off from reality, has the illusion that she is a kind of savior. She longs to leave the life she has known and to create a new world on her own. Thus, Hester creates something new and beautiful out of the scarlet letter "A." She believes that her own artistic skills can transform the "A" into something other than it is. She proudly dons her dull, gray clothes but labors over the "A"—the symbol of her desire to become something she is not.

The great irony of imitating an abstract ideal or desiring another is that they both are forms of self-centeredness. As Girard says, "a self-centered person thinks he is choosing for himself but in fact he shuts himself out as much as others" (298). "Desire according to another" may be termed blindness, a sickness, the tendency to see only ourselves and not others. This form of desire may be seen as a vain projection or abstract ideal to be imitated. It is the *vaniteux*, the imitator, according to Girard, that "cannot draw from his own desires but must borrow from others" (6). The Romantic *vaniteux* wants to be "an original." Ironically, the Romantic *vaniteux* blindly follows "a desire according to another," believing all the while that he or she is autonomous, original, and independent. This desire according to another robs Hester of all originality and affects everything about her. Hester is blinded by an unrealistic vision of Dimmesdale, just as

Emma Bovary (Flaubert's *Madame Bovary*) and Mathilde de la Mole (Stendhal's *The Red and the Black*) are blinded by the idea of romance they read in novels. Emma and Mathilde blindly follow ideals that are unrealistic, ideals not based on the way things are but on mediated desires. Tess, in Hardy's *Tess of the D'Urbervilles*, follows a desire to have a "name" and so suffers greatly. Thus, Hester follows, as do other Romantic protagonists, an abstract ideal that takes hold of her imagination.

Hester sees her relationship with Dimmesdale as an impossible ideal. Hester tells Dimmesdale, "what we did had a consecration of its own," raising her relationship with Dimmesdale to a mediated desire (213). Hester has a "mind of native courage." She follows a blind ideal, separated from the world. She wanders "without rule or guidance, in a moral wilderness" where "shame, despair, and solitude" are her teachers (218). Drawn to the "A," she continues to follow its course even after Dimmesdale's death. The darkness of the "A" becomes a kind of addiction for Hester, who is led by the power of mimetic desire to return to the community:

But there is a fatality, a feeling so irresistible and inevitable that it has the force of doom, which almost invariably compels human beings to linger around and haunt, ghost-like, the spot where some great and marked event has given the color to their lifetime; and still the more irresistibly, the darker the tinge that saddens it. (85-86)

Hester's darkened desire to be a martyr takes her out of normal human relations. She follows a powerful desire. Love, however, is a powerful force and needs a guide. She remains beautiful like nature but equally untamed: "Nature—that wild heathen Nature of the forest, never subjugated by human law, nor illumined by higher truth" (222). Hester remains determined but never illumined by truth or "true love." She longs to take the path of love but lacks moral guideposts along the way.

Following the desire to be a martyr for all, she takes the brunt of the guilt on her own shoulders: "Hester Prynne yet struggled to believe that no fellow-mortal was guilty like herself" (94). Thus the "A" becomes a powerful mediator for Hester that continually burns in her "red-hot with infernal fire" (94). Hester becomes bound like Prometheus by her pride and must suffer in isolation. Only now and then does she experience a vision of freedom, a means of escape from the imprisonment of mimetic desire:

> But sometimes, once in many days, or perchance in many months, she felt an eye—a human eye—upon the ignominious brand, that seemed to give a momentary relief, as if half of her agony were shared. The next instant, back it rushed again, with a still deeper thorn of pain, for, in that brief interval, she had sinned anew. (93)

Although the "A" is not a "real," physical force, it becomes the means of her imprisonment. Hester paces in a confused world of mimetic desire that masks her own identity, leaving her a fallen woman, alone and caged.

Hester is caught in a desire-filled triangle with Dimmesdale and Chillingworth. There, she falls under the spell of the "A." Hardy's protagonist Tess is also torn between men: Alec, a kind of Dionysian force; and Angel, an Apollonian figure. Hester is pulled between Chillingworth's monomaniacal quest for revenge and the guilt he inflicts upon her and Dimmesdale's buried grief and self-inflicted torture, which also move her to feel guilt and pity. As she tries to negotiate both, her identity is fused with the "A." She allows both men and society to force the image of the "A" upon her. Similarly, Wharton's Countess Ellen Olenska is caught between the count and Newland, Tess is torn between Alec and Angel, Flaubert's Emma Bovary runs back and forth between Charles and Rudolphe, and Stendhal's Mme. de Rênal vacillates between the passion of Julien and fidelity to her husband, M. de Rênal.

The "fallen woman," exemplified by Hester Prynne, Emma Bovary, and Tess Durbeyfield, is not permitted personhood. Although she becomes a victim of mimetic desire by her own choosing, the world presents an unrealistic vision of becoming, an unrealistic vision of happiness, desire, and passion that borders on the unattainable. The "A" pulls her into a realm where she believes she is an angel and thinks she has a vision beyond everyone else's; she has a vain illusion that she is "the destined prophetess," "the angel and apostle of the coming of a new revelation" (287).

As the infernal mimetic triangle is played out between Hester, Dimmesdale, and Chillingworth, a stern New England community, filled with "steeple-crowned hats" and clothed "in sad-colored garments," projects its own "Utopia of human virtue and happiness" (51) and thus forms a breeding ground for mimetic desire. Hester becomes an object of mimetic desire for the community, a scapegoat for its own sinfulness. The puritanical community believes it is possible to label sin externally. This same social structure is a cage that, like the ornamented opera box of the Wellands in Wharton's *The Age of Innocence*, holds all together under the name of social convention but is actually a prison. While the community appears to be interested in the common good, it is really only interested in self-gain and in keeping the "evil one" at a distance. This New England society fails to see that sin is also a redemptive force and that redemption can only occur when sin is recognized as a universal sickness. The community thus pulls up the wheat with the weeds, rejecting sinners such as Hester publicly and denying its own diseased, sinful state.

Lurking along the desolate seashore while gathering herbs and tormenting Dimmesdale with stories of weeds growing from a sinful heart, Roger Chillingworth plays to Dimmesdale's weaknesses (Dimmesdale's mediated desires) and then relishes the pain and agony that Dimmesdale endures. Dimmesdale allows Chillingworth to become a destructive force. The narrative voice states:

> Had a man seen old Roger Chillingworth, at the moment of his ecstasy, he would have had no need to ask how Satan comports himself, when a precious human soul is lost to heaven, and won into his kingdom. (151)

Chillingworth seeks revenge through the "A." He becomes obsessed with the punishment of the "A" and does a devilish dance when he realizes the powerful effect it has had on Dimmesdale. The scarlet letter "A" is an intricately woven fabric of desires.

Dimmesdale also becomes a victim of the "A's" mediated desire: "[A]bove all things else, he loathed his miserable self" (158). He becomes a victim of his own desire to be miserable. He states to Hester in the forest:

> Hester, hast thou found peace? Whatever of good capacity there originally was in me, all of God's gifts that were the choicest have become the ministers of spiritual torment. Hester, I am most miserable! (208–209)

Dimmesdale is a miserable man who torments himself. He is what Girard would term a "hero of internal mediation" who, "far from boasting of his efforts to imitate, carefully hides them" (10). Dimmesdale continually desires to be free of the unspeakable sin, yet the "A" constantly rekindles his desire. He lives a life based on an idealistic vision of holiness that he imitates outwardly while secretly disclosing his internal desires. He seeks love and passion in Hester and then spends most of the novel desiring to be wretched—to be the sinner.

Ultimately, Dimmesdale shuns the power of the mediator. He, like other literary characters led by mimetic desire such as Don Quixote, Julien Sorel, and Raskolnikov, rejects his former ways and experiences a "clarity of vision" (Girard 291). Don Quixote rejects his vision of knight-errantry, Julien Sorel rejects his ideas of revolt, Raskolnikov rejects his superhumanity, and Dimmesdale rejects his masochistic desires. Each of the protagonists ultimately releases or denies his "fantasy inspired by pride" (Girard 293). As Dimmesdale returns to town after his interview with Hester, he changes—he experiences an internal revolution, "a total change of dynasty and moral code" (236), in which he now is enticed at every step to do something strange—some "wild, wicked thing or other" (237). He emerges from the forest as a new man, much like the blind man in Chapter IX of the Gospel of John and in the ninth chapter of Acts, when Paul is struck by a lightning bolt and thrown from his horse, blinded. These dramatic blind epiphanies represent, as with the blindness Oedipus imposes upon himself, "seeing" for the first time. Although Dimmesdale passes into the abyss, Chillingworth withers from revenge, and Hester wanders through a spiritual wilderness, hope eventually appears: "on a field, sable, the letter A, gules," a sign of rebirth and renewal (278).

Works Cited

Girard, René. *Deceit, Desire, and the Novel: Self and Other in Literary Structure.* Stanford: Stanford UP, 1987.

———. *Things Hidden Since the Foundation of the World.* Trans. by Stephan Bann. Baltimore: Johns Hopkins UP, 1965.

Hawthorne, Nathaniel. *The Scarlet Letter.* New York: Modern Library–McGraw-Hill, 1984.

Lukács, Georg. *The Theory of the Novel.* Trans. by Anna Bostock. Cambridge: MIT, 1971.

A TALE OF TWO CITIES
(CHARLES DICKENS)

~~~~~~~~

"'Recalled to Life': Sacrifice and Renewal in *A Tale of Two Cities*"
by Arthur Rankin,
Louisiana State University, Alexandria

In his study of narrative structure and reading practices, Peter Rabi-nowitz points out that readers pay attention to openings and clos-ings as areas that allow for rich interpretive moments: "Placement in such a position does more than ensure that certain details will remain more firmly in our memories. . . . [O]ur attention during the act of reading will, in part, be concentrated on what we have found in these positions" (59). Rabinowitz's comments on reading practices are especially pertinent when thinking of Dickens's novels. Consider the well-known openings of such novels as *David Copperfield*, *Bleak House*, *Great Expectations*, or even *A Christmas Carol*. In all of these novels, Dickens gives his readers profound images that color how they will interpret the unfolding of the novel. We see Pip turned upside down by Magwitch, who magically transforms Pip's life. The novel then follows Pip's painful transformation from a sympathetic urchin to a dreadful snob to a true gentleman. Like *Great Expecta-tions*, the famous openings of the other novels—the overwhelming mud of *Bleak House*, David Copperfield's wondering who shall be the hero of his tale, or Jacob Marley's connection to a doornail—all set in place the means that readers need to direct their understanding of the novel's message.

A Tale of Two Cities also fits this model. Along with the famous opening comparison between England and France on the brink of the revolution, most readers can recall Sydney Carton's well-known last words at the novel's close. The sacrifice that Carton makes at the novel's end demonstrates that renewal is possible even amid the hopelessness represented by the relationship between England and France at the novel's opening. Sacrifice and renewal color the novel and give it, as Hilary Schor argues, "prophetic vision" (76). For instance, even though Carton faces the guillotine, he sees the possibility of his namesake leading a better life: "I see that child who lay upon her bosom and who bore my name, a man winning his way up in that path of life which once was mine" (361). Carton's sacrifice is significant; without it, the novel fails. As Robert Alter has pointed out, Dickens concerns himself with "mankind's potential for moral regeneration" (96). The sense of humankind's moral potential based in our capacity to act for the benefit of others underscores the idea of renewal in the novel. This sense of renewal, though, is tied to sacrifice.

Consider two recent studies of the novel. First, Jennifer Ruth's "The Self-Sacrificing Professional: Charles Dickens's 'Hunted Down' and *A Tale of Two Cities*" focuses on the urban professional intervening in the domestic sphere. She argues that these professionals embody "the rationality of the father and the disinterested sympathy of the mother" (287). In what manner does Sydney Carton exhibit these characteristics? We see, for instance, that he has a keen and observing eye (rationality) and can take in his environment when others are at a loss to do so (disinterested sympathy). Indeed, he is the one to observe Lucie as she faints in the courtroom during Darnay's trial:

> Yet, this Mr. Carton took in more of the details of the scene than he appeared to take in; for now, when Miss Manette's head dropped upon her father's breast, he was the first to see it, and to say audibly: "Officer! look to that young lady. Help the gentleman to take her out. Don't you see she will fall!' (73)

This scene reveals Carton's concern for others—specifically Lucie—a concern that will ultimately arise in his later actions. Furthermore, Ruth reveals the sympathetic essence of Carton's character and its relationship to the sense of hope and renewal that the novel expresses. She states that Carton "purposely sacrifices himself for others" (296). Here, the word that should strike us is "purposely," because Carton's deliberate sacrifice allows Darnay to be recalled to life at the end of the novel as his father-in-law, Dr. Manette, is at the beginning of the novel. Additionally, Carton's sacrifice also redeems his blighted life.

Second, consider Simon Petch's argument that Carton's sacrifice "fulfils absolutely the professional ideology of service" (para. 16). If Petch is right, then Carton's sacrifice exists as a cipher similar to the French aristocracy that can only serve its own desires, without concern for the lives of others. That is to say, if Carton is merely fulfilling a professional obligation, then his sacrifice is not freely given, and renewal cannot occur. Yet Dickens takes great pain in directing his readers' attention to Carton's final words: "It is a far, far better thing that I do, than I have ever done; it is a far, far better rest that I go to than I have ever known" (361). Carton realizes that his sacrifice has sanctified his life even to the point that people witnessing his execution see him as "sublime and prophetic" (360).

The problematic nature of Sydney Carton has occupied critics for some time. In his study of the novel John Kucich points out that Carton appeals to readers because he is not bound by the same code that exists for his professional colleagues such as Lorry and Stryker: "Carton appeals to us through his freedom from convention and from constraint" (61). While Carton appears to be liberated from the social obligations that direct the lives of the other characters, we see in his conversation with Lucie that he sees his life as blighted by its outward forms, imprisoned by the "constraints" that give value to Lucie's life:

> 'Be comforted!' he said, 'I am not worth such feeling, Miss Manette. An hour or two hence, and the low companions and low habits that I scorn but yield to, will render me less worth such tears as those, than any wretch who creeps along the streets. (146)

Garrett Stewart sees Carton's role as a "suffering stand-in for the readers as well as for his private double and the Darnay circle" (118). Stewart further argues that Carton's sacrifice functions as an apocalyptic representation about the "Day of Judgment" (109). What the work of these critics reveals is an ongoing need to uncover Carton's importance to the novel.

When we see Carton as a stand-in for the "readers," as Stewart does, then we can understand Dickens's purpose—didactic though it may be. Carton is like us: imperfect, beaten down by life, cynical, but ultimately hopeful that life does have a transcendent meaning. Herein lies his power as a sacrificial figure. Carton can rise above his cynicism, and with him, so can the readers. At the end of Chapter 13 we can discern something of the renewed man that Carton will become by the end of the novel. He tells Lucie:

> 'O Miss Manette, when the little picture of a happy father's face looks up in yours, when you see your own bright beauty springing up anew at your feet, think now and then that there is a man who would give his life, to keep a life you love beside you!' (147)

Dickens takes great care here to reinforce the renewal that Carton's sacrifice will bring. While Carton is willing to trade his life to keep Lucie's home safe, he also exists here as a guardian spirit over the child she had with Darnay. His sacrifice makes possible the renewal that is shown in the generations represented by Lucie's children. We see, then, as Jennifer Sims argues, that "Sydney Carton embodies stability" (219).

Carton's role as a stabilizing force takes on significance when we examine several earlier scenes in the novel. Images of darkness pervade these early scenes. Consider Jarvis Lorry's coach ride. Jarvis Lorry and his "three fellow-inscrutables" (17) are shrouded against the cold night and trudging through a vast expanse of mud striving to reach the summit of Shooter's Hill. There is little trust between the passengers because anyone could be in "the Captain's pay" (11), as Dickens informs the readers. The threat of being robbed and an aura of mistrust tinge the scene with a sense of impending doom. Part of this sense of doom occurs because, as the opening of the novel reveals, "there was scarcely an amount of order and protection to justify much national boasting" (8). Darkness, disorder, and danger prevail in the world of the novel—soon to be outdone by the rampaging violence of the revolution in France. The sacrifice of a good person like Sydney Carton is necessary to illuminate such a dark world. Indeed, Philip Allingham argues: "the personal suffering and sacrifice of a good person contributes to the improvement of condition (as well as an increase in moral perception) for the survivors" (4).

This "moral perception" Allingham points out is clearly connected to Lucie. When we first meet her, however, she, too, is surrounded by an all-encompassing gloom. Since the name Lucie relates to light, readers can observe that her presence, like Carton's sacrifice, may bring light to overcome the overwhelming dreariness of the novel's early chapters. However, funeral black surrounds her when she first enters the novel:

> It was a large, dark room, furnished in a funeral manner with black horsehair, and loaded with heavy dark tables. These had been oiled and oiled, until the two tall candles on the table in the middle of the room were gloomily reflected on every leaf; as if *they* were buried, in deep graves of black mahogany. (23)

The two candles struggle to emit any light, emphasizing the dead state of the world that underscores the opening chapters. Like her father, who has been buried in a dark prison, Lucie inhabits a grave-like environment. The difference, though, is that Lucie's light (represented by her golden hair) will inspire Carton to surrender his life for a greater good.

The image of darkness is intensified by Dr. Manette's presence. He has been buried so long in prison that the light rushing in when Lucie and Jarvis enter blinds him momentarily. In fact, he never fully recovers his sanity. Lucie's first sight of her corpse-like, "parchment-yellow" (42) father and her reaction to him highlight her goodness and correlate to her effect on Sydney Carton, who is emotionally corpse-like: "He recoiled, but she laid her hand upon his arm. A strange thrill struck him when she did so, and visibly passed over his frame" (45). Still, Lucie comforts her father as she does her child later in the novel when she awaits news of Charles's French trial: "She held him closer around the neck, and rocked him on her breast like a child" (47). These episodes reveal Lucie's power to recall the dead to life and take on a mythic quality as similar actions inspire Carton.

In the darkness that dominates the opening of the novel, then, Lucie functions as the life-giving ray of golden light that, Isis-like, gives rebirth. Dickens intensifies the mythological tone of the novel and its connection to both Lucie and Carton in the Gorgon's Head chapter. Here we encounter fully the vileness of Monsieur the Marquis, whose death brings such tumult into Lucie's life and leads finally to Carton sacrificing himself for her and her family. The irony of the marquis's death is that he is the most corpse-like person we meet, and his face returns to its true gorgon-like quality in death. Moreover, the darkness in the chapter that initially serves to cover the murder of Monsieur the Marquis is truly a reflection of the despair that the French aristocracy has caused by its excessive living. The rage and vengeance kindled in Madame Defarge is an extension of the oppression generated by the aristocracy. As we find out after Darnay's second trial in France, Monsieur's monstrous actions have brought about death and anguish for Madame Defarge's family.

In her quest to eradicate the Evrémonde family, Madame Defarge, like Medusa, seeks to victimize Charles and Lucie's daughter. The threatening violence in her soul is a manifestation of the intense gloom and darkness that underscore the novel. Indeed, Madame Defarge seems most like the Fates in her incessant knitting that appears to spin out and end the lives of her intended victims. In her study of the novel, Linda Lewis points out, "The unforgettable Madame Defarge, witch of Sainte Antoine, angel of Revolution, goddess of retribution, and historian who preserves a text of the revolution, is the principal allegorical figure in the novel" (31). The terms Lewis employs to describe Thérèse Defarge reveal her status as a mythological trope in the novel and place her in opposition to Sydney Carton. While Madame Defarge exists as a force of dark destruction in the novel, Carton, especially after recognizing her spy, becomes the chief agent of light and redemptive rebirth in the story.

This connection between the two characters signifies the heart of the novel because Carton has suffered as has Madame Defarge, yet his suffering ultimately leads him to give himself as the chief sacrifice of a noble cause. Unlike Madame Defarge, who experiences her own form of decapitation, Carton transcends his origins. Lucie, the main character in the novel with whom they share a relationship, enlightens Carton while only enraging Thérèse Defarge. We observe the adamantine soul of Madame Defarge create as profound a chaos as the French aristocracy has. In fact, she is most like Monsieur the Marquis because she has her servants obeying her every command and fulfilling her every wish, just as he does. Of course, his wishes relate to decadent, cruel, and selfish desires, but the two characters have something in common: Both inhabit and increase the domain of darkness that haunts the novel.

As the novel progresses, we perceive that one form of brutal government simply supersedes another, making it difficult to tell them apart. However, in the context of the violent and shadowy second half of the story, light does shine through. While the novel opens in a world shrouded in gloom, it closes in a world where hope and true nobility struggle against the reigning Terror. Sydney Carton personifies the struggle against the forces of nihilism that threaten Lucie, Charles, and their family. Consider the titles of the chapters where we see Carton in ascendance: "The Substance of Shadow," "Dusk," and "Darkness." Here Dickens develops the earlier theme of a small light in the darkness that we witness when Lucie first appears in the text. The change, conversely, is that now Carton is the ray of light. The dissipation of his youth now comes as he wins the poker hand of life against the mob. His winnings release the Darnay family and signal the triumphant rebirth of hope that underscores the novel's close.

In Carton's ramblings through the Paris night, we glimpse a reworking of his earlier nocturnal movements. Just as we find that he was often at work rather than seeking gratification, in these closing chapters we observe his attempt to liberate Darnay and help Lucie's family escape the Terror. As the three Jacques were, Carton becomes the perfect spy capable of blending into the nocturnal world of Sainte Antoine. While on these rambles, he discovers Madame Defarge's plot to destroy Lucie and her daughter:

> 'They are in great danger. They are in danger of denunciation by Madame Defarge. I know it from her own lips. I have overheard words of that woman's, to-night, which have presented their danger to me in strong colours. I have lost no time, and since then, I have seen the spy. He confirms me. He knows that a wood-sawyer, living by the prison-wall, is under the control of

the Defarges, and has been rehearsed by Madame Defarge as to his having seen Her'—he never mentioned Lucie's name—'making signs and signals to prisoners. It is easy to foresee that the pretense will be the common one, a prison plot, and that it will involve her life—and perhaps her child's—and perhaps her father's—for both have been seen with her at that place. Don't look so horrified. You will save them all' (329–330)

The above passage is lengthy, it is necessary to show it in its entirety, because it represents the moment in the text when Sydney Carton experiences his transcendent rebirth from dissipated wastrel to heroic human being. His impassioned words reflect this change. His life training in law comes to the fore as he gives witness in his own personal trial. Although he asserts that Jarvis Lorry will save the Darnay clan, it will be Carton's substitution of his life for Darnay's that allows the other characters to escape Paris and return to life in London.

Readers experience in the character of Sydney Carton a profound sense of renewal, a sense that hope can be rekindled with a heroic sacrifice, that the world can be made better. The small band of travelers escaping the wrath of the Terror mimics the opening of the novel when Jarvis Lorry travels by coach to take Lucie to Paris. While darkness shrouds the first journey, optimism infuses the second. In his well-known biography of Charles Dickens, Edgar Johnson writes, "*A Tale of Two Cities* has been hailed as the best of Dickens's books and damned as the worst" (979). Johnson goes on to state that the novel "is neither" (979). Puns on the opening aside, the novel confirms for its readers that while sacrifice is sometimes necessary, renewal is always possible, as we see in Carton's last prophetic vision: "I see a beautiful city and a brilliant people rising from this abyss, and, in their struggles to be truly free, in their triumphs and defeats, through long years to come, I see the evil of this time and of the previous time of which this is the natural birth, gradually making expiation for itself and wearing out" (360).

Ultimately, then, Carton's vision and his deep sense of peacefulness that so impresses the crowd watching the executions become the dominant images impressed upon the reader. The conclusion of the novel guides the reader toward an understanding of the importance of sacrifice. Additionally, the movement of the novel's action from darkness and misery to Carton's triumphant nobility calls readers' attention to his sacrifice for his friends, which shines like a golden light, reflecting hopefulness amid despair and optimism overcoming cynicism.

WORKS CITED

Allingham, Philip V. "*A Tale of Two Cities*' (1859): A Model of the Integration of History." *The Victorian Web* 13 October 2007. <http:www.victorianweb. org>

Alter, Robert. "The Demons of History in Dickens's *Tale*." *Modern Critical Views: Charles Dickens*. Ed. Harold Bloom. New York: Chelsea House, 1987. 93–102.

Dickens, Charles. *A Tale of Two Cities*. Ed. Andrew Sanders. Oxford: Oxford UP, 1988.

Johnson, Edgar. *Charles Dickens: His Tragedy and Triumph*. New York: Simon and Schuster, 1952.

Kucich, John. "The Purity of Violence: *A Tale of Two Cities*." *Modern Critical Interpretations: Charles Dickens's* A Tale of Two Cities. Ed. Harold Bloom. New York: Chelsea House, 1987. 57–72.

Lewis, Linda M. "Madame Defarge as Political Icon in Dickens's *A Tale of Two Cities*." *Dickens Study Annual* 36 (2006): 31–49.

Petch, Simon. "The Business of the Barrister in *A Tale of Two Cities*." *Criticism* 44.1 (2002): 27–42.

Rabinowitz, Peter J. *Before Reading: Narrative Conventions and the Politics of Interpretation*. Ithaca: Cornell UP, 1987.

Ruth, Jennifer. "The Self-Sacrificing Professional: Charles Dickens's 'Hunted Down' and *A Tale of Two Cities*." *Dickens Studies Annual* 34 (2004): 283–299.

Schor, Hilary. "Novels of the 1850s: *Hard Times, Little Dorrit*, and *A Tale Of Two Cities*." Ed. John O. Jordan. *The Cambridge Companion to Charles Dickens*." Cambridge: Cambridge UP, 2001. 64–77.

Sims, Jennifer. "Dickens's *A Tale of Two Cities*." *The Explicator* 63.4 (2005): 219–222.

Stewart, Garrett. "Death by Water in *A Tale of Two Cities*." *Modern Critical Interpretations: Charles Dickens's* A Tale of Two Cities. Ed. Harold Bloom. New York: Chelsea House, 1987. 107–120.

THE TEMPEST
(WILLIAM SHAKESPEARE)

᠅

From *Shakespeare's Mystery Play:*
A Study of "The Tempest"
by Colin Still (1921)

INTRODUCTION

Colin Still, in this series of excerpts from his book-length study of *The Tempest*, "contends[s] that the Play deals primarily with certain permanent realities of spiritual experience; . . . and that it may be regarded as an account of Initiation . . . [:] the renouncing of 'the world, the flesh, and the devil' in the upward struggle 'out of darkness into light.'" Thus, for Still, the play is an allegory for spiritual rebirth, "a reversal of the Fall of Man." Throughout his analysis, Still expounds upon the allegorical meaning and significance of Shakespeare's plot, characters, and images, arguing that they contain allusions to both Christian and pagan initiation rites and rituals of renewal and rebirth.

᠅

[I] contend that there are abundant grounds for the opinion that *The Tempest* is not a pure fantasy, but a deliberate allegory—not a work in which the Poet gives free rein to the caprice of imagination, but a

Still, Colin. *Shakespeare's Mystery Play: A Study of* "The Tempest." London: Cecil Palmer, 1921.

work in which a clear and dominant idea transcends the nominal story
and determines the action, the dialogue, and the characterisation.
[. . .]

I contend that the Play deals primarily with certain permanent realities of spiritual experience; that it expresses the universal
psychology of upward endeavour in the same allegorical terms as are
employed in all authentic myth and ritual; and that it may be regarded
as an account of Initiation in so far as Initiation (whether ceremonial
or empirical) is understood to signify the renouncing of "the world,
the flesh, and the devil" in the upward struggle "out of darkness into
light." Furthermore, I maintain that actually the Poet has reproduced
with extraordinary fidelity both the substance and the form of the
Christian and of the non-Christian traditions; that if this fact be not
due to deliberate design, it must be due to some necessity inherent
in the essential theme of the Play; and that this same fact not only
supports my interpretation of the Play, but also renders any other
interpretation inadequate or inadmissible.
[. . .]

In the New Testament account of the Baptism of Christ we read
how, coming up out of the water, He went straightway up into the
Wilderness, where He remained fasting for forty days; and, being
hungry and thirsty, He was tempted by the Devil, whom He resisted;
whereupon angels came and ministered unto Him.

This myth, for such we may call it with no irreverence, is by no
means peculiar to the life-story of Christ. It is related in some form of
all the great religious teachers. It is to be understood, I think, not in
the literal sense, but as an allegory in objective or environmental terms
of a purely subjective experience. It is, in fact, an account of the Lesser
Initiation; and, indeed, it has manifestly all the essential features of an
Ascent through WATER and MIST to AIR.
[. . .]

What does the Lesser Initiation, in its psychological aspect,
comprise? It comprises the renunciation of worldly and passional
things and the achievement of that state of divine inspiration which
is the prototype of the mythical Lost Estate of Man. Rising from
the plane of EARTH, through and beyond the plane of WATER, the
consciousness reaches the plane of MIST. That is to say, the aspirant
renounces material and passional things and concerns himself with

intellectual speculation. But MIST is the plane of error and illusion. Being partly emotional and partly rational, it is the plane of imperfect thinking; for here the influences which rise from the passional plane (as Mist rises from Water) darken and obscure the reason, causing the aspirant to follow many false paths in his search for Truth. After a long period ("forty days") of these fruitless wanderings, the seeker grows weary. The passional inhibition and the sense of isolation from the ordinary life of men are now realised in all their bitterness, while the compensating rewards are yet withheld. The seeker is desolate and disappointed: his long abstinence from normal worldly satisfactions seems to have been endured in vain. He hungers for the bread of fellowship and he thirsts for passional indulgence.[1] He is assailed by Desire, tempting him to abandon his quest. This is the testing time for the seeker after Truth. He must hold fast to his purpose. Desire, if it be resolutely resisted, will depart from him, leaving him to pursue his way in peace.[2] When at last this triumph over Desire has been accomplished and all the darkening clouds of prejudice, sentiment, custom, and the like have been surmounted, the consciousness reaches the next plane. It passes out of MIST into the pure dry AIR—out of error and doubt and temptation into serene and dispassionate reason. The aspirant now learns in some measure the Truth he seeks. This partial apprehension in the AIR of reason of the Truth whose complete apprehension is possible only in the AETHER of intuition is [. . .] represented in tradition as a hearing by the ear of a distinctly speaking Voice that bears witness of the mystery which is not yet seen by the eye.

All this is undoubtedly implied in the myth of Christ's Sojourn and Temptation in the Wilderness.

[. . .]

In like manner, Aeneas crossed the River Styx, passed through the purgatorial region, and finally came to a pleasant place (Elysium) where he received a spoken discourse from his father Anchises— precisely as the Children of Israel crossed the Red Sea, wandered in the Wilderness, and came at last to the Promised Land. Of the same kind is the pilgrimage of Dante up the Mount of Purgatory to Eden, and that of Christian through the Valley of Humiliation to the Land of Beulah.

All these stories employ the same allegorical medium to express the same subjective experience—namely, the rising of the consciousness above sensuous or passional things, the long wanderings in the lonely wilderness of speculation in quest of Truth, and the coming at last to that serenity of pure reason in which the voice of inspiration is heard. And, since the psychological state thus finally attained is the prototype of the mythical Lower Paradise, or Eden, the Gospel myth—like these other stories it resembles—is an account of self-redemption conceived as the recovery of the Lost Estate of Man. It deals with a reversal of the process implied in the myth of the Fall.

[. . .]

To this traditional allegory, which we find in both mythology and ritual, the story of the Court Party thus far conforms unfailingly. For, after a symbolical immersion in the sea (WATER), the King and his company pass into a desolate place that is also a place of expiation—in short, a purgatorial wilderness (MIST). Here they wander in search of "the lost son," and, after prolonged and fruitless seeking, they realise that they are wandering in a maze of straight and crooked paths:

> GON. I can go no further, Sir,
> My old bones ache: here's a maze trod, indeed,
> Through forth-rights and meanders!
>   (Act III., Scene 3.)

Every genuine philosopher knows from his own experience what follows upon this realisation. Confused in the maze of speculation, discouraged by failure, his spirit dulled and depressed by weariness, the seeker passes through doubt to a sense of the hopelessness of his quest for the "lost Word" of Truth. So in the Play:

> GON. Here's a maze trod, indeed,
> Through forth-rights and meanders! By your patience,
> I needs must rest me.
>   ALON. Old lord, I cannot blame thee,
> Who am myself attached with weariness
> To the dulling of my spirits. Sit down and rest.
> Even here I will put off my hope, and keep it

No longer for my flatterer: he is drowned
Whom thus we stray to find.... (*Ibid.*)

The constancy of the seeker after Truth is now severely tested.
His unavailing search is mocked by his own passional nature, by the
WATER whence he has risen. As Alonso says of the Court Party:

The sea mocks
Our frustrate search on land.... (*Ibid.*)

Relaxing his efforts in weariness and failure, the seeker becomes
a prey to desire. He is haunted by doubts and fears and unclean
thoughts, which crowd upon him like evil creatures in the darkness.
He is troubled by memories of sensuous delights, memories that
make a sweet appeal and beckon him back to forbidden things. He
is tempted to abandon his purpose and return to the commoner and
easier concerns of mankind. And upon the issue of this temptation
depends the issue of his high endeavour.

As this experience is part of the discipline imposed upon the
philosopher in the course of empirical initiation, so likewise it was
represented as befalling him who sought for Truth by the way of
formal or ritual initiation into the pagan Mysteries. I contend that
it was ceremonially depicted by the candidate's encounter with
"monstrous apparitions," and that in the Play it is figured by the
Court Party's encounter with the "strange shapes."
[...]

First let it be observed that the temptation of the aspirant may
be described in at least three different ways. We may say—(i) that
he is assailed by desire, or (ii) that he becomes obsessed by unclean
thoughts, or (iii) that he hears the sweet compelling summons to
sensuous indulgence. There is, of course, little essential difference
between these three conceptions, for they all refer to the same phase
of psychological experience. Nevertheless, in the process of allegorical
elaboration the three produce somewhat divergent results. Temptation myths fall, in fact, into three main classes, typical of which
are—(i) the struggle with the Dragon, (ii) the encounter with horrid
Monsters, and (iii) the hearing of the Sirens' Song.
[...]

[In] *The Tempest*, we find therein a remarkable synthesis of the several conceptions with which I have been dealing. For the Court Party, being despondent after prolonged and fruitless search for "the lost son," is beset by certain strange creatures which resemble those of ancient myth and ritual in that they are "of monstrous shape"; and, moreover, these creatures act the part of the Tempter. Making their appearance when the King and his company are wearied by their wanderings in the desolate isle, the "strange shapes" present a banquet and "invite the King, etc., to eat." So, in the symbolical myth of the Gospels, Christ wandered in the Wilderness; and, being hungry, He was accosted by the Tempter, who sought to turn Him from His purpose by *inviting him to eat*:

> If thou be the Son of God, command these stones that they be made bread.

To which Christ made the obvious reply of a steadfast seeker after that divine inspiration which is the word of God:

> Man shall not live by bread alone, but by every word that proceedeth out of the mouth of God.

In the Poet's version of this temptation, Ariel intervenes. He causes the banquet to disappear when the Court Party approaches it. There is, of course, a seeming inconsistency in the suggestion that the King and his company, who would have eaten of the banquet had they not been deprived of it by Ariel, have now successfully withstood (as every initiate must) the symbolical temptation to eat. This difficulty is dispelled by a correct appreciation of the part of Ariel, [. . . who] may be said to play at this point the restraining part of Conscience, which upholds the initiate against temptation.
[. . .]

In the Wilderness the aspirant not only hungers; he also thirsts. After long abstinence, he craves for those sensuous satisfactions of which the pursuit of his purpose has deprived him. In symbolical terms, he "thirsts" for the sensuous WATER. It is this experience that is represented in the pagan mythology by the hearing of the music of the Sirens; and in the Gospel myth it is implied in the statement that the Tempter offered Christ all the glories of kingship.[3] The story of the Court Party corresponds to the former of these two versions of the same essential idea, although the latter is also suggested by the plotting of Sebastian and Antonio. Like the mythical Sirens, the Strange Shapes in the Play make "gentle acts of salutation" to the accompaniment of "marvellous sweet music." They are monstrous and unnatural in form; yet they seem at the first encounter to be pleasing and attractive in their manners, a curious combination of qualities peculiar to the mythical Sirens:

> Though they are of monstrous shape, yet note
> Their manners are more gentle-kind than of
> Our human generation you shall find
> Many, nay, almost any. (*Ibid.*)

Their seductive appeal being frustrated by the intervention of Conscience (Ariel), these Strange Shapes do not become fierce and violent, as the mythical Dragon (Desire) is often and quite properly said to do: they only "dance with mocks and mows," wherein they aptly resemble siren memories which one strives to ignore.
[. . .]
Alonso's resumption of the search for "the lost Son," following the bitter accusing speech of Ariel, is the closing feature of the third Scene of the third Act; and the Court Party does not reappear for some time, although we are given to understand that in the interval these men, stung by the lash of Conscience, suffer remorse and sorrow in full measure. In the final Scene (V. i) we witness the completion of their Lesser Initiation; for we see them pass from this purgatorial subjective state to the happy state of purity and self-mastery which is the Lower Paradise or Elysium.

The Scene opens with Ariel reporting to Prospero on the state of mind of the King and his friends. Being sent to fetch them, Ariel presently returns with the Court Party.
[. . .]
[. . . The] Court Party is now passing from the subjective Purgatory to the subjective Elysium—that the consciousness is now rising from the MIST of error and illusion to the AIR of clear reason:

> And as the morning steals upon the night,
> Melting the darkness, so their rising senses

>   Begin to chase the ignorant fumes that mantle
>   Their clearer reason.
>   (Act V., Scene 1.)

The psychological change here referred to is explicitly an upward movement of the consciousness out of the "fumes" of error into the clear and unclouded reason.[4] In terms of the symbolism, it is an ascent out of MIST into AIR; in terms of the allegorical tradition, it is an ascent out of Purgatory into Elysium. It is directly likened by the Poet to a change from a state of darkness to a state of light. . . .

[. . .]

The first main object of the Lesser Initiation has now been achieved. The Court Party has undergone that subjective change which is allegorised in ancient myth and ritual as a passage through the Wilderness or Purgatory to Eden or Elysium. In their own psychological experience these men have brought back the Golden Age of happy innocence—to which, indeed, we find Gonzalo expressly aspiring at an earlier stage in the Play:

>   Had I plantation of this isle, my lord, . . .
>   I would with such perfection govern, sir,
>   To excel the golden age.
>   (Act II., Scene 1.)

Like Dante, at the close of the *Purgatorio*, they have recovered from the consequences of the Fall, and have regained the Lost Estate of Man.

[. . .]

Now, when the initiate has come at last to Elysium, he finds that for which he seeks during his "wanderings." And indeed, it is only when the King and his company have risen out of the darkness of error (Purgatory) into clear and unclouded reason (Elysium) that the ostensible purpose of their wanderings is fulfilled by the finding of "the lost son" Ferdinand, who is discovered when Prospero throws open the entrance of the cell.

But my whole argument throughout this section has been to the effect that what is really implied in the wanderings of the Court Party, as in the ritual wanderings of the pagan aspirant, is the quest for Truth. How, then, is Truth found in Elysium?

[. . .]

Mythologically, as in Dante's *Divina Commedia*, the Greater Initiation consists in an ascent from Elysium (AIR) to the Celestial Paradise (AETHER), where a glimpse of divine things is obtained—precisely as in psychological experience Truth is fully revealed only when the seeker, "closing his eyes" to the external world, has mounted from the plane of reason (AIR) to the plane of intuitional perception (AETHER).

I contend that the story of Ferdinand in the Play is an account of this Greater or "Ocular" Initiation; and that, although it is told concurrently, it continues and completes the allegory presented in the story of the Court Party.

When we first see Ferdinand, his passion and the wild waters have already been simultaneously allayed by the sweet music of Ariel:

> Sitting on a bank,
> Weeping again the king my father's wreck,
> This music crept by me upon the waters,
> Allaying both their fury, and my passion,
> With its sweet air.
> (Act I., Scene 2.)

In other words, Ferdinand has already passed through emotional tumult to that tranquillity which is the subjective Elysium. That he has passed through "Hell" is implied in the special and seemingly gratuitous reference contained in Ariel's initial report to Prospero:

> The king's son, Ferdinand,
> With hair up-staring (then like reeds, not hair),
> Was the first man that leapt; cried, "Hell is empty,
> And all the devils are here." (*Ibid.*)

But this Hell-like scene has been wholly transformed when Ferdinand first appears. He is now following after Ariel, who is singing a song that we may fairly take as describing the pleasant place to which Ferdinand is led when the wild waves of his passion have been stilled:

> Come unto these yellow sands,
>   And then take hands;

> Court'sied when you have, and kissed
>   The wild waves whist:
> Foot it featly here and there;
> And, sweet sprites, the burden bear. (*Ibid.*)

The transformation of his environment is thus as complete as that of his mood. Moreover, it closely resembles the change Aeneas experienced when he passed up from Purgatory to Elysium; for Virgil expressly says that the mythical Elysium is a pleasant place where "happy spirits dance and sing upon the yellow sands."[5]

In the mythological as well as in the subjective sense, then, Ferdinand is in Elysium. Here he meets Miranda, as Dante meets Beatrice in Eden. Both Miranda and Beatrice represent (as I have shown) that Immaculate Woman who, as the beloved of the aspirant, is a personification of Wisdom. Like the Woman Wisdom, Miranda is "wondrous" and unique, peerless and perfect, precious beyond compare. Like Wisdom, she comes to toil with her lover in his trials, and ultimately becomes his bride.

[. . .]

Like the pagan candidate for the Greater Initiation (who had already made a ritual ascent to Elysium in the preceding ceremony), Ferdinand has to accept the discipline of ascetic diet and arduous labours. His labours, it is interesting to note, consist in carrying a heavy burden of wood—as Christ, before His crucifixion and death, was made to carry the Cross.[6] These preliminaries having been completed, Ferdinand then undergoes the experience which constitutes the supreme initiation.

[. . .]

[. . . In] the supreme psychological experience, the ecstatic "closing of the eyes" (or mystical swoon) in a temporary death to this world precedes the arrival of the consciousness upon the plane of complete and instantaneous knowledge, which is the plane of revelation, so, in mythology, the passage through the fiery circle precedes the aspirant's arrival in the Celestial Paradise, where a glimpse of divine things is obtained. [. . .]

Such is the case with Ferdinand [. . . who] is now in that mythical Celestial Paradise wherein the perfected Soul, emancipated from the

cycle of incarnations, lives for ever; and indeed, at this very moment
he exclaims:

> Let me live here ever:
> So rare a wonder'd father and a wise
> Makes this place Paradise.
>   (Act IV., Scene 1.)

Furthermore, we are expressly given to understand that this beholding
of the gods is directly related to and confirms his "contract of true
love" with Miranda. In other words, it is an apocalypse; for it marks
his union with the Wisdom or Truth that is fully acquired only
through revelation.

[...]

With the philosophical speech of Prospero, which ensues
upon the vision and of which the purpose is to awaken Ferdinand
from the dream of the earth-life and its transient material splen-
dours, the "revels" of the Greater or Ocular Initiation according
to the pagan model are ended. I have left a certain amount of the
textual evidence contained in the story of Ferdinand for consideration later in a separate section dealing with Miranda; and hence
the brevity of the present section, as compared with that relating
to the Court Party. But enough has, I think, been said to show
that, if this part of the Play be treated as continuing the allegory
embodied in the story of the Court Party, we find in the two narra-
tives a full account of that Pilgrimage of Perfection which is called
Initiation.

[...]

The self-redemption of man consists in his recovery of the Lost
Estate of inspired reason. To achieve this, the aspirant must expiate
the original sin by a triumph over precisely the temptations by which
the Fall was compassed. He must overcome that insidious Tempter
who is Desire. I have already dealt extensively with this ordeal, but
the consequences of failure have yet to be considered. Failure to resist
the Tempter involves not only failure to achieve "Initiation," but also
another lapse to EARTH. And this further lapse necessarily corresponds exactly to the original Fall.

It is now my intention to show that the story of Stephano and Trinculo expresses this conception with singular and suggestive precision, and that the Play is thus completed as a mythological cycle by the inclusion of a version of the Fall; but, as a preliminary to this demonstration, the case of Caliban must first be considered.

Much has been written on the subject of Caliban. He may be said, in fact, to present one of the most difficult problems of the Play. The proposition which I now submit is that *in Caliban we have a personification on mythological lines of the Tempter who is Desire.*

I have already dealt at some length with the aspect of the Tempter as Desire, and also with the various forms in which he is represented. In the *Genesis* story the Tempter is described simply as a Serpent. But the typical form which he assumes in myth and legend is that of a monstrous Serpent or Dragon, as in the myths of Cadmus, of Perseus, and of St. George. This creature is native to water, whence he emerges to assail his victim. And since the conception of the Tempter, as Desire, is entirely subjective in significance, the water whence the monster emerges must be understood to be the emotional WATER in the human composition.[7]

[. . .]

Caliban has, therefore, four important points of resemblance to the Monsters of mythological tradition and initiation ritual; for—(a) he is native to water, (b) he resides, or is encountered, out of water, (c) he is of mixed species, and (d) he figures the Tempter. True to the tradition, he is met with by Stephano and Trinculo when, emerging from the water, they have wandered on the shore—that is to say, he is met with when in the course of the Reascent they have passed through WATER into MIST. This MIST is the Purgatorial Wilderness, the place of temptation and expiation. It is also, as we have seen, a place or state of darkness; so that Caliban is quite truly described by Prospero as—

This thing of darkness . . .
　　　　　(Act V., Scene 1, line 275.)

This may be no more than a verbal coincidence. It is, perhaps, a remark that is conventionally moral rather than deliberately symbolical. In any case, the Tempter is pre-eminently a "thing of darkness." Indeed, he is the Prince of Darkness.

[. . .]

In so far as the Play corresponds to the pagan rites, Prospero may be regarded as the counterpart of the hierophant, or initiating priest. But in the wider scheme I have latterly been treating he figures the prototypical Supreme Being, whom, indeed, the pagan hierophant was deemed to represent.

We have seen that the expulsion of the dragon Caliban from the Cell of Prospero is a version of the Fall of Satan from Heaven; which must imply that Prospero is equivalent to God. We have seen, too, that he stands in relation to Stephano and Trinculo precisely as the Lord God stood to Adam and Eve. Consider now the seemingly limitless range of Prospero's power

> I have bedimmed
> The noontide sun, called forth the mutinous winds,
> And 'twixt the green sea and the azured vault
> Set roaring war. . . . The strong-based promontory
> Have I made shake, and by the spurs plucked up
> The pine and cedar. Graves at my command,
> Have waked their sleepers, oped and let them forth
> By my so potent art. (Act V., Scene 1.)

These are superhuman works. In fact, Prospero claims quite definitely that he possesses the power of mighty Zeus himself, for not only does he say that he can make lightning, but he declares that he has actually employed the god's own thunderbolt:

> To the dread rattling thunder
> Have I given fire, and rifted Jove's stout oak
> With his own bolt. (*Ibid.*)

For what purpose, save that of allegory, does the Poet thus exalt him to the very topmost pinnacle of superhuman power? Furthermore, although the storm which beset the "men of sin" is repeatedly stated in quite unequivocal terms to have been decreed and created by Prospero,[8] his minister Ariel expressly attributes it to Destiny and the powers of retribution:

> You are three men of sin, whom Destiny
> (That hath to instrument this lower world

> And what is in 't) the never-surfeited sea
> Hath caused to belch you up. . . . I and my fellows
> Are ministers of Fate. . . .
> The powers, delaying, not forgetting, have
> Incensed the seas and shores, yea, all the creatures,
> Against your peace . . . and do pronounce by me
> Lingering perdition, worse than any death
> Can be at once, shall step by step attend
> You and your ways; whose wraths to guard you from,
> Which here, in this most desolate isle, else falls
> Upon your heads, is nothing, but heart's sorrow,
> And a clear life ensuing. (Act III., Scene 3.)

Here it seems to be plainly intimated that Prospero himself is that Omnipotent Judge whom sinners cannot evade, who can pass sentence of "lingering perdition," but whose mercy can always be won by repentance.

[. . .]

He represents the Supreme Being whose benign influence governs the lives of men. Sorrow and misfortunes he does, indeed, ordain; yet his sole purpose is thereby to bring sinners to repentance:

> They being penitent,
> The sole drift of my purpose doth extend
> Not a frown further. (Act V., Scene 1.)

His very name is suggestive of that Beneficent Power which works for the true happiness of mankind (*prospero* = "I make happy"). Against him the dragon Caliban conspires with Stephano and Trinculo, as the fallen Satan conspires among men against the God he hates. Cast out by those whose thoughts are set on their own temporal ends, Prospero does not at once restore himself and maintain (as he could do) his sovereignty by a pitiless use of his superhuman power; but ("delaying, not forgetting") he patiently achieves his own reinstatement by leading them through tribulation to penitence and amendment. This done, he is all-forgiving, and gently bids them "Please you, draw near."

I have argued that *The Tempest* is an account of Initiation, conceived as a reversal of the Fall of Man. And what, in essence, is the Fall but

the dethroning of the Most High from the human heart? In the Play we have a Ruler of supernatural power who has been exiled and forgotten by "men of sin"; and, with Prospero as with God Himself, the means whereby he regains his rightful kingdom are precisely the means whereby those who had dethroned him achieve Initiation.
[. . .]

From no standpoint is the Epilogue, which is spoken by Prospero in the first person, consistent with his part in the drama. It can be reconciled neither with his nominal character as the magic-working Duke of Milan nor with his allegorical character as the Supreme Being; and those commentators are undoubtedly right who insist that Prospero here represents Shakespeare himself. But, while I agree so far, I dissent from the ordinary view that this closing speech contains simply the Poet's intimation that his labours as a dramatist are ended. I suggest rather that Shakespeare, having written a profound allegory, designed the Epilogue for the express purpose of pleading for *release* in the special sense of *interpretation*.
[. . .]

[The] Poet not only needs, but is at this moment invoking, the spiritual aid of his readers to enforce the real and secret purpose of *The Tempest*; and, looking back upon his allegory and recognising its many outward imperfections, he may well say that "his ending is despair" unless the appeal he now makes to us "pierce" so that we forgive the faults in a full appreciation of all that he attempted.

> As you from crimes would pardoned be,
> Let your indulgence set me free.

Yet again, in closing, he asks us to release him. His words are at once a plea and a challenge. All the evidence points to the conclusion that what he asks for is interpretation; and, if the case I have formulated through these many pages be rejected, I know not in what manner his appeal may be answered.

NOTES

1. That the "thirst" which the aspirant suffers is a thirst for the passional WATER, is obvious enough. As for the "hunger," I need

only refer to the universal practice of breaking bread together as the outward symbol of worldly fellowship. This fellowship is one of the worldly pleasures which must be renounced by the aspirant to initiation.

2. Cf. *Jas.* iv. 7: "Resist the Devil, and he will flee from you." Similarly, Apollyon left Christian when the latter resisted him in the Vale of Humiliation. Both the Devil and Apollyon are figures for Desire—that same insidious Serpent which caused (and causes) the Fall from the Elysian AIR of reason, and which must be overcome as a condition precedent to a return thither in the Second Degree of Initiation.

3. Temporal power and glory gratify man's love of display. Desire for them (ambition) is desire for sensuous satisfactions, and may be symbolically described as a "thirst" for the sensuous WATER. Thus Prospero, speaking of his brother, remarks:

> So *dry* was he for sway. . . .
>
> (Act I., Scene 2, line 112.)

Ambition lures men to spiritual death or bondage, like the music of the Sirens. Every true initiate must resist it. By rigid self-discipline he must become utterly indifferent to the sweet satisfactions of temporal power and glory. No otherwise can he be successful in his quest for Truth.

4. "Fumes" are, of course, mist or cloud. Bacon, of whose familiarity with the symbolism I have already given presumptive evidence, describes an error as a "fume." He writes: ". . . For that is the *fume* of those that conceive the Celestial Bodies have more accurate influences upon these things below than indeed they have . . ." (Essay on *Viciss. of Things*).

5. Cf. *Aen.* vi. 643–4:

> Contendunt ludo, et fulva luctantur arena,
>
> Pars pedibus plaudunt choreas, et carmina dicunt

6. *St. John* xix. 17. Nevertheless, the other Gospels affirm that the Cross was carried by one Simon, a Cyrenian. I do not press the comparison between the case of Ferdinand and that of Christ according to St. John. But I may here point out that as Christ's Baptism and Sojourn in the Wilderness represent respectively the First and Second Degrees of Initiation, so His Death and Resurrection represent the Third Degree.

7. Note that there are two mythical Dragons, the higher and the lower. The higher Dragon is native to the WATER ABOVE (FIRE), which is the element of intuitional wisdom; hence the higher Dragon is held to be sacred, as by the Chinese. It is the "Serpent of Wisdom." But the lower Dragon, being native to the passional WATER BELOW, is evil. It is the Tempter who is Desire—"the great dragon, that old serpent, which is the Devil, and Satan."

8. Cf. I. 2. 1–2; I. 2. 26–9; I. 2. 194–5; V. 1. 6.

THEIR EYES WERE WATCHING GOD
(ZORA NEALE HURSTON)

❧ ～

"Resistance, Rebirth, and Renewal
in Zora Neale Hurston's
Their Eyes Were Watching God"
by Deborah James,
the University of North Carolina at Asheville

These sitters had been tongueless, earless, eyeless conveniences all day long. Mules and other brutes had occupied their skins. But now the sun and the bossman were gone so the skins felt powerful and human. (1)

Zora Neale Hurston's writing—anthropological and literary—aimed at giving voice to a community which society often rendered as "tongueless, earless, eyeless conveniences." Within her texts, African Americans, particularly ordinary working people, live and breathe. That gift of life in her texts is perhaps her most important contribution to American letters. And nowhere is that talent displayed more ably, more poetically, than in her most celebrated work, *Their Eyes Were Watching God*. While its major focus is the life of its main character, Janie, it also brings to life again a community that is vital despite the enforced enclosure of race. Within the communities she constructs, African Americans have agency; they have lives full of laughter, work, envy, love, resentment, sometimes violence, pride, curiosity—a whole range of human activity and concerns. They also have a lively, expressive language augmented by Hurston's own gifts

229

of poetic expression. This novel demonstrates how people, collectively and individually, create their lives—resisting external categories and achieving renewal. Janie, the protagonist of the novel, is Hurston's most significant portrait of an individual who achieves renewal through her ability to resist the definitions of others and her openness to the sometimes-painful process of rebirth.

Since its reappearance on the American literary landscape in the 1970s, critics and readers of *Their Eyes Were Watching God* agree that the novel chronicles Janie's self-discovery. She has several key relationships within the story—first with her grandmother, the other three with each of the men she marries. Discussions of the text identify Janie's marriages as crucial junctures for her—the moments when her discoveries about herself are most apparent and intense. From this vantage point, her most important lessons would seem to be lessons about love—understanding what love is *not* through her first two marriages, initially to Logan Kellicks, then to Joe Starks (or Jody as Janie called him). Janie finally learns what love *is* during her last relationship with Tea Cake (Vergible Woods). If, however, this is the only concern of the novel, all that it offers its readers, it would have ceased to be of critical interest some time ago. In fact, some early reviewers, Richard Wright and Sterling Brown for example, dismissed her tale as worthless because it seemed to ignore the political and social realities of the times and to be limited to only these domestic concerns. What these readers missed was Hurston's implicit challenge to the stereotype of the day that said black people were incapable of true romance because, as a race, they were limited in human feelings and understanding. Fortunately, this issue has virtually vanished for contemporary readers.

But there is more to the novel than this exploration of romantic love. As eminent African American literary critic and scholar Henry Louis Gates observes, a wide range of critics continue to discover new aspects of the novel that they contemplate and discuss with delight if not always in agreement (Gates, *Their Eyes* 164). For example, while most contemporary readers agree that Janie does gain valuable knowledge about the nature of love through her experiences with the men in her life, some critics, such as Mary Helen Washington (Washington, "I Love . . .") argue that Janie's self-discoveries are limited by her relationships with men. While Janie's relationships provide experiences through which she learns and grows, they are not the full measure of that growth. Janie's discoveries result in renewal because of everything she learns about life and the courage with which she seeks to live it on her own terms. On her return to Eatonville, she shares her tale and her hard-won understanding with her best friend, Pheoby.

> It's a known fact Pheoby, you got tuh go there tuh know there.
> Yo' papa and yo' mama and nobody else can't tell yuh and show yuh. Two things everybody's got tuh do fuh themselves. They got tuh go tuh God, and they got tuh find out about livin' fuh theyselves." (192)

Through her experiences, Janie discovers that in order to achieve real knowledge she must resist external limitations and expectations, becoming a full participant in shaping her own life. Thus she is reborn as a whole person.

Early on, Janie demonstrates her resistance to external definition in the episode where she fails to recognize herself in a photograph as the one black child among the other children who live on the estate. Although that failure has some troubling connotations (i.e., is Hurston suggesting some negative response to being identified as black?), it actually signals her resistance to the stigma associated with the racial stereotypes of the day. As she relays this incident to Pheoby, she explains her response in terms of the freedom and equality she experienced as a child and how it differed from the typical experience of blacks in the pre-civil rights era. Her surprise about her racial identity does not seem linked to any personal negative feelings about it. Rather, as the rest of the novel attests, it indicates the difference between how Janie thinks of herself (not limited in terms of race and class) and how other people see her and expect her to respond. Janie's resistance to the facts of her poverty and race, to what those *should* mean in terms of her feelings about her "place," forecast her reaction to her grandmother's efforts to provide security for her by way of marriage. From the beginning, Janie's judgments and desires are shaped by her own feelings about the circumstances of her life rather than by others' expectations. This leads to a deep rift between Janie and her grandmother.

When Nanny observes Janie's sexual awakening (kissing Johnny Taylor across the fence), she is catapulted into action for Janie's safety. Janie, however, understands neither how she is endangered nor what the nature of the danger is. Everything seems to be happening too abruptly. Like a dreamer awakening, Janie is temporarily blinded by the glories of a new world, in which sensuality, sexuality, and love seem to equal marriage. But Nanny, born into slavery, victim of her master's lust and her mistress's rage, knows how vulnerable Janie is from this moment on. She argues that Janie must have the protection of marriage and the security of possessions to prevent what Nanny believes will otherwise be her inevitable fate.

> Ah don't want yo' feathers always crumpled by folks throwin'
> things in yo' face. And Ah can't die easy thinkin' maybe de
> menfolks white or black is makin' a spit cup outa' you . . . (20).

These terrors have no reality for Janie though. In her mind, Nanny has transformed almost unaccountably into someone forcing Janie to submit to her will against Janie's own instincts. And while she tries to accept Nanny's vision as her own, it does not fit. But Nanny does not comprehend Janie's view, dismissing it as insubstantial and naïve. Janie longs for "things sweet wid mah marriage . . ." (24). Nanny instead insists that marriage to Logan Kellicks is the perfect protection. He is an older man—settled, a widow, and, most importantly, a landowner (sixty acres). While Nanny's fears for Janie are real and her efforts to provide for her are loving, her refusal to take into account Janie's feelings confuses and angers Janie. In Janie's view, her marriage to Kellicks diverts her from her own fledgling attempt to explore her world and herself. In marrying Logan, Janie allows her life to be dictated by Nanny's view, with negative consequences. Later in life Janie even decides that,

> She hated her grandmother and had hidden it from herself all
> these years under a cloak of pity. She had been getting ready
> for her great journey to the horizons in search of *people.* . . . But
> she had been whipped like a cur dog, and run off down a back
> road after *things* (89).

To Janie, Nanny's well-intentioned protection, in fact, aborts her first attempts to achieve womanhood.

While Janie's resistance to Nanny's plan for her life has been almost entirely intuitive (she has little experience on which to base her fears), in her union with Logan, she begins to acquire lived experience on which to base her growing understanding. First, however, she must resist Logan Kellicks himself, the next threat to her development.

Like Nanny, Logan tries to impose his view of what she should be on Janie. Though he initially seems smitten with her (i.e., chopping wood for her, etc.), when she fails to immediately reciprocate, he becomes angry. He thinks she should be grateful that he has rescued her from what he sees as the humiliation of her poverty. When she refuses to behave with gratitude, he begins to demand servitude, first demanding that she chop her own wood, then purchasing a mule specifically for her to help him plow the field. Ironically, this is the fate that Nanny thinks she has protected Janie from.

> So Janie waited a bloom time, and a green time and an orange time. But when the pollen again gilded the sun and sifted down on the world she began to stand around the gate and expect things. What things? She didn't know exactly. . . . She knew things nobody had ever told her. . . . The familiar people and things had failed her so she hung over the gate and looked down the road towards way off. She knew now that marriage did not make love. Jamie's first dream was dead, so she became a woman. (25)

Janie begins to understand through her own experience with Logan what she does not want. Moreover, she has proof that she should follow her own instincts, so when Joe Starks arrives, representing the horizons she wants to explore, it takes very little time for her to decide to leave Logan. Thus she embarks on her first reinvention of herself. But she does not simply leave Logan to attach herself to Joe. In fact, the morning she walks off, she is poised on the brink of self-discovery: "A feeling of sudden newness and change came over her. . . . Even if Joe was not there waiting for her, the change was bound to do her good." (32)

Joe's arrival has reawakened Janie's previous yearnings, especially her desire for a relationship in which she can know and be known more fully. Once again she is disappointed. Like Nanny and Logan, Joe is intent on Janie enacting the role he has assigned her. He is unwilling to consider her concerns or feelings in any real way. He is convinced that he knows best. Janie must again resist someone else's idea of who she should be in order to derive a clearer understanding of who she is.

In fact, Janie's most sustained resistance occurs within the boundaries of her marriage to Joe. In the beginning, she thinks she has found a partner with whom to share her exploration of the world. Joe Starks is a man with a vision; he is heading to a black town in its infancy to be part of its growth and development from the ground up, and he is taking Janie with him. But Joe believes he must tell her what she *should* think, what she *should* feel despite Janie's assertions that women think too. In a heated exchange, he tells her that women "just thinks they's thinking." (71) Janie retreats into silence—but silent resistance rather than submission.

> She found that she had a host of thoughts she had never expressed to him, and numerous emotions she had never let Jody [Joe] know about. Things packed up and put away in parts of her heart where he could never find them.... She had an inside and an outside now and suddenly she knew how not to mix them. (72)

So Janie's first response to Joe's domination is to preserve her true self from him in silence. Her outside self does what Joe demands, while her inside self remains hidden from him. It is during this sustained silence that she begins to observe more carefully the contrast between this outside, which conforms in some measure to expectation, and the inside, which harbors her real feelings. In this silence, the gap between the two states of being grows.

But such a split cannot be maintained forever. One day, when Joe derides her in front of the usual crowd in the store, something snaps. She retaliates by scorning him publicly, describing his impotence: "When you pull down yo' britches, you look lak de change uh life" (79). Janie moves from passive resistance to open rebellion, using the voice she has discovered to devastating effect. But even when Joe faces death, he will not *hear* Janie.

> "Listen, Jody, you ain't de Jody ah run off down de road wid. You'se whut's left after he died. Ah run off tuh keep house wid you in uh wonderful way. But you wasn't satisfied wid me de way Ah was. Naw! Mah own mind had tuh be squeezed and crowded out tuh make room for yours in me."
>
> "Shut up. Ah wish thunder and lightnin' would kill you" (86).

Though her attempts at reconciliation fail, she has her say. More than that, though, in the aftermath of Joe's death, she once again takes stock. Janie achieves one level of self-knowledge when she left Logan. At Joe's death, she gains another. The young girl is now completely gone, replaced by a handsome, confident woman, able to present her "starched and ironed face, forming it into just what people wanted to see" (87). This mask becomes a protective cover while a new Janie develops within this cocoon.

The community sees from her what it expects to see, while Janie enjoys her first real freedom. She begins this process of renewal by first divesting herself of the head rags that symbolized Joe's domination. But she continues by questioning herself deeply. She asks herself what she really wants, then listens in stillness for the answer. It is in this process that she discovers her antipathy toward Nanny. In this stillness, she discovers ". . . a jewel down inside herself" seeking its mate in some undiscovered other (90). In this state of contemplation, Janie also discovers how much she enjoys her own freedom. Although the first two relationships in her life had looked like freedom, each became a different kind of bondage. So Janie is very cautious about avoiding that mistake again. She is also coming to the end of her willingness to even provide the outside demanded by others. When Pheoby presses her to consider remarrying, Janie responds:

> "Tain't dat Ah worries over Joe's death, Pheoby. Ah jus' loves dis freedom."
>
> "Sh-sh-sh! Don't let nobody hear you say dat Janie. Folks will say you ain't sorry he's gone.

> "Let 'em say whut dey wants tuh, Phoeby. To my thinking
> mourning oughtn't tuh last no longer than grief" (93).

Thus between Jody's death and her next relationship, Janie emerges as
a new woman, ready and able to make her own decisions about her
life. She knows the consequences of allowing other people to dictate
the terms of one's own life. It is in that state of readiness that she has
her most life-altering encounter. She meets Tea Cake, her mentor and
the other whose internal jewel matches hers.

From the beginning, Janie's relationship with Tea Cake is unlike
the previous ones. This relationship is marked by play, a level of
mutual honesty and self-disclosure that Janie's previous relationships
lacked. Though she's cautious about her new freedom, her banter with
him during their first meeting is easy and relaxed. It is Janie who sets
the boundaries of their relationship early on. She decides when and
where she engages with him. Even her efforts to avoid the eyes of the
town at first give way very soon to their evolving relationship. Janie's
anxiety that he is a young man out to make a fool of her is quelled
by Tea Cake's accurate reading of her fear. He sets out then to prove
that his interest in her is genuine and not limited to either property
or sex.

A turning point in their relationship comes after he has returned
to her after having disappeared earlier with the two hundred dollars
she had hidden as security in case he abandoned her on the road.
Upon his return, he describes to her in detail what he has done with
the money; she asks why he did not take her with him. Like Logan,
but especially like Joe, he voices the idea that she is too refined to
be exposed to low life. Not only does she resist this view openly, but
she also tells him that from that moment on she expects to "partake
wid everything. . . ." (124). Tea Cake accepts this idea and tells her,
"Honey since you loose me and gimme privilege tuh tell yuh about
mahself, Ah'll tell yuh . . ." (125). Thus Tea Cake begins his role as
guide for Janie, sharing all the dimensions of his life with her and thus
inviting her to do the same. Janie participates in everything as much as
she chooses to. Tea Cake does ask her to do things for him: to go with
him "on the muck" (work in the Florida Everglades), to live on only
what he can provide for them, to work side by side with him in the
fields. The difference is that he invites her into his life, the better to

know him. In fact, he presents the idea of working the fields together as a way for them to spend even more time together. Janie accepts. When Mrs. Turner befriends Janie only to try to turn her against Tea Cake, he asks Janie to keep her away from the house, but he does not blame her when she is not completely able to avoid the association. It is a sign of the severity of his illness toward the end of the novel when he demands that she stay in his sight and begins to accuse her of disloyalty.

With Tea Cake Janie tries to inhabit a new identity, one not limited by class or external expectations. In fact, at one point she thinks,

> ... of the old days in the big white house and the store and laugh(ed) to herself. What if Eatonville could see her now in her blue denim overalls and heavy shoes? The crowd of people around her and a dice game on her floor! She was sorry for her friends back there and scornful of the others. The men held big arguments here like they used to do on the store porch. Only here, she could listen and laugh and even talk some if she wanted to. She got so she could tell big stories herself from listening to the rest (134).

She learns other skills besides—she can fish and hunt and shoot. She is also a good cook. But most of all, she feels free to be herself—without constraint, without pretense.

Her relationship to Tea Cake can be said to be problematic, especially to the contemporary eye. Tea Cake "slaps her around" when he finds out that Mrs. Turner is trying to set Janie up with her brother. He tells the other men that he does this not because of Janie's behavior but to show Mrs. Turner that he controls his home. So even within this love match, Janie is not altogether free of the violence and controlling behavior that some men consider their right where women are concerned. Yet, on the muck, she is free to work or not, to dance, laugh, fight, cry, think, make love—to give expression to a full range of emotions. This freedom stems from Janie's sense of self-sufficiency, from her confidence in her ability to take care of herself. She still has the home and store that Joe's death has left her and money in the bank. She returns to this place readily after losing Tea

Cake. But in her life with him she experiences a sense of completion, of being deeply loved and of loving deeply.

At the end of the day, however, Janie has only herself and her hard-won knowledge to rely on. In the last view of Janie that Hurston provides, she is again taking stock. But this time when she looks inside, she thinks, "Here was peace. She pulled in her horizon like a great fish-net. Pulled it from around the waist of the world and draped it over her shoulder. So much of life in its meshes. She called in her soul to come and see" (193). Janie is unafraid of the journey. She knows who she is now for sure.

WORKS CITED AND SELECTED CRITICAL READINGS

Gates, Henry Louis. "*Their Eyes Were Watching God*: Hurston and the Speakerly Text." *Zora Neale Hurston: Critical Perspectives Past and Present*. Henry Louis Gates Jr. and K.A. Appiah, eds. New York: Amistad Literary Series, 1993. 154–203.

———. "Zora Neale Hurston: 'A Negro Way of Saying.'" Afterword. *Their Eyes Were Watching God*. New York: Perennial Classics, 1998. 195–205.

Hurston, Zora Neale. *Their Eyes Were Watching God*. New York: Perennial Classics, 1998.

Wall, Cheryl A. "Zora Neale Hurston: Changing Her Own Words." *Zora Neale Hurston: Critical Perspectives Past and Present*. Henry Louis Gates Jr. and K.A. Appiah, eds. New York: Amistad Literary Series, 1993.

Washington, Mary Helen. "Introduction." *Their Eyes Were Watching God*. New York: Perennial Classics, 1998. ix–xvii.

———. "'I Love the Way Janie Crawford Left Her Husbands': Emergent Female Hero." *Zora Neale Hurston: Critical Perspectives Past and Present*. Henry Louis Gates Jr. and K.A. Appiah, eds. New York: Amistad Literary Series, 1993.

❧ *Acknowledgments* ❧

Alighieri, Dante. "To Can Grande della Scala." *Dantis Alagherii Epistolae: The Letters of Dante*. Trans. Paget Toynbee. Oxford: Clarendon Press, 1966 (First published 1920). 160–211.

Bergsten, Staffan. "The Later Quartets." *Time and Eternity: A Study in the Structure and Symbolism of T.S. Eliot's* Four Quartets. Stockholm, Sweden: Svenska Bokförlaget, 1960. 206-44. © 1960 by Berlingska Boktryckeriet Lund. Reprinted by permission.

Brockbank, J.P. "The Damnation of Faustus." *Marlowe: Dr. Faustus*. Woodbury, N.Y.: Barron's Educational Series, 1962. 51–60. © 1962 by J.P. Brockbank.

Butler, H.E. "Introduction: The Sixth Book of the *Aeneid*." *The Sixth Book of the* Aeneid. Oxford: Blackwell Publishing, 1920. 1–18.

Guerard, Albert J., "The Journey Within." *Conrad the Novelist*. Cambridge, Mass.: Harvard UP, 1958. 1–59. © 1958 by the President and Fellows of Harvard College, renewed 1984 by Albert J. Guerard. Reprinted by permission.

Holland, Norman N. "Realism and Unrealism: Kafka's 'Metamorphosis.'" *Modern Fiction Studies* 4.2 (Summer 1958): 143–50. © 1958 by Johns Hopkins University Press.

Rudicina, Alexandra F. "Crime and Myth: The Archetypal Pattern of Rebirth in Three Novels of Dostoevsky." *PMLA* Vol. 87, No. 5 (Oct. 1972), 1,065–1,074 © 1972 by Modern Language Association. Reprinted by permission of the Modern Language Association of America.

Steinbrink, Jeffrey. "'Boats Against the Current': Mortality and the Myth of Renewal in *The Great Gatsby*." *Twentieth Century Literature*, Vol. 26, No. 2 (Summer 1980), 157–70. © 1980 by Hofstra University. Reprinted by permission.

Still, Colin. *Shakespeare's Mystery Play: A Study of* The Tempest. London: Cecil
    Palmer, 1921.
Tolkien, J.R.R. "Beowulf: The Monsters and the Critics." *Beowulf: The Monsters
    and the Critics*. Darby, Pa.: The Arden Library, 1978, 1936. Copyright ©
    1983 by Frank Richard Williamson and Christopher Reuel Tolkien as
    Executors of the Estate of J.R.R. Tolkien. Reprinted by permission of
    Houghton Miflin Harcourt Publishing Company. All rights reserved.
Wilcockson, Colin. "The Opening of Chaucer's General Prologue to *The
    Canterbury Tales*: A Diptych." *Review of English Studies* 50: 345–50.
    © 1999 by Oxford University Press. Reprinted by permission.

Index

A

Adêlê Ratignolle (*Awakening*),
20–21

Aeneid, The, "Book 6" (Virgil), 1–12
Dante and, 5, 11
Elysium and theme of rebirth, 1,
5–6
Greece and Rome compared, 4
haunting beauty and melancholy,
5
heart of poem, 2–4
Introduction, 1
judge of dead duties as undefined,
9
lack of completion and Vergil's
death, 9–10
metempsychosis doctrine, 10–11
Pythagoreanism and, 6, 11
twilight beauty overall, 5
underworld spirits in, 7–8
uniqueness of, 11
Albany (*King Lear*), 151
Alcée Arobin (A*wakening)*, 13, 20
Alena Ivanovna (*Crime and
Punishment*), 63
Alighieri, Dante. *See Divine Comedy*
(Dante)
Amy *(Beloved)*, 29
Angelou, Maya, 135–143
Arnsberg, Lilane K., 135–136

Augustine, 57, 79, 94
Augustus (*Aeneid*), 3, 4
Awakening (Chopin), 13–23
lack of sympathy for Edna, 20
plot of, 13–14
provocative ending of, 14–15,
22–23
See also *specific names of characters
(e.g.*, Edna Pontellier)

B

Baby Suggs *(Beloved)*, 26, 30
Bailey (*Caged Bird*), 135, 139
bastards, in Elizabethan drama, 145
Beloved (Morrison), 25–33
Beloved as mystical incarnation,
25, 28, 31–32
epilogue, 31
hair combing as metaphor, 25
healing of human psyche and,
33–34
infanticide as metaphor, 26
plot of, 25–27
power of language and, 29
religious context and, 26–27
remembering slavery and,
26–27
sexual imagery and, 30
and suspension of disbelief, 26